CASE STUDIES of AMERICA CORPORATIONS

Zeros and Heroes of Business

The Book for People Who Wish to Understand
and
Why the Others "Just Don't Get It"

by
Dr. Thurman Richard White

WESTVIEW PUBLISHING CO., INC. – NASHVILLE, TENNESSEE

© 2006 by Dr. Thurman Richard White, Ed.D. MA, BS, AS

No part of this book may be reproduced or transmitted in any form or by any means, electronic or mechanical, including photocopying, recording, or by any information storage and retrieval system without the express written permission of the author. Short excerpts may be used with the permission of the author or publisher for the purposes of media reviews.

First edition June 2006

ISBN 0-9773179-5-1

Printed in the United States of America on acid-free paper

Layout by Westview Publishing Co., Inc.

Cover art by Dr. White

Cover design by Hugh Daniel

Westview Publishing Co., Inc.
P.O. Box 210183
Nashville, Tennessee 37221
www.westviewpublishing.com

DEDICATION

I want to dedicate this book to children all over the world. We all begin our lives as children and experience the formative years developing into adulthood. As a child growing up to be an adult, one of many heroes that I have modeled my life into adulthood is George Washington Carver. His quote should be taught to all the children of the world. It is the first step to becoming a true hero.

"How far you go in life depends on your being tender with the young, compassionate with the aged, sympathetic with the striving, and tolerant of the weak and strong. Because someday in your life you will have been all of these."

George Washington Carver

ZEROS AND HEROES OF BUSINESS

CONTENTS

Dedication iii

Acknowledgements vi

Introduction vii

Part One – Systems Thinking 1
   Three Models 3
   Terminology And Why Study Science Management 23

Part Two – Validation Thinking 43
   Communication & Information Anxiety 45
   Statistical Thinking – What To Do In The
      Absence Of Information 75
   Business Ethics & Leadership 109

Cases Studies 115
   The Educational System – Institutional Learning 117
   Organized Religion – Another Human Enterprise System 130
   Federal Express – Zapmail 152
   Mediclaim Incorporated – The Arkansas Medicaid Bid 187

Summarization Structure & Conclusions 237

ACKNOWLEDGEMENTS

It would be difficult to sufficiently thank all those who helped in the design and preparation of this book. This project's accomplishments are a result of the many honest heroes I have had the privilege of knowing and working with. Heroes have taught me that those who really deserve praise are the people, while human enough to enjoy power nevertheless pay more attention to justice than they are compelled to do by their situation. Much gratitude goes to the managers of business organizations that are committed to ethics.

I wish to thank my wife Teresa, for her invaluable and constant support. Her guidance and encouragement during the development of this project was the feedback that directed the completion of this book. I wish to thank my parents, Dr. Richard P. White and Ethel Mae White as well as my Uncle Thurman Miller (my mother's older brother) and his wife my Aunt Mary; for showing me that what a person has been is history, what a person is is philosophy, but what a person ought to be is ethics. My mother named me Thurman Richard, giving me the two names of my heroes in life.

My Uncle Thurman served in World War II as a medic with the 2nd Battalion 60th Infantry 9th Division. He also was a pharmacist and business owner of four (4) pharmacy stores and served as President for two years with the Indiana Pharmacy Association. I have detailed my father's outstanding career in this book in the case concerning the educational system.

Ethics is like the stars in the sky. We never reach them, but like the mariners of the sea we chart our course by them. Ethics is an integrated part of our lives. It fits well into the Total Quality Management programs because ethics is about what we ought to be and directs individuals to be practitioners of self-improvement. Ethics reveals the character of any person and gives a brand name to the individual. Incorporating ethics in the work place delivers trust that people can appreciate. Divorced from ethics, leadership is reduced to mere management practices and organizational political techniques.

INTRODUCTION

Throughout the history of business practices in the United States, we have been inundated with many books concerning the way we ought to conduct business. Most of these books contain *schools of thought* that promise positive results if one follows better business practices. These books pretend to understand and explain business practices of corporate America; however, these books lack the science that explains and differentiates good and/or bad business practice outcomes. This book is structured differently. It is about my personal business experiences as an insider working with both the amazingly brilliant business people as well as the galactically inane. The case studies sited in this book relate to personal experiences and the application of science management. The reader will not be inundated with espoused theoretical commentary brought about by an armchair philosophy or academic conjecture. The case studies in this book contain interoffice memorandums and other related items pertaining to the business practices of several fortune 500 companies as well as State Medicaid bids in the area of healthcare computer technology. The reason for the inclusion of these business documents is for the reader to test the inferences for statistical significance and have the reader draw their own conclusions concerning management practices. This is not outside looking in; it is about inside speaking out.

During my lifetime I have experienced being an employer and business owner as well as an employee and manager in a variety of organizations. As a result, I have studied the best practices of many business organizations. I have also completed four college degrees during my working career. At the Universities I attended, I became disturbed reading all of the business management books and materials that propagated and spawned more incompetent managers. These metaphorical books absolutely have no meaning and only fuel the fire for managers to continue mismanagement practices. Books such as "Who Moved My Cheese" are only for candy-land managers supporting a fantasy organization that breed both petrified employees and supports narcissistic self-entitlement ideology. These business books that are designed to "get in touch" with people's feelings destroy a person's ability to think and factualize management decisions based on an objective measure. During my doctoral studies, I was required to read "Who Moved My Cheese" while attending a leadership/management class. The professor told the students that we would open the class with a discussion of the book. In an emotional yet philosophical way, the professor asked what he felt was a deep and intellectual question. The professor pointed to me and asked, "What is change?" I responded, "Where I come from, change is three quarters, two dimes, and a nickel." When asked to explain my absurd answer I responded, "In order to become familiar with science management and become heroic in any organization; one must commit to abandoning the method of factualizing based on feelings. The book "Who Moved My Cheese" offered no substance or ideas concerning the development of better management practices when change occurs in the business arena. When we allow feelings to factualize outcomes, then rival explanations occur and definitive answers are lost. Due to the non-factual decision making practices taught to managers, concept errors occur. The book "Who Moved My Cheese" is full of concept errors and offers no methods for correct managerial practices, especially when it comes to managing change in a business organization." Concept errors occur as a result of availability errors or concepts that move beyond one's complexity horizons. An availability error is nothing more than a strong disposition to make judgments or evaluations in light of the first available idea that comes to mind. Many managerial books are filled with availability errors. Many of these books that are sold in the market place advocate a management style by situational leadership. These books become the employees most feared and revered list of prioritized practices that act as a non-creative cookbook for management. It should be obvious to members of any organization that the first priority of a manager is to match the employee's talent to a role that will foster development for the employee, manager, and company. Placing non-talent into a role only places several points of failure that predestines the employee to frustration and creates chaos in any enterprise. Managers who don't know how to manage become misfits of the organization. Misfit managers often create the illusion of progress by *restructuring* the territory, *reorganizing* the department, or *replacing* employees. The misfit manager is so busy driving their own agenda; they often fail to ask employees what processes are in place that can be improved. These managers fill the void with pseudo-positive sounding rhetoric, such as "If you are at the end of your rope, tie a knot in it and swing." Or "if you have a lemon in your life make lemon-aid" and "now that you are an employee in this company, you need to become more of a corporate man." What does all this mean? These statements are clever but are void of any real meaning and direction for employees to resolve real issues. These misfit managers are narcissistic people filling the voids with non-informative statements. Managers that use the words *team player* are in reference to "don't tell on me for sexually harassing the women in our office" or "don't rat me out for all the bad things I have done." Only self-serving people are team players. People who work well together are team-workers. There is a difference in team players and team workers. Team workers have accomplishment to tout and have a history of resolving issues as a team. Team players live too much of their life perpetuating problems and not living solutions.

People make decisions everyday. The decisions we make and the filters we choose to reach an understanding are a product of what we learn and experience. Why do mangers rarely consider and listen to an employee's idea, but when the President of a company presents ridiculous ideas, the manager listens intently? How we make decisions becomes a permanent arrangement in our daily activities and continues throughout our lives. Many of the problems with the educational system, governments, business, and any active organization are a result of the process we choose to make decisions. What was the process when we decided to buy one automobile and not another? Why do we decide that this religion is better for me than

INTRODUCTION

another? Why do people decide to live in this country as opposed to another? Why are some people Republican or Democrat? The decisions we make now determine the future outcomes of our lives. Why do we select certain clothes to wear that expose our skin to carcinogens or select one food group over the other? These decisions drive the very basis of who we are and what we become. Often the decisions people make are a result of an availability error. If something is available, feels good, and easy to accept or implement; then the convenience satisfies the decision rather than laborious due diligence to find the facts. Heroes find the facts first and the correct feelings follow. Zeroes put feelings first and then fallacies follow.

Business curriculum in our schools, colleges, and universities include several courses that prepare managers and leaders to be better practitioners. The most well known curriculum degree program is the MBA (Masters of Business Administration). An MBA curriculum in many universities includes courses on behavioral psychology of the organization, the latest management fads, business statistics, accounting, finance, and ethics. These same core courses are included as essentials to complete an associate degree, bachelor degree, or certification in business management and/or administration. During the early to mid 1900's, the leading theories of business management had been intuitionism, emotivism, naturalism, and personal realism, just to mention a few. Today's successful business curriculums have replaced the old *schools of thought* with *science* management. Business books written today have begun to borrow and incorporate the language and structure of science. Science words such as paradigm, systems thinking and other science terminology are becoming the language of business people in corporate America.

This book is structured with three models designed to illuminate the reader in the areas of business science, behavioral psychology, and ethics. The book then defines the method and vocabulary of the three models and includes a section on statistical thinking. Behavioral psychology often includes the art of communications with others. Many books have been written concerning transactional analysis and how to be better communicators. The section titled information anxiety is designed to illuminate the reader with a tool to challenge information exchanged during the communication process. When applicable, the reader will be able to use these definitions and models more specific with people in any enterprising organization. Examples are presented in the book as well as real case studies. This book clarifies what it means to be scientifically minded as it relates to business practices. The three models represent the processes that make hero managers be known as great leaders and differentiate why other manager/leaders are zero people. Outstanding managers, in general, are unable to explain their process. However, they subconsciously follow the rules as outlined in the three models.

PART ONE:
SYSTEMS THINKING

ZEROS AND HEROES OF BUSINESS

THE THREE MODELS

The three models are *structuring understanding*, *follower readiness*, and *good decisions verses bad decisions*. The first model, *structuring understanding*, identifies three ways that people structure their reasoning and understanding. The second model *follower readiness*, identifies the willingness of people to follow leaders of an organization. The third model, *good decisions verses bad decisions*, identifies two types of people in an organization, heroes and zeroes.

First Model – Structuring Understanding

There are essentially three categories that structure and guide people's understanding. These are pathways for a person's logical reasoning. Usually, people follow one of these thought pathways when reaching conclusions. Decisions are all about passing judgment on an issue under consideration or a particular person or group's ideology. People make decisions everyday all over the world, the method in which people reach and act on their conclusions has origins in one or all of these three categories. The categories to structuring understanding are *science*, *the school of thought*, and/or *a movement*.

To illustrate these categories of ways people structure understanding, we will use the subject of ecology; however, it works as a tool for any subject or ideology under consideration. Ecology is the study of the relationships between organisms and their environments. Therefore, we will categorize Ecology as a logical pathway represented as a *science*, a *school of thought*, and a *movement*. Here are the general characteristics of the categories.

Ecology as **science** is studied using the scientific method. Observations of an ecosystem yield data that is analyzed, organized, and experimentally investigated. These experimental activities are restricted to advance objective knowledge on the subject. Ecology the science validates the observations and presents a class of characteristics of plants and animals. Knowledge is gained through direct experience. Theories that are developed explain findings and raise questions. Others easily reproduce observations, conduct experiments, and reasonable provisional agreement is confirmed. The individual or a team of investigators directly experiences discovery of new ideas and the accumulation of knowledge. The observer participates in the accumulation of knowledge. Just as it is with obtaining a patent in the business world, one must teach to others how to practice the trade. In other words, a working model exists that others can duplicate and repeat the process producing similar outcomes and results. People, who are active in constructing their understanding with science, are being informed rather than feeling informed.

When Science is used to structure our understanding, understanding is brought about by the following steps:

1) First, it starts with a curiosity to discover new things.
2) Second, it involves a passion to investigate thoroughly with an objective measure.
3) Third, results of new discoveries are verified and universally accepted.
4) Fourth, the power of the new discovered theory is the theory's ability to predict unknown possibilities and the theory's universal application to resolve problems.

Ecology, *the school of thought*, does not gain knowledge through direct experience; rather it is a construct to teach others what was gained from someone else's direct observations of an ecosystem. Ecology as a school of thought is presented as an academic subject. This offers a student a lens through which the student indirectly views the scientific world. Knowledge is gained indirectly using a disciplined set of techniques (curriculum and educational construct) to interpret the ideas of those who directly made the observations. So ecology the school of thought involves the students, their textbooks, and a professor that explains the subject of environmental interactions in the ecosystem. Nobody is or was a participant in direct observation. The teacher and student do not necessarily obtain new knowledge; rather it is dictated by the teacher. Theories are generally presented as conclusions rather than a tool to guide questioning. Students are taught the findings of scientist, not the scientific method.

Ecology, *a movement,* would be evident when people put patches on their clothing and carry signs to march on Washington D.C. Such individuals are typically willing to follow charismatic leaders where no knowledge of science or a school of thought is required. The appeal of the leader is emotional and prolong studies of the facts are unnecessary. Fear of ecological disasters or the wish to live in pristine environments may motivate many to support any claims of the leader. Earth Day is an emotional commitment to improve our environment, but requires no definitive knowledge of how. The followers of movement leaders gain very little knowledge on their own. Knowledge is subjective and gained mainly from the group leader. There are no strategies developed by the leader for followers to acquire or apply knowledge on their own. Interpretation of incomplete data is subjective. Followers are not to question the leader. When people join a movement they are subjective in the thought process. Due diligence concerning alternative views or compromises are suppressed by the leader of the movement. Leaders are not concerned with teaching a person to duplicate or practice the trade. Movements are not interested in others practicing a trade; rather the followers practice and support the fanaticism of the leader. Movement people do not correct the errors of their predecessors, they perpetuate them. Based on so called good authority (what the leader says), people will structure their understanding. Their thinking is akin to mob rule.

PART ONE: SYSTEMS THINKING

Which one of these *systems of understanding* do individuals often use when structuring an impression concerning people's behavior and/or issues? Each of these three systems represents a filter process that people use to increase their knowledge and understanding when making decisions and arriving at conclusions. Which system of thought do people more often incorporate concerning race issues? Are beliefs about other people factual conceptualizing with science through investigation based on unbiased first hand experience, or did a conceptualization occur with school of thought or movement?

To summarize, *Science* has parsimony. Parsimony values a theory's ability to compress a maximum of information into a minimum of formalism. An example of parsimony is Einstein's equation for the relationship of mass and energy ($E=mc^2$). The first rule of science in relation to impact studies is the ability for the experiment (study) to be replicated with the same results. The science community must be able to repeat the study and get the same results. This reduces conflict with others with provisional agreement among a group of people actively participating in the investigation of the experience. When one constructs understanding with science, one is being informed rather than feeling informed.

When we deal with a *school of thought*, we have theories that lack parsimony and are unable to be tested universally. This causes conflict of opinion. Theories and ideas that are spawned by school of thought are left opened to interpretation. As a result, many theories lack unity and provisional agreement among many people. So rival explanations are generated and ideas remain open to a wide variety of interpretations. There is never closure to resolving issues and debate is the preferred format for problem resolution. In general, during the debate, the winner is the one with the most ammunition. The winner has an arsenal of espoused theories and ideas. There is a difference in espoused theories and theories that are put into practice. An espoused theory is adopted and given loyalty by a minority of people in a group, but it lacks practical application for the majority of people in a group. Many ideas are presented as sound intellectual practices, but these are what I call *the educated error*. Information obtained by school of thought makes one feel informed but does not provide the tools to question or enhance our information of reality.

An example of science verses school of thought is illustrated in the movie "The Wizard of Oz." One of the people who traveled to meet the Wizard was the scarecrow. The scarecrow wanted a brain so he could think. He actually received the ability to think during a crisis, not when the Wizard gave him the diploma. If you remember, Dorothy was being held captive in the castle of the evil witch. The scarecrow said, "I have a plan." This requires a brain. At that moment the scarecrow received the brain he had asked of the Great and powerful Wizard of Oz. Later when the scarecrow was in front of the Wizard after implementing his brainstorm at the witch's castle, the Wizard gave the scarecrow a symbol of getting a brain, the diploma. At this moment, the scarecrow said something that sounded intelligent, but was inaccurate. The scarecrow said, "the sum of the squares of an isosceles triangle is equal the square of the opposite side." Sounds real intelligent, but his attempt to quote the Pythagorean Theorem failed. The intelligent information that the scarecrow shared with us was incorrect expect when the equal sides are at a 90-degree angle. So, the scarecrows statement is true and only true if the equal sides are at a right angle and this is not a general rule but a specific one. Amazing, it was after an educational institution recognized the scarecrow that he sounded intelligent but made an educated error. The statement sounded intelligent but astonishingly incorrect.

MODEL #1 – STRUCTURING UNDERSTANDING

Science ============➔	**School of Thought** =======➔	**Movement**
1) objective	1) subjective	1) dogmatic
2) rational	2) speculative	2) belief
3) verified results	3) plausible results	3) unverified results
4) facts	4) authority	4) assumptions
5) empirical data	5) incomplete data (opinions)	5) void of content
6) evolutionary	6) convolutionary	6) revolutionary
7) has parsimony	7) lacks parsimony	7) no parsimony

The model contains arrows that point from one category of understanding to another category of understanding in a direction of understanding degradation. Once an understanding with science has been reached, often the other two categories will take certain characteristics and elements of sound science but reject the important objective measures taken to verify results. The school of thought categories and movement often reject the use of direct experience that uses objective measures. As we move from the use of science to guide our understanding, our credibility gap begins to widen with respect to making decisions. The result is misunderstandings. When communication between people occur using one category to another, it is inevitable that misunderstandings will arise. This is a result of understanding incompatibility. When observing people in a controversial discussion, it will be an incoherent discussion when people have these categorical differences of reasoning and understanding. Many people do not develop a disposition imbedded in science understanding. So argument and disagreement is the result when two or more people are presenting their position if one is conceptualizing with school of thought and talking to another who conceptualizes with science methods.

Generally, when examining the reasons why people arrive at a conclusion, their understanding originates from one of these categories. Many people reach a conclusion based on what they consider to be sound reasoning and judgment. However, people devote a great deal of time reasoning with what they were taught. Most people categorically base their decisions and structure an understanding with school of thought. Reviewing this as a statistical model it would look something as diagrammed using the bell shaped curve. The bell shaped curve is familiar to many people. Known characteristics of the normal curve make it possible to estimate the occurrence of any value in a normal distribution. One standard deviation above and below the mean is about 68%, two standard deviations above and below the mean are about 95% of the values in the sample space. In this model, the three categories of understanding that are most associated with the percentage of the population are labeled. Approximately, 68 to 95 percent of the people center their decision-making practices with school of thought. For the most part, these people have learned to reason in most situations using school of thought as their primary tool to understanding.

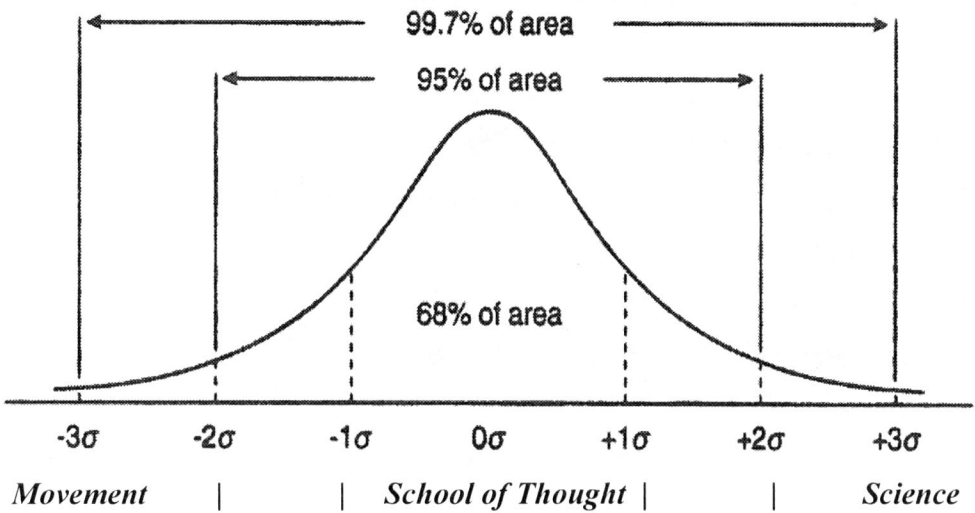

The reader may question whether this model is scientific. I originally considered the model for my doctorate dissertation study. Even though my academic advisors declined the idea of this model, I did a separate study of my own concerning these categories of understanding while doing research on leadership and ethics. This study was important to me due to an aphoristical expression by Claude Bernard, a French scientist of the mid-nineteenth century. He is also known as the father of modern physiology. Bernard devoted considerable thought to the personal characteristics required to do dispassionate research, and decided that the kind of reasoning needed for the purpose does not exist as an innate quality of the human mind. Claude Bernard expressed his aphoristic summary with the following statement:

"Man is by nature metaphysical and arrogant. Accordingly, man thinks that the idealistic creations of his mind, which correspond to his feelings, are identical with reality. From this it follows that the experimental method is not really natural to man, and that only after lengthy wanderings in theological and scholastic discussions has he recognized at last the sterility of his efforts in his direction."
~ Claude Bernard

Claude Bernard stated the differentiating factor that separates science reasoning and understanding from movement and school of thought reasoning and understanding. When we factualize with our feelings, we are reasoning with the movement and/or school of thought category. We are not being scientific with our understanding when we reject the facts and allow our feelings to become identical with our reality. Think about it. Claude Bernard's statement, even though it is aphoristically expressed, is a science statement. Why do I regard this aphoristically expressed statement about human beings as scientific? Because Bernard gave us a short concise statement (a principle) expressing his wise and careful observations of the many people he interacted with during the many years of developing modern physiology. As such, this prompted me to do a study which concluded that 68 to 95 percent of the people in organizations I researched correspond their feelings (not facts) to be identical to their reality. Very few people have the disposition, to apply an experimental method to solve problems or reach sound conclusions concerning daily issues. More often people innately reach for feelings to determine factual details of situations. This step in a reasoning process (our feelings are our reality) produces availability errors. An availability error occurs when a strong disposition to make judgments or evaluations is enlightened with the first available idea that comes to mind. Everyone loses when people begin to factualize with their feelings. First understand the facts and the correct feelings will follow. Never put feeling before the facts.

Visualize the bell curve provided in this book and calculate for yourself the number of people that factualize with their feelings. As you interact with people in your organization, listen to talk radio/television, interacting with people, and/or study articles of information (clinical studies/news papers/etc.); you will determine that the scientific and rational mind is often missing and feelings are substituted for the facts. Heroes list the facts and find an objective measure to minimize their feelings. When anyone lacks the use of an objective measure, we widen the gap between fact and feeling. When we are scientific and we are using an objective measure, we remove the superstitions, the doubts, fears, and the speculations.

These categories also serve as a tool to determine the origins of a person's reasons for advocating one idea over the other. These three categories serve as a method (tool) to explain why people associate with a certain belief, theory, business strategy, or any general philosophical construct that are advocated as truths. If you observe and investigate others, you will see that people arrive at conclusions in one of these three general categories. People who are heroes practice the *science* when making decisions, making improvements, and reaching an understanding that involves critical thinking. Heroes can be counted on to structure their reasoning and understanding with *science.*

PART ONE: SYSTEMS THINKING

STORIES TO PONDER

Story #1 - Chicken Little

You may remember the story of Chicken Little. It goes like this. Chicken Little was minding his own business in the farmyard. He happened to walk under an oak tree and an acorn fell on his head. Chicken Little then panicked and decided that the "sky is falling!!!" Chicken Little then began to run around to all the other farm animals, interrupting what they were doing, and insisted that he be heard concerning this catastrophe. Chicken Little continued to be hysteric and would not listen to others. Chicken Little insisted that the sky was falling and campaigned to shove his idea down everyone's throat. No one in the farmyard could talk to Chicken Little, but Chicken Little could talk to them. Not listening to others and with no regard to others views, Chicken Little continued to recruit everyone into the SKY IS FALLING MOVEMENT.

Who cares about the people that are referred to as chickens with their head cut off. A chicken without a head can't talk. The Chicken Littles in an organization do a great deal of damage. The Chicken Littles in organizations generate rival explanations. Rival explanations are a result of different patterns of thought in conjunction with our method of understanding (usually movement and/or school of thought); permit a different number of alternative explanations that are unfounded in science understanding. Chicken Little did not take time to collect his thoughts and structure his understanding. Chicken Little reacted to a feeling that subjectively factualized the event into hysteria about the sky is falling. Chicken Little failed to investigate the situation and list the facts of the matter. As a result of emotion driving the situation, feelings (availability error) factualized his situation.

There are so many people like Chicken Little that are frustrating others with their lack of knowledge. Chicken Little factualized with his feelings. It was obvious to Chicken Little that the gases in our atmosphere had solidified into matter and was breaking apart before our very own eyes. When we factualize an event without the use of an objective measure we begin to believe in weird things. We begin to believe in superstitious things that are absolutely absurd. We become superstitious, because we did not take the time to do an objective analysis and test our hypothesis.

"Great minds have purposes, others have wishes. Little minds are tamed and subdued by misfortune, but great minds rise above them."
~ Washington Irving

Analyzing Mr. Irving's statement helps us to understand what went wrong with Chicken Little. There was no purpose with Chicken Little rather a subdued mind that resulted in hysteria. We see what happens to our minds when we factualize with our feelings. Purpose is defining the facts in our life. Misfortunes and wishes are only ideas brought about when we allow our feelings to dictate our circumstances and goals. We must do the right thing first (listing the facts) and our appropriate feelings will follow.

Story # 2: Cargo Cult Culture

While reading Richard Feynman's book, "The Pleasure of Finding Things Out" I read an interesting illustration of faulty reasoning. Some of us may have read or studied this in Anthropology or other books. During World War II, in the Solomon Islands, the natives did not understand airplanes, which came down during the war and brought all kinds of goodies for the soldiers. The natives benefited from the supplies brought to the soldiers. The natives were given food, water, clothes, and other extra supplies that were brought by the airplanes. When the war with Japan ended, the airplanes quit coming to the island. As a result, the natives began an airplane cult. They made artificial landing strips by lighting fires every night along each side of the airfield. This was to imitate the landing lights that they knew brought the airplanes down to the island. The natives also built wooden boxes that looked like control towers and built earphones out of coconuts. They used bamboo for antennas. They even built wooden radar domes and continued to practice aviation as they had seen the American's so eloquently demonstrate for years. All this action was in hopes of luring back the airplanes that brought them the goods. The planes did return one day, but the people in the planes were not soldiers with the goodies. They were scientists that had come to observe the native's activities.

Was the scheduled flight to the Solomon Islands a coincidence or did the activities of the natives work to achieve the goal (bring back the airplanes and get the goodies back)? The natives felt that their actions worked. It obviously brought back the airplanes with the goodies. Their hard work finally paid off? The proof in their activities was the return of an airplane. I hope you can see that the native's application of a school of thought lead them to believe in a false positive. A false positive results when we misidentify a cause and effect relationship (*post hoc*). False positives waste our time, energy, and money (example: a rain dance will end a drought).

The natives were only imitating the action of aviation science, but they are not pursuing the science of aviation. It took a great deal of work to carve and fashion wood in a way that imitated sound aviation practices. However, this activity does not mean we are actually finding something new. The natives mimicked aviation science. They did not discover new ideas or apply an objective measure to verify their results. All the work was not directed to the discovery of new and improved aviation science, rather it was diverted into the practice of a new cult. They are imitating the action. The natives did not verify progress with facts; it was their feeling of achievement that determined a benchmark of their progress. Their belief only strengthened their false positive conclusion.

PART ONE: SYSTEMS THINKING

There is no doubt in the scientific mind that the activities had nothing to do with bringing the airplanes back to the island. The case is closed when we investigate with an objective measure. These tools we use to measure must be calibrated from time to time, but true progress is achieved when we remove the rival explanations and replace it with provincial agreement based on an objective measure.

Story #3 - On a Texas Farm

Sometime back a group of people were imported to work on a Texas farm. These people had come from a small village where motor vehicles were still largely unknown. One day these workers were riding in the back of a speeding truck, driven by a Texas farmer going to a different work location on the farm. While the truck was still moving, the workers traveling in the truck thought they came to the place where they should get off. Without giving it thought, they simply stepped off the back of the speeding truck. Fortunately, it was a soft dirt farm road, not a paved highway, but even then the results of their method of disembarking were remarkable. They went bounding, spinning, sliding, and cart wheeling along the dusty rode for quite a distance before gravity and friction working together finally brought them to an astounding halt. None of the workers were seriously injured. In fact, by the time the terrified driver got back to them they were laughing uproariously about the whole thing. The truck driver in explaining the incident later put the blame on their never having ridden in trucks before. The truck driver's answer is an example of an availability error. Remember, an availability error is nothing more than a strong disposition to make judgments or evaluations in light of the first available idea that comes to mind.

Well the truck driver presented an obvious answer, but not necessarily the right one. The amazing circus tumbling act on this Texas farm road had been caused by ignorance of a natural law and understood by physicist around the world. A law that operates the same weather a truck, a boat, an airplane, or any moving body is involved. Sir Isaac Newton gave us the law and it goes like this: "A body in motion tends to remain in motion until acted upon by an outside force." When the workers stepped off the back of the truck they were going the same speed as the truck itself and sharing horizontal velocity in this frame of reference. The outside force was gravity, which pulled them down to the road still traveling at the same speed and ... well you get the idea. They had been hurt, confused, frightened, and turned upside down because of their ignorance of the laws of physics. They could have been killed!

Just as with the example of the workers, all over the world there are millions of people who are being hurt, confused, frightened and whose lives are turned upside down because they don't understand which laws of science is appropriate for the basis of successful outcomes. People will nod their heads and say "yes that's certainly true" and then go their way and never realize, for the most part, how close they came to truth so great and all enveloping that their every thought and action is effected by it. I am sure that you find it remarkable that a majority of the people have to learn things the hard way, generation after generation. It's only natural to think that if a great discovery were made in a particular generation all the succeeding generations would know about it and utilize it for their own good. But to a large extent such is not the case. This is true with inventions and discoveries, which obviously affect our lives, but it is frequently not true when it comes to the great laws, which determine the successful outcomes of our individual destinies.

As it is with the Texas farm illustration, there is an obvious answer but not necessarily the right one. Knowledge of Newton's law of motion would have prevented the workers from their unconventional disembarkment from the moving vehicle. When we use further investigation, we can determine that a system of physical laws was at work that is world renown. It is obvious that a block of steel will not float. All one has to do is experiment for themselves. Take a large block of solid steel and put it in the water. It sinks and does not float. Well, wood floats! So what would possess the United States Navy to build big boats out of steel? We just tested steel to determine if it would make a good material for floating. This is how sound science can make a difference. When we investigate and test we encounter new and wonderful ideas. What separated Sherlock Holmes from his contemporaries was his patient ability to thoroughly investigate beyond the obvious. The fictitious detective never *missed a detection* that other detectives did. Never be satisfied with a surface observation when explaining outcomes.

If all this is true about science structuring our understanding, then why do things go wrong? The axioms of science are not statements of facts. They are the rules, which single out the classes of problems to which they apply. We must investigate to determine how we are to proceed in the theoretical consideration of any problem. When we apply the rules, an objective measure must be identified and incorporated in the measurement process. An axiomatic system that classes problems is worthless in authentication of results without an objective measure. Just as with the illustration of Cargo Cult Culture, managers mimic a science. There have been many studies done in which people make observations and they make lists and they do statistics, but this alone does not become established science or established understanding. They are merely an imitative form of science like the South Sea Islanders making airfields. Learn from science that you must doubt the experts that talk in *schools of thought or movement*.

Second Model – Follower Readiness

Leadership and employee performance is a complex affair. A great deal of effort has been devoted to discover what makes an enterprise organization effective. Most of the studies have been working conditions and general psychological patterns leaders approach with respect to followers in the organization. Many organizations spend a great deal of time and money evaluating employees. No doubt about it, psychology is here to stay.

PART ONE: SYSTEMS THINKING

When asked, many leaders and employees of the organization can tell you what personality type they are (A or B). During my doctoral studies, all candidates were required to take three courses titled "Leadership and Organizational Behavior I, II, and III." Doctoral candidates learned how to administer multiple intelligence tests, how to test for personalities most dominant in a person, how to test for culture influences on behavior, and many other tools to understand a person's psyche. One of the many psychologists we studied was the legendary Stanford psychologist, Lewis Terman. He helped hundreds of gifted children and showed America that it's okay to be smart.

Terman used IQ tests to qualify youngsters for his genius study, now the longest-running survey in history. In Terman's own writings, his ardent promotion of the gifted few was grounded in an elitist ideology. Especially in the early years of his career, he was a proponent of eugenics; a social movement aiming to improve the human "breed" by perpetuating certain allegedly inherited traits and eliminating others. IQ scores would dictate not only what kind of education a person received but what work he or she could get. The most important and rewarding jobs in **business** and government would go to the brightest citizens. Terman grouped **businessmen** and surrealists together. While championing the intelligent, he pushed for the forced sterilization of thousands of "feebleminded" Americans. Later in life, Terman backed away from eugenics, but he never publicly recanted his beliefs.

There are other psychologists that have influenced organizations with respect to performance evaluation of others. Many management/leadership books that have been written have borrowed the theories and language of these most noted social scientists and psychologists. So a brief review of these psychological *schools of thought* is necessary to better understand the many psychological concepts that people value in the organization.

Freud's form of psychology is called analytical psychology, and his most important discovery was the unconscious mind. His theories are based on the belief that feelings, thoughts, and emotions that are too difficult to deal with consciously are stored in the unconscious by one of many defenses. The goal of therapy is to get in touch with the repressed material through a process called "free association" as well as through dream interpretation. This therapy is used in order to free the person of unconscious thoughts and feelings that may have adversely affected behavior.

Ivan Petrovich Pavlov opened the way for new advances in theoretical and practical medicine. He experimented and showed that the nervous system played the dominant part in regulating the digestive process. This discovery became the basis of modern physiology of digestion. Pavlov made known the results of his research in this field, which is of great importance in practical medicine. Pavlov's research into the physiology of digestion led him to create a science of conditioned reflexes. A series of experiments, using food as stimuli distanced from animals, caused Pavlov to reject the *subjective* interpretation of psychic salivary secretion. Sechenov's hypothesis was based on a psychic activity of a reflex nature, not necessarily permanent but a temporary or conditioned one. This discovery of the function of conditioned reflexes made it possible to study all psychic activity *objectively*, instead of resorting to *subjective* methods. Pavlov showed others that it was now possible to investigate by experimental means the most complex interrelations between an organism and its external environment. His work was more *scientific* than *school of thought*, but often his scientific discoveries are not taught by educators of psychology and are presented as a *school of thought*. He received a Nobel Prize for his work.

Behavioral psychology was the next step in the evolution of psychology and was developed by B.F. Skinner. The fundamental belief of this *school of thought* is that every human being consists of particular behavior patterns. When a particular behavior is not desired, the idea is to inhibit that behavior through a process called "operant conditioning." This process consists of removing the unwanted behavior by giving negative feedback whenever that behavior is exhibited. Eventually, through negative and positive reward, the person learns to cease unwanted behavior. In essence, you get the behavior you reward.

The next *school of thought* was founded and developed by Carl Rogers and Abraham Maslow. This humanistic psychology, developed out of a response to the view of the human being as more than just unconscious desires and conditional behavior, as analytical and behavioral psychologist proposed. The common theme with these guys is that each person comes into the world with a desire to self-actualize ones potentials as human beings. Many of us are familiar with Maslow's hierarchy of needs that has been applied to all areas of life, from organizational management to self-fulfillment.

There is a predominant school of thought that has developed from the proceeding ideas concerning human behavior. Carl Jung, a contemporary of Freud, broke from the collective unconscious. Through Jung's use of symbols and his extensive explorations into the philosophies and religions of the East, he found that there are collective symbols, archetypes, and spent most of his life working with clients through the application of particular archetypes into their lives. Jung is considered to be one of the first applicators of transpersonal philosophy/transpersonal psychology. Transpersonal psychology goes one step beyond by incorporating the idea that there is more to a person than what can be seen, felt, or experienced on a conscious or unconscious level.

There is more to psychology than just these ideas, but these are the more predominant *schools of thought* in our society. These schools of thought are convoluted and lack parsimony. All this need for self-identification, self-actualization, and self-association (in touch with our feelings) is an absolute myth. How does all this foster development with our co-workers, families, and friends? To apply these theories of behavior requires years of education in the esoteric language of psychology. You would also need to become very familiar with the psychologist's

PART ONE: SYSTEMS THINKING

acronym zone (REM, ESP, etc.). I have always asked the question, "Why do we get so deep in the practice of such complicated psychological exercises?" Leaders who are heroes remove the psychological schools of thought. Heroes interact and evaluate the nature of people according to the next model introduced in this book. This model is called "Follower Readiness."

This may be a familiar picture or model to you. I have modified it to help us understand more about our readiness level to follow leaders and follow their ideas. This model is a guide to watch what people do and listen to what they say. However, we should pay more attention to what people are doing rather than focusing only on what people are saying. Actions speak loader than words. So, I recommend that we listen to what people say, but more importantly, watch what people do.

Let us look at the model in the figure and think about our willingness to follow leaders and our leader's willingness to participate in their own leadership practices. This model will also serve as a tool to identify our relationship with others as well as make decisions to participate in the ideas and practices of others.

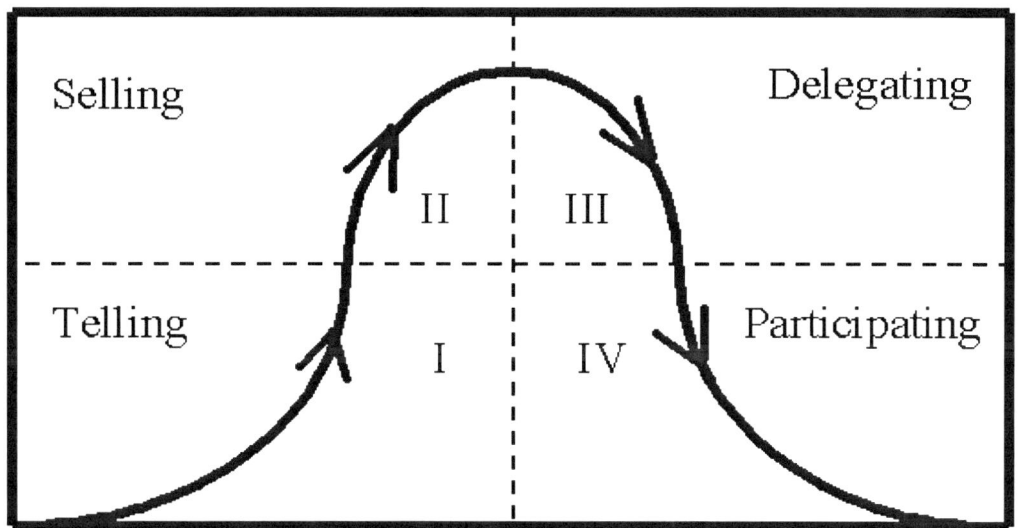

Quadrant 1: Telling

These four quadrants represent stages in the growth development of our lives. Quadrant one is the telling stage of our development. Just as it is when we have little children, adults must tell toddlers not to touch the hot stove. We tell children not to go out in the street and not to get in front of a moving automobile.

When a new employee comes to an organization, we TELL them that this is how we do things in our organization. The new employee is usually TOLD by others, who have been working for the organization, how to do things as well as TOLD what the expectations are. Most relationships begin with the telling stage. When we meet people for the first time we tell them our name and tell them something about ourselves.

Quadrant 2: Selling

The next stage of development as people grow to follower readiness is to be SOLD on the concepts that they have been TOLD to do. Just as children have been TOLD not to touch the hot stove, they begin to follow the idea without direct experience of feeling the burns as a result of not following what they are told. They are SOLD on the concepts of not touching the hot stove. As adults, we do not have to remind the child/teenager, that hot stoves can burn you. They are SOLD on the concepts of practicing safety in the kitchen without feeling the consequences of skin touching the hot stove. This is one of the differences in intercession and interfering. We do not have to directly experience everything that is commonly known to cause damage to ourselves. The experience is taught to others vicariously to prevent damage to a child. We are not interfering with the child's experience to learn new things. This will be discussed more in the statistics section concerning tampering with processes.

Even with people in any organization, after they are TOLD what to do, they may grow to the understanding of why it is important to follow procedures and certain processes. These people are SOLD on these various concepts TOLD to them by leaders in the organization. Employees or members of a family that are in this stage of readiness level will not have to be TOLD or reminded that this is what they are suppose to do. They begin to follow concepts without question.

Quadrant 3: Delegating

The next stage of development as people grow in their follower readiness is their ability to be delegated responsibilities. Just as children have been TOLD/SOLD not to touch the hot stove, they begin to follow the idea without direct experience of feeling the burns as a result of not following what they are told. They are SOLD on the responsibilities parents told them to do. Now the child can be delegated to act as the parent to turn off the stove. These concepts of responsibilities are DELEGATED to the child. The child begins to share in the responsibilities of sound safety processes concerning a hot stove. As parents, we can trust our children to be in our homes making parental decisions in our absence. When a child is approached by others to do something wrong such as illegal drug use, in the parent's absence the child will say "No!"

In the business organization, people who are DELEGATED responsibility, begin performing many of the tasks that they were TOLD/SOLD by their leaders/managers. Once we demonstrate that we are SOLD on the concepts, TOLD to us, we can now be trusted to have leaders delegate to us new opportunities. We are given the power and authority to act as the leaders we follow. We have the readiness level to act alone in the same manner as our leader.

Quadrant 4: Participating

The next stage of development as people grow in their follower readiness is PARTICIPATION. Just as children grow up and parents continue to delegate responsibilities, the child becomes a young adult and starts to participate with the parents. The parents of the child will name one of the children as executor of the estate and conversations between child and parents are more of a participatory nature. They all share in the decision making process of the family. The adult child participates in decisions concerning the elderly mother living at home or moving to assisted care living. The parents are asking the adult child to share in their decisions and want to hear the ideas of the young adult.

In the organization, people who are participating in the decisions of the organization are the executive officers, board members, and principle owners. These people share and participate in next year's business plans. People who participate are not generally interested with the opinions of those who are in the telling and selling stage of follower readiness.

Summary of Follower Readiness

If you like what you have been TOLD (good or bad) eventually you become SOLD on the concepts. If you TELL a child they will amount to nothing, and if they become SOLD on that concept, then you have a child that has become convinced that they will amount to nothing and will PARTICIPATE in becoming nothing. This model serves as the ultimate test whether to follow anyone who champions an idea, cause, or process. It helps people determine whom they should follow and who are the real leaders. It is real simple, watch to see if they are willing to PARTICIPATE in their own ideas and plans for others.

Example: Abraham Lincoln once said, "I know no man that is for the institution of slavery that is willing to become a slave themselves."

This statement by Abraham Lincoln is simple but very direct. In summary, the statement asks the question, are you willing to participate in your own ideas? John Kennedy made a similar statement, but in the opposite direction; "Ask not what your country can do for you, ask what you can do for your country." This statement directs the participation in the other direction. Am I asking my country to have the willingness to give to me, but I do not have willingness to give to my country? In essence, I am asking others to do something for me that I am not willing to do for myself or others. The intent to dictate to others things that we are unwilling to do ourselves is a sign of a ZERO not a HERO.

When John Cade (Psycho-Pharmacologist) investigated lithium carbonate for its effectiveness as an antimanic agent, he tested animals with lithium urate. Cade determined with confidence that he had found a good antimanic agent. He was so confident in his process of analysis that he administered the drug on himself first before taking the drug to others. He did not tell others that they had to use his drug; rather he participated in his own practice before imposing his beliefs on others. Many other medical researchers have also demonstrated their own willingness to follow their own ideas and participate in the analysis in such a manner as John Cade did. If a drug company advocates that a drug is working well, then how often is this drug administered to family members and used by the developers? If we really think the institution of slavery is a great idea, then why are the advocates not willing to participate and become slaves on their own plantations? History has documented the actions of the slavery advocates, not once were any advocates willing to become slaves themselves and serve others. They only wanted to be served, not serve others. If a leader tells you to work in this nuclear reactor and speaks to you with confidence that it is safe for you, then they should be willing to work along side with you and the other workers.

This model also explains why an organization follows processes that produce unexpected outcomes that create failure. Leaders and managers that are not participating often tell, sell, and delegate unverified results (bad ideas). So the downside of this model demonstrates why people will follow unverified results, first by telling unverified results, then sold on unverified results, and then delegate to others unverified results. This is how an organization becomes a Cargo Cult Culture.

Even evil and immoral leaders such as Hitler knew how to motivate people to a high follower readiness level. This model illustrates why people are willing to follow evil. During the Nuremberg trials, people who were running from justice simply used the model to explain that they were told to do monstrosities. They acted like they never participated in any atrocity. People whose follower readiness remained in the telling stage of development feel justified that they only did what they were told to do. These people think that remaining in the telling stage is safe and frees them of responsibilities. Followers of evil, generally blame the person doing the telling. They rarely are willing to take responsibility for following what they were told to do. But the people on trial have actions documented that demonstrated they were sold on these concepts and were delegated to carry out inhuman acts for their leaders. As a result of being told what to do, these people act as the victim and not the perpetrator. The truth is that the people who were on trial participated in something evil. When we are told to do something, we need to stop and *tell* ourselves, am I treating others in the same way I would want to be treated? We need to tell ourselves statements that will move us as well as others to a follower readiness that will foster development in the direction of good rather than bad deeds. We need to strive to follow good ideas and not bad ones. Model two is a practical way to identify the learning levels that occur over time in an organization for good or bad. But how do we determine what is good and bad so we will know our direction of follower readiness will foster development?

Third Model − Intent

Self-Interested or Other Oriented?

An investigation of business ethics starts with the identification of two kinds of people, Zeros or Heroes. A hero person loves people and uses things. A zero person loves things and uses people. Here is a model to determine intent. When leaders use people to fulfill love for things, we all loose including the leader. Self-interested people never think about what is common knowledge and beneficial to others during a decision making process. Zero people in general are not other oriented, heroes are.

Loves People ⬅========= **TARGETED INTENT** ============➡ *Uses People*
Uses Things   *Loves Things*

For a clearer understanding of leadership, model three distinguishes between the concept of leadership and the leader role of a manager. Many people of an organization have experienced a zero leader who is in the role of a manger. Model three is not an explanation of people who unfortunately have neurological damage, chemical imbalances, or suffer from mental diseases. Model three illuminates the difference between character ethic and character flaws that are a result of an individual's targeted intent. Managers, teachers, and many employees in organizations are not qualified to diagnose physical mental illnesses. People must be willing to submit themselves to a battery of tests in a clinic that specializes in the recognition of chemical imbalances. When dealing with people who are questionable concerning their behavior, people must not jump to conclusions. However, watch what people do. If it appears that they are a self-centered/self interested person, then they are more often looked upon by the organization as a zero person. Unless a doctor/physician note can be produced explaining the behavior disorder, people in the organization will most often rule that the self-centered/self interested person has character flaws.

One important aspect that is generally missed when zero people with character flaws decide to target acceptable behavior is the misconception that zero people often have concerning the idea of forgiveness. Forgiveness does not mean forgetting. Forgiveness is a process that can and will be monitored over time. Forgiveness involves the three Rs. The three Rs are Repent, Repeat-not, and most important Repair. Repent means to have a true change of mind and heart, Repeat-not is the historical actions that others can see with changed actions (a person can be counted on to not repeat the problem). Then a Repair of the relationship is met with an agreeable compensation that will foster development. These three steps of forgiveness are very important when fixing troubled relationships. If there is an active contribution that benefits the individual as well as others in the relationship, then others in the relationship should not abandon the individual who is in active repair.

Generally relationships that have gone for the worse are due to unshared values. When zero people begin to act like heroes everyone will witness the change; however, when building back the relationship it is important that all can count on sharing values. Sharing values is very important to building relationships. Contrary to what has been told by so called experts of relationships concerning relationships that end in a separation, the real reasons relationships fail or are successful is due to shared values. Even though some social engineers theorize that divorce is a result of economic issues, or the couple was too young to be married, or incompatible; the real reason people separate is due to shared values. If having money could have saved the marriage, then why do rich movie stars get a divorce? If marring too young is the issue, well I have several friends who married the day after high school graduation. They were both teenagers, no college completed, and no income. But, they are still in their marriage 30 years later. If we think about all the reasons people give for getting a divorce, you will understand that it comes down to not having shared values. Even if a married couple both do drugs and never take care of the children, they will stay together because they share values. When one of the parents decides to stop doing drugs, and the other person in the relationship continues to do so, then the relationship is in jeopardy to disseminate. The relationship is no longer sharing values.

So a hero is a person who loves people and uses things. As a result for their love for people, they protect the organizations relationships with shared values. A hero does not use people for the love of things. When we use people to fulfill our love of things, we become selfish and self-serving. A hero is a person that will not allow any organization or enterprise to become self-serving. Knowing this, what can we say about the present and past movements of the sixties? Take a close look at the feminist movement that had begun to grow and develop during the 1960s. Many women did benefit, but has it become a self-serving organization during future decades? Is the majority of the activity in the organization directed toward politically positioning the cause and creating the illusion of progress to help others? What are the facts or are we factualizing with feelings of hate for others? When people in an organization are other oriented and loving people, and not loving things, everyone benefits and becomes heroes. When organizations are incapable of bringing back customers to corporate relationships, it is usually because zero people of the organization do not take an interest in repairing broken relationships. Of the three Rs, repairing is the most important and the most difficult to achieve. If our customer is of the self-interested type, we need to burn the bridges in the relationship. Anytime an organization discovers that people within the organization or customers are incapable of sharing values, then consideration must be taken to terminate the zero relationships and nurture the hero relationships that have shared values with the organization. Hero people don't need zero people as stakeholders of the organization.

Summary Conclusions to the 3 Models

John Coffey, a fictitious character in the book and movie "The Green Mile" was the hero. He exemplifies a person that wanted to repair bad outcomes. Sometimes it was too late to "Take it Back." He was part of the solution and was not the instigator of the problem. He was a good person who understood while others "just didn't get it." But John Coffey never held this against anyone. The book as well as the movie makes one think of all the heroes that are so misunderstood in our world and often go unrecognized. It is a true miracle that there are more good people in this world than bad people. People, who are concerned for others, are usually paying more attention to justice than they are compelled to do when bad situations arise. Bad people need good people to fulfill their objective, but good people don't need bad people to fulfill their objective. John Coffey talked about how bad people will use the love that good people have for each other against them. Bad people force others into a situation that removes alternate decisions. Bad people want to remove a person's freedom to choose.

The models serve to illuminate if shared values exist in a relationship. If everyone in the organization values conceptualization with *science*, but a small fraction of people have to be *told* to quit *participating* in a *movement* conceptualization, subsequently everyone in the organization is not sharing values.

Heroes oppose the idea of reaching an understanding with school of thought or movement strategies and tactics. Heroes are never seen judging others subjectively. Heroes participate in their own ideas. Heroes continue to target their intent to consistently practice the science, are participators, and love people. Heroes emphasize that science is the action of starting with a curiosity to investigate the truth and continually practice being informed rather than feeling informed.

These models also illuminate zeroes that are promoting evil. Zero people that lure children into their car to kill them follow these models. They tell children and sell them on what appears to be a good idea. These perpetrators will say "My doggie is lost will you help me find my dog?" They are selling the child on the value of participating in what appears to be a good act. Children who are instructed to challenge the sincereness of the perpetrator will simply say, "The appropriate thing to do is to ask for my parents' participation in this endeavor."

People's reactionary experience is illustrated with three basic stories to ponder. Managers that lack real experience with leading people will mimic processes and then defend their uncreative behavior. These are the "fake it until you make it" managers. Heroes intently listen to other's experiences and determine the validity of the experience. People can pretend to be who they are not, but not always. A person can *tell* people they are a surgeon. But probing deeper, people can determine the validity of the statements with questions concerning the real experience of performing surgery once this person is *delegated* the task to perform. It is important that we share with others our experiences with how a process works better or worse. People who have had real experience can share the real results. As others listen to the experience of making a home repair or any other process, others can perform the action of the person sharing the experience and can validate with the repeated experience. When people begin to test another person's experience, then the people who have *participated* can compare results. The results will be similar if people continue to probe into the shared knowledge of the experience. The stories to ponder presented in this chapter 1) Chicken Little, 2) Cargo Cult Culture, and 3) the Texas Farm; can assist in understanding the shared experience.

Chicken Little – Shared experience was not founded in what really happened. As a result Chicken Little factualized with feelings. Chicken Little felt informed but did not use science as the act of being informed.

Cargo Cult Culture – The people are sharing their reality (experience), but the experience is only mimicking others who fostered development based on reality.

Texas Farm- The shared experience was founded in what really happened but had an inadequate analysis of the cause and effect.

When people conceptualize with science, people begin to actively share values and become participants in the experience. In summary, heroes understand that improvements are never made with school of thought and movement reasoning. These armchair pseudo-scholastic zeroes talk the talk but rarely walk the walk. The models are not the panacea to everyone's problems and are not representations of how to fix relationships nor do they prevent bad outcomes in business practices. The models should not be used during a professional evaluation of people in a business enterprise. There is nothing wrong mentally with a person who has to be told to do something. These models illuminate the conceptualization of how people in the organization generally differentiate heroes that are leaders and zeroes that act as a leader in a management role.

Terminology and Why Study Science Management

After my eight-grade year of school, I took Introductory to Physical Science during the summer. This was a suggestion of my Mom's to take the class in order to move forward with high school credits before my freshman year of High School. This class consisted of students from different high schools as well as different grade levels (Freshmen, Sophomores, Juniors and Seniors). During our first experiment, the teacher instructed the students that we will need water for this experiment and we will need to heat the water with a Bunsen burner. He also instructed the students that we needed to get cold water because cold water reaches its boiling temperature faster than warm or hot water. Some students objected and said that hot water reaches the boiling point faster than cold. As the debate continued between those students who insisted hot water would boil faster than cold and vice versa (rival explanations), the teacher said that the laws of thermodynamics states that heat transfers from hot to cold faster than hot to hot. The teacher also reiterated that he had a Masters Degree in Physics and he was the authority concerning the thermodynamics of water.

When the class was finished for that day, I asked the teacher if I could stay after class and test which hypothesis was correct. Does cold water reach a boiling point quicker than warm water? I also respectfully requested that my teacher stay and work with me. My teacher reminded me that his hypothesis was already tested. He also informed me that it would be a waste of time to perform an experiment and nobody would be staying after school hours to do experiments. The next day, we had extra time in class to study, catch up on homework, or study for the test coming up. I decided to use this time to test whether cold or hot water reaches the boiling point quicker.

I took two similar beakers from my laboratory desk and went to the rest room to fill equal amounts of water in the separate beakers. One beaker I labeled warm water beaker and the other cold-water beaker. I then filled the beaker labeled cold water with cold water from the bathroom faucet. I also filled the beaker marked warm water with warm water from the warm water faucet. I then turned on the hot plate so the temperature of the hot plate used to heat the water would be at the same temperature for each beaker. I used equal thermometers to measure and record the initial temperatures of the water. I then recorded the time for cold water to reach a boiling point and then recorded the time it took for warm water to reach a boiling point. To everyone's surprise, warm water comes to a boil quicker than cold water. My teacher couldn't believe it. He insisted that my experiment was rigged. I asked him to repeat the experiment with me. We repeated the experiment ten times changing thermometers, beakers, and hot plats; only to record data that verified the results of my initial experiment. Unless proven otherwise, cold water does not reach a boiling point quicker than hot water. Afterward, it was very disappointing that the teacher as well as students continued to insist that cold water when heated reaches the boiling point quicker than warm.

Moral to the Experience: In spite of the evidence demonstrated during experimentation, some people are unwilling to abandon their misapplication of a true scientific concept. The concept that heat will travel faster from a location of high heat concentration to a location of lower heat concentration (colder in temperature) may not have an appropriate application. A brief look into thermodynamics helps to determine why there are rival explanations.

Thermodynamics is the study of the conversion of energy between heat and other forms, mechanical in particular. There are many processes that convert energy from one form to another. For example burning wood converts chemical energy (in the wood) to heat; turning a hydroelectric generator converts the kinetic (motion) energy of the water into electrical energy. There are two laws that can be reviewed to help understand processes like these: The first law of thermodynamics says that energy is conserved, it is neither created nor destroyed but can change form. The second law of thermodynamics says that systems always tend to states of greater disorder -- this is another way to say that the entropy always increases. In terms of energy conversions this means that they can never be 100% efficient. Some portion of the energy involved in a conversion will inevitably be lost to the surroundings as heat.

With respect to this experiment performed with water, when applying the laws of thermodynamics it is necessary to begin with the definition of what is a "system". In the confines of thermodynamics, a system is any region completely enclosed within a defined boundary. Everything outside the system is then defined as the surroundings. Although it is possible to speak of the subject matter of thermodynamics in a general sense, the establishment of analytical relationships among heat, work, and thermodynamic properties requires a relationship be established to a particular system. This includes distinguishing between properties of material within a system and properties of its surroundings. In accordance with their definition, thermodynamic properties apply to systems which must contain a very large number of ultimate particles. Other than this there are no fundamental restrictions on the definition of a system. The boundary may be either rigid or movable. It can be completely impermeable or it can allow energy or mass to be transported through it. In any given situation a system may be defined in several ways; although with some definitions the computations to be performed are quite simple, with others they are difficult or even impossible.

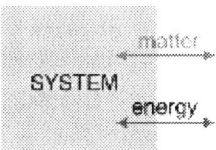

SURROUNDINGS An open system is one where both matter and energy can freely cross from the system to the surroundings and back. Example is an open test tube.

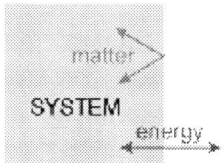

SURROUNDINGS A closed system is one where energy can cross the boundary, but matter cannot. Example is a sealed test tube.

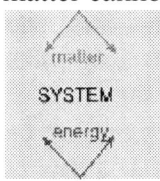

SURROUNDINGS An isolated system is one where neither matter nor energy can cross between the system and the surroundings. At present, scientists believe the universe itself is an isolated system (as there are no surroundings to exchange matter or energy with).

It is often impossible by means of thermodynamic methods alone to make heat transfer calculations if a system is defined so that both heat transfer and diffusional mass transfer occur simultaneously through the same area on the boundary of the system. For processes in which mass transfer takes place only by bulk stream flow this problem can be avoided easily by a proper definition of the system. In a flow process of this type the system is defined so that it is enclosed by moveable boundaries with no stream flows across them. Heat transfer then always occurs across a boundary not crossed by mass. So it becomes apparent that thermodynamics only applies to irreversible processes with respect to a systems definition. The second law of thermodynamics is not an absolute law, but is a statistical law.

Science History

More often, students are taught what scientists have found, not necessarily the methodology. A review of science history better illustrates the four aspects of science: 1) curiosity, 2) an objective experimental method, 3) intense investigation, and 4) testing (verifying results with an objective measurement) summarizes the essence of what science is.

Prior to the Renaissance, science was concerned only with the observations. What you see is what you get. Aristotle was a very careful observer of nature and a brilliant theorizer and so were many of his contemporaries as well as scholars prior to Aristotle's era. The fact that Aristotle was considered such an authority most likely impeded rather than help scientific progress. Progress in science did evolve during this time but beliefs concerning many subjects were based on what you were *told* by a so-called authority, rather than what was observed. This is the crucial difference. This difference is our connection to the Renaissance. During the Renaissance, knowledge was based on perception and this perception must be *tested* to make sure it is clear and distinct. So the scientist added steps to the scientific method. Testing of one's observations was a crucial step added to the scientific method (during the Renaissance); because it was discovered by many Renaissance scientist, that our observations may trick us. As a result, we fail to have an accurate explanation of an observed phenomenon. Renaissance scientist began to incorporate an objective method to test observations, so science has its true birth during the Renaissance. Thus, science developed and included a method that verified observations objectively rather than subjectively. Think about it. If you didn't know that the Sun was stationary relative to the Earth and that the Earth revolved around the Sun, what would your senses tell you? As you observe the time the Sun rises and until it sets, you see the Sun moving across the sky. There is no sensation of the Earth turning on its axis or moving in orbit around the Sun. So why question something that seems to be so apparent and self-evident?

As with many branches of science prior to the Renaissance, thermodynamics had its starting point in the subjective impression of people. These subjective impressions were the concepts of hot and cold. Prior to incorporating an objective measure, an old man could sit in a tub of very hot water and state that this feels great. If the old man were in his eighties, nerve endings are not as sensitive as it would be to an 18-month-old baby. The temperature of the water may be soothing the pain of the eighty year old's arthritic, but the temperature of the water may be uncomfortable to the young child's skin because of the more sensitive nerve endings. So what happens when the child joins the old man in the water? A difference of opinion arises between the one with a lower sensitivity feeling and one who has over sensitive feelings. How do we know who's opinion should be acted upon? What temperature is best for which age group? If you saw people in a hot tub, would you test the water first before submerging yourself? In order to make a decision; an objective method must be presented when comparing temperatures. When a column of mercury is substituted for the subjective estimate of the degree of warmth, we have facts that become a reliable measurement. Anyone who has performed experiments knows that often our objective measurements do not always confirm our subjective intuition. This is because our subjective intuition is often affected by influences of psychological or physiological factors.

So what has all this got to do with science management? Many of the new enterprise organizations, as well as the old enterprise organizations have began the science rhetoric and claim to know science (as did my teacher), but are not managing scientifically. We hear the words "Quantum Leap", "Paradigm", "Paradigm Shift"

PART ONE: SYSTEMS THINKING

"Systems Thinking", and many other words stolen from the science community. Many of the people using such terminology are obviously just like the scarecrow in the Wizard of OZ, as illustrated on page 5. The scarecrow's attempt to quote the Pythagorean Theorem sounded intelligent, but was incorrect. Others have used science terms to truly bring enterprising organizations closer to science management. It is necessary to understand these terms and system concepts, because these ideas are becoming increasingly used in business books as well as businesses all over the world. I have read hundreds of books concerning business, math, and science. Here is a starting list of books that I have found to be the most useful to me as well as to others endeavoring in any human enterprise. These books have assisted many people in a wide variety of organizations in the development of becoming better systems thinkers, better managers, and a better person. Heroes practice what these books teach.

The 7 Habits of Highly Effective People
by Stephen Covey

Stephen Covey discusses why techniques for quick fixes are not effective and that life patterns of habits foster long term results. Of the seven habits, habits 1, 2, and 3 are character habits that will move one toward introspection into one's self. Habits 4, 5, 6, and 7 are the outward habits to others expressing one's character ethic. These habits must be learned in this order. A habit is based on a principle that one internalizes. Internalizing means to know what to do and requires knowledge, skills, and attitudes. If a person lacks knowledge and lacks the skills, then a habit cannot be formed.

Habit 1 - Be Proactive

Proactive means choosing your own response. This is the habit of our life integrating one's walk the talk. This means taking responsibility for your own life. Your behavior becomes a product of your own decisions based on values, not feelings.

Habit 2 - Begin with the End in Mind

This habit suggests that the individual writes a mission statement, philosophy, and value system. Don't be tied to your past history, draw on your own consciousness. This is the leadership habit that sets the criteria of our purpose in life.

Habit 3 - Put First Things First

This is the management habit. When we put first things first, we can manage ourselves. Covey explains the difference in IMPORTANT and URGENT in this section. Important means habit 2 and taking the time for direction. Urgent means it is pressing on you and even though it may be a waste of time, we need to attach our mission statement to the situation to check the alignment of our goals.

The next four habits concern our "other oriented" behavior toward others. One should be happy of the success of others. If we are truly happy, then you have developed habits 4 through 7.

Habit 4 – Think Win/Win

This is the habit of communicating with others and having a commitment to communications until we agree. Many of our communication problems exist as a result of a flawed paradigm (p. 206). From our character ethic we can build and maintain great relationships. From our relationships flow the agreements that give definition and direction to Win/Win.

Habit 5 – Seek First to Understand, Then to be Understood

This is the habit of collective dialog. We should listen to others first. Once the listener understands, then people can relax. Don't push irrelevant issues, rather be patient and most of all be respectful.

Habit 6 – Synergize

This is the habit of thinking of new and better solutions. We need that internal security system that becomes true to our value system. Balance your courage and your considerations. Maturity is when one realizes interdependency.

Habit 7 – Sharpen the Saw

This habit is tied to a story concerning a man who was so busy sawing wood he did not stop to sharpen his saw. We should make sure in our life that there is harmony with our mission statement. This is accomplished as follows:

- After you learn it, teach it.
- When you agree to teach something to others, you make a commitment to change your role.
- If you want to change people's behavior then change people's pictures of their roles.
- Experience the paradigm shift.
- Your attitude and behavior is a function of your paradigm of how you see the situation.
- It isn't what happened to us that affects our thinking; rather it is our interpretation of the situation.

PART ONE: SYSTEMS THINKING

Concluding Thoughts on Covey:

The issue is not submission to laws or commandments, but rather how we should treat others. Because of Covey's introduction of paradigms many organizational issues could be immediately resolved if people have the ability to recognize flawed paradigms. Heroes recognize flawed paradigms and practice the 7 habits. This is why a hero participates (Follower Readiness-Model #2).

The Fifth Discipline
by Peter M. Senge

When one is trying to make sense of the world, or an organization, an enterprise, or even a small group of people, it helps to think in terms of systems. The modern systems thinkers have identified system archetypes, these archetypes are sort of the building blocks of complex systems. People like Peter Senge, Jay Forrester, and Arie de Geus have led the way in modern thinking about systems. Another systems thinker was one of America's founding fathers, James Madison.

The Fifth Discipline is an excellent place to begin with science management thinking. The tools for systems thinking introduced in the book are especially designed for understanding dynamic complexity. They help in seeing the underlying structures and patterns of behavior that are obscured in the fury of daily events. Dynamic complexity occurs when "cause and effect" are not close in time and space and obvious interventions do not produce expected outcomes. This book explains in detail with excellent examples, why everyone should practice the art of being a learning organization.

Drawing on the Right Side of the Brain
by Betty Edwards

Betty Edwards' book has not only been used by artist in training, but it has become a companion to several business organizations. This book applies much of the most recent developments in brain research that relate to drawing as well as provides information concerning the science of learning. The new insights she brings concerning the use of drawing techniques, accurately describe the paradigm shift that Stephen Covey wrote about in the book *The Seven Habits of Highly Effective People*. Betty Edwards calls these paradigm shifts the "Ah-Ha!" She illustrates that many problems in industry, art, and education can be solved by turning the process or picture drawing up-side-down. I highly recommend that you read this book and work the exercises. This book is an excellent companion to read with *The Fifth Disciple* and *The Seven Habits of Highly Effective People*.

Who's Afraid of Schrodinger's Cat?
An A-Z Guide to All the New Science Ideas You Need to Keep Up with the New Thinking
by Ian Marshall and Danah Zohar

This book contains a collection of mini-essays that are both readable and a useful overview of modern science. This book will help build a better science vocabulary and correct many misconceptions of the use of science terminology. This book is an illuminating and indispensable reference guide for one to become scientifically minded. It will assist to understand the concepts, consequences, and implications of state of the art science.

Out of the Crisis
by W. Edward Deming

Edward Deming, in my opinion, is one of the most misunderstood geniuses of all times in our American enterprise. This book explains the principles of management transformation and how to apply these principles. Deming provides an innovative plan that helps businesses protect investment, ensure future dividends, and provide more jobs by improving products and services. Deming's management philosophy is action oriented. It is important that managers use the science of statistics to define what measurements have meaning to the organization. The most important point of the Deming philosophy of science management is one's ability to understand when processes are being tampered. Organizations must understand the principle of intercession. There is a difference between interfering and intercession. Often people try to intercede, but fail because they identified the wrong problem and interfered with others. Managers rarely intercede; they more often interfere (tamper with processes).

Understanding Statistical Process Control
by Donald J. Wheeler & David S. Chambers

Donald Wheeler and David Chambers are Deming disciples. Their book, Understanding Statistical Process Control, is a way of thinking to make statistical ideas relevant, understandable, and useful. This book covers the fundamental concepts of the control chart, the very heart of the science practice of systems improvement. They cover the right ways and wrong ways of computing control chart limits, as well as explore the myths about control charts. There is an excellent discussion of why three-sigma limits are action limits and include several advanced topics on how to interpret skewness and kurtosis, as well as the effect that variation has upon a balanced system. This book provides the tools needed to investigate and accurately use mathematics to understand systems and their periodic equilibriums.

Innumeracy – *Mathematical Illiteracy and its Consequences*
by John Allen Paulos

All of John Allen Paulos' books are excellent reading material. This is a mathematician that can write. I recommend this book as a starting point to understand why so many people know so little about mathematics. This book presents several case examples that demonstrate people's inability to deal rationally with numbers and the probabilities associated with numbers. Innumeracy results in misinformed governmental policies, inaccurate risk assessments in all types of organizations, poor personal decision-making practices, and why people become superstitious rather than scientific. I have bought this book for many of my friends. It makes a great gift for any occasion.

The Power of Logical Thinking
by Marilyn Vos Savant

Marilyn Vos Savant presents many hard facts about the flaws of reasoning that occur in the practical lives of people. Her book is brilliant and has easy lessons in the art of reasoning and why we need to arm ourselves with the power of logical thinking. She has many examples of how our own reasoning process can work against us and she has examples of how statistics can be misleading. This book also contains a section concerning the fallacies about facts. If you are interested in studying the art of making sound judgments and making the best decisions, this book is the best beginning.

Calculated Risks: *How to Know When Numbers Deceive You*
by Gerd Gigerenzer

Cognitive scientist Gerd Gigerenzer emphasizes the importance of becoming statistical thinkers. His book illustrates that many people have not taken the time to learn statistical thinking. Most people just do not have a good understanding of risk and uncertainty. In order to assess risk, everyone should have basic statistics. He gives real examples of several real documented cases ranging from the risk of an automobile accident to the certainty or uncertainty of some common medical screening tests. Astonishingly, doctors and lawyers don't understand risk any better than anyone else. Gigerenzer reports a study in which doctors were told the results of breast cancer screenings and then were asked to explain the risks of contracting breast cancer to a woman who received a positive result from a screening. The actual risk was small because the test gives many false positives. But nearly every physician in the study overstated the risk. Yet many people will have to make important health decisions based on such information and the interpretation of that information by their doctors. In the tradition of *Innumeracy* by John Allen Paulos, German scientist Gerd Gigerenzer offers his own take on innumeracy. This is an excellent companion book for John Allen Paulos' book as well as Marilyn Vos Savant's book. All three books use concrete examples from the real world. This book will make you think about ever trusting again the words of anyone placed in authority. This book demonstrates that even people who claim to be experts are not qualified to make sound statistical judgments.

These books should be added to everyone's personal library. Before you read another book, you will need to arm yourself with the tools to make sound judgments concerning the content of what you read. Once you begin conceptualizing with the tools of science, you will be able to validate the truth content of all the information you obtain by reading or listening. You will save valuable time and money that had been wasted on principles that will never foster development in an organization. I also suggest reading the books these authors list as their references. Begin the journey to conceptualize with science rather than school of thought or movement. Leave the world of unfounded knowledge and misconceptions and begin to approach the truth. You may not learn what everything is, but you will definitely know what is not the truth. You will be able to recognize the lies, deceit, and fallacies of managers in any organization. If you don't start standing on true facts and knowledge, you will fall for anything.

Science Terminology - Paradigm and Paradigm Shift

The first word and concept to define is *paradigm* and *paradigm shift*. What actually is a paradigm? What actually is a paradigm shift? Stephen Covey's book *The Seven Habits of Highly Effective People* did an excellent job defining these scientific concepts. I studied it intensely during my master degree program as well as my doctoral studies. I have read the book five times. I will also recommend several other books in this section that should be read by every person affiliated with the human enterprise. We will first begin with *The 7 Habits of Highly Effective People* as well as Betty Edward's book *Drawing on the Right Side of the Brain*. I highly recommend that everyone read these books and do the artistic exercises in Betty Edwards's book. I will synthesize the knowledge of the two books to explain why they are important to define paradigms and paradigm shifts. Both authors did an excellent job to move people from school of thought to a higher level of science understanding concerning paradigms.

In science, a paradigm is an example or a model that best describes what we agree to be the real system. It is commonly used among the scientific community to mean a theory or frame of reference. Paradigms assist scientist in the development of a model that is representative of the natural world. Paradigms are also useful in conceptualizing the invisible world such as the mechanics of the atom. If we can make a model of an airplane that is functional, then we should be able to extend the valid results to make it real. Model airplanes were flying long before people actually started to build and fly in real airplanes. Models establish a reference of visualizing something that becomes much bigger. Models can be tested to validate and authenticate real systems.

The word paradigm was first made prominent by the science philosopher Thomas Kuhn in his now classic book *The Structure of Scientific Revolutions*. Thomas Kuhn used the word paradigm to describe the overall framework of the basic assumptions used by scientist as scientist analyze and interpret data brought about by theoretical as well as laboratory experimentation. In the theoretical sciences, a paradigm mathematically models a scientific experiment. Math equations are used to govern variables to produce data to test predictions and assumptions. Modeling is less expensive and is used during trial and error studies. If we take the assumption that a body is moving, it is compelled to do so by the application of some force. This assumption of force and the moving body is couched within the larger paradigm of Newtonian classical mechanics and therefore is assumed that all movements are governed by laws of cause and effect. Cause and effect is an example of a Newtonian paradigm.

Stephen Covey's definition of paradigm is that we should see paradigms as maps.

"We all know that 'the map is not the territory.' A map is simply an explanation of certain aspects of the territory. That's exactly what a paradigm is. It is a theory, an explanation, or model of something else."

Stephen Covey's definition is accurate. His definition describes what a paradigm is to the scientific/business management mind. So according to Covey, our paradigm is simply an explanation of certain aspects of something else.

Thomas Kuhn, explained that within science itself, science knowledge does not always proceed through the gradual accumulation of knowledge. Sometimes this knowledge is not evolutionary, but revolutionary, or a paradigm shift to a very different sort of vision. Kuhn points out in his book that the classical physics of Newton's laws of motion, plus his law of gravity, predicted the movements of the known planets. But, sometime in the middle of the nineteenth century, scientist noticed small discrepancies in the observed orbit of Uranus. This was based on the assumption (the paradigm) that some other body must be exerting a force on Uranus's movements. As a result in 1846 scientist discovered an additional planet Neptune. The overall paradigm of Newtonian science easily absorbed the new discovery. A new scientific fact and discovery was added, but scientific assumptions remained unchanged.

Kuhn demonstrated that scientist cling to their assumptions and paradigms, inspite of the evidence presented in the data that challenges the old paradigm. The new data are generally ignored or explained away as "experimental anomalies," until the evidence for some new perspective becomes overwhelming. Thus in the case of planetary orbit abnormalities, small discrepancies in the orbit of Mercury could not be explained in the same way as similar discrepancies in Uranus's orbit. No new planet was exerting gravitational force on Mercury. The discrepancies could only be explained using a new science. Albert Einstein's new paradigm expressed in his theory of General Relativity made sense of the odd orbit of Mercury. This odd orbit could not be explained with Newtonian physics. Relativity theory represented a paradigm shift. This required scientist to adopt a radically new set of assumptions to understand the new data. Thus the second scientific revolution had begun.

Relativity required scientist to give up their deeply held philosophical schools of thought and many familiar categories of analysis to adopt an entirely new way of viewing the physical world. This is what Betty Edward's book is all about *Drawing On The Right Side of The Brain*. Betty Edward's teaches people how to create professional drawings. She has several examples in her book of students whose drawings were very child like and unprofessional. These adults were embarrassed by their drawings. Betty Edward's developed a technique to improve a person's artistic drawing skills. She has several methods for her student's to become better artist. Her technique is for the artist to view the world from different perspectives. One very effective technique that she uses is to simply take a picture, turn it upside-down, and then have the student's draw the upside-down picture. From this new perspective, the student draws the upside-down picture, after completing the drawing, the student turns their drawing right-side up. To the student's amazement, their drawings are a great improvement. This technique forces the Ah-Ha that every artist experiences when creating.

The "Ah-Ha!" everyone experiences during this process is a paradigm shift. Betty Edwards explains that we can all become better artists if we first start with turning the picture we are attempting to draw, upside-down. Turning the picture upside-down presents a totally new perspective of the subject we are drawing. It also forces the left side of the brain (analytical/language mode) to remove itself from the task at hand. The left brain mode decides that upside-down pictures are inappropriate for the analytical task at hand, so then the visual/perceptual right side of the brain kicks in. This shift in consciousness is experienced when driving on the freeway. Unless we are conscious of time, we begin to look at the country side and all this visual/perceptual information becomes inappropriate for our analytical brain and we begin to subconsciously start to innovate and problem solve with our right brain.

Betty Edwards has two illustrations of new business practices brought about by solving problems with our right brain. People who come up with new ideas, often invert (turn upside down) the business process and "Ah-Ha!" the problem is solved. In 1838, the American inventor Elias Howe turned his attention to devising a sewing machine. After perfecting various features, he remained with one major problem, the needle. Needles had always had a point at one end and an eye at the other end to hold the thread. Howe's problem, how could such a needle pass through a piece of cloth and come back up again in a continuous action without the machine letting go of the needle? Howe could not visualize a needle in any other way until one night he dreamed of being attacked by savages carrying spears that had eye-shaped holes near the tips. Ah-Ha! Howe awakened from his dream and immediately whittled a sewing machine needle with the hole at the pointed end of the needle. He turned the picture (process) upside-down (paradigm shift in business).

Henry Ford did the same thing when he noticed that workers at his car manufacturing facility were walking all over each other when the workers were attaching parts to the cars that sat still on the floor. The workers came to the cars to do the assembly. This process caused confusion to the workers as they competed for time and space to attach their part to the car frame. Henry Ford turned this picture upside-down. He decided to have the workers stand still and he would bring the car to the worker rather than the other way around. Henry Ford turned this process upside-down and a new paradigm was discovered, the assembly line process.

In Gerd Gigerenzer's book, <u>Calculated Risks</u>: *How to Know When Numbers Deceive You,* he illustrates how information may be inverted to test for what is being implied by a statement. Here is an example from his book concerning DNA evidence presented against a person in court.

Prosecuting Attorney said, "The probability that this DNA match has occurred by chance is 1 in 100,000."

This statement presented in a courtroom to convict a criminal can be very incriminating and decimating. This statement presents evidence in terms of probabilities that implies that we can all be certain that this person and only this person could have committed the crime. Now imagine the same statement rephrased, inverted and expressed in terms of natural frequencies using the same information

"Out of 100,000 people, 1 will show a match."

What is being implied? The statement now makes us ask, how many people in any given population of millions could have committed the murder? This brief exercise is considered a paradigm shift. We shifted our information interpretation in terms of probabilities (very certain he was the only one who could have committed the murder) to interpreting the information in terms of natural occurrences. Inverting the information and data contained in our paradigm opens new doors to explore alternatives. This is the difference with people who are rational (Heroes) and those who are irrational (Zeroes).

Paradigm shifts are not an easy quick fix to problems and processes. Paradigms are a long term commitment to prevent acting with quick fixes. In physical science part of the Correspondence Principle states "in order for a new theory to be valid, it must account for the verified results of the old theory. Any organization should continually strive to have the most complete understanding and knowledge of present paradigms of the organization before proposing the new paradigm when implementing change. Flawed paradigms will tamper with processes. Hero managers produce proactive insights with their paradigms. Heroes have the ability to be descriptive as well as predictive with respect to the enterprising goals of the organization.

Science Terminology - Systems Theory

Modern science has described the functioning of the human body, microorganisms, computers, and even corporations in terms of a set of rules. The human body is composed of several systems. There is the nervous system, the vascular system, and related organs (heart, lungs, kidneys, liver, brain, etc.). Scientist have made it possible to analyze the structure and functioning of an organ at ever finer levels in terms of the organs biochemical and cellular composition. Some organs secrete biochemical substances that act on other organs and in turn receive chemical messages that indicate more or less of this secretion is required. According to systems theory, it is not necessary to understand the detailed cellular makeup of the organ in question to describe the approximate dynamics of the overall process. Scientists need only to understand qualitatively how the organ responds.

General systems theory enables the dynamic of natural systems as well as organizational systems to be modeled. A System is the state or condition of harmonious orderly interaction in a group of interrelated interdependent elements forming a collective entity. Systems are generally characterized and modeled (diagrammed) with having an input element, output element, storage element, and feedback element (positive & negative feedback).

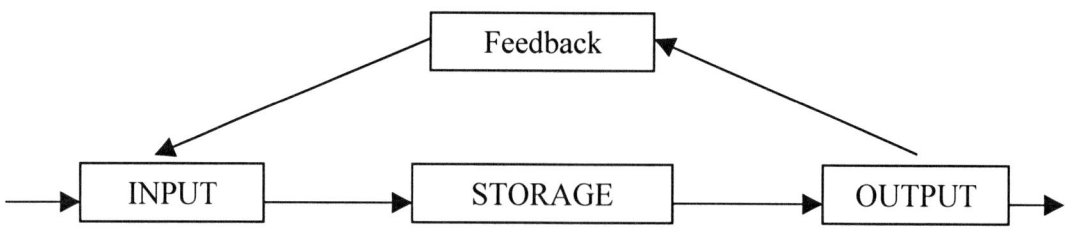

Systems theory analyzes the internal dynamics of an organization in terms of information flow or the various sequences involved in a production process. Using statistics, these processes can be determined to be capable. I will discuss process capability more in the statistics section of this book. Many systems can be identified and diagrammed with other subsystems by using connections. Once the interconnected boxes are diagrammed, it becomes apparent where lines of interaction and communication are missing. These lines that connect the boxes are referred to as feedback loops. Negative feedback stabilizes a system each time a process deviates from a prearranged norm or is out of control statistically. In general, the simplest systems consist of two boxes interconnected by arrows, representing enhancing effects (positive feedback) or diminishing effects (negative feedback). So using our two box system, there are three possible systems within this simple system. If both arrows are positive, the two boxes are cooperative or coevolutional. Coevolution stresses the advantages of cooperation in nature and the interdependence of plants and animals. If one arrow is positive and the other negative, then we have a predator-prey system. The predator-prey relationship is an endless circle of growth and decline that produces a stable equilibrium. Two negative arrows give a competitive system. A competitive system is a chance process that is goal directed. The goal is not the survival of an individual, but the survival of a particular group or species.

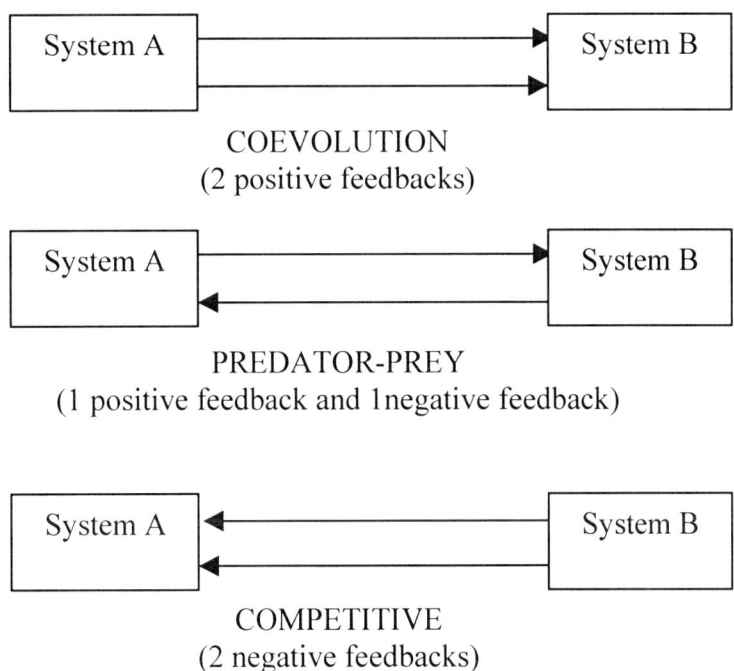

The tools for systems thinking introduced in Peter Senge's book *The Fifth Discipline* is especially designed for understanding dynamic complexity. They help in seeing the underlying structures and patterns of behavior that are obscured in the fury of daily events. Dynamic complexity occurs when "cause and effect" are not close in time and space and obvious interventions do not produce expected outcomes. Peter Senge explains what systems theory, systems thinking, and systems design is. NASA designed a management system prior to designing rocket systems. Senge explains why a management system is so important and why every organization should design a management system before designing anything else.

To summarize, a System is the state or condition of harmonious orderly interaction in a group of interrelated interdependent elements forming a collective entity. Systems are generally characterized with having an input element, output element, storage element, and feedback element. When we think of design, we conceive, invent, and contrive to form a plan for an intended goal and purposeful outcome.

Science Terminology - Systems Design

A systems design starts from a problem to be solved and uses the field of feedback control to organize and form a collective entity of harmonious orderly interaction in a group of interrelated interdependent elements to contrive a plan for an intended outcome and purpose.

The purpose of systems design is to select and plan a system that meets the requirements necessary to deliver the problem solution. Typically, various logical design models of the proposed system are created to show what the system will do, and what outcomes the system will generate. These logical design models are useful in verifying that the desired outcomes of the system do in fact meet the system requirements. Once the logical design models have been verified, physical design models are begun. Physical design models are usually detailed diagrams and specifications that describe the physical characteristics of the system and the environment in which it will operate.

Science Terminology - Systems Thinking

When a person is trying to make sense of the world, or an organization, or even a small group of people, it helps to think in terms of systems. One example that comes to mind is from nature. If coyotes aren't getting enough to eat, they have smaller litters, which makes for less coyotes, which means there is more food to go around, so that litters may again get bigger, etc. The modern systems thinkers have identified system archetypes - sort of the elementary building blocks of complex systems. Here are several examples of archetypes.

1) *The reinforcing loop* archetype – Is exemplified as the vicious circle that occurs when a family breaks apart, the children are scarred by this, they are less able to cope, they get less well-educated, they resort to escapes like drugs or promiscuity, the next generation has a worse upbringing, they are less able to function, they spiral down into poverty and brokenness.

2) *Escalation* archetypes - Is exemplified by the arms race. One party in a system takes an action, which is perceived by the other as a threat. The second party takes an action to defend itself against the perceived threat. That reaction is perceived as a new threat by the first party, which then takes further steps to defend itself.

3) *Tragedy of the Commons* archetypes - Is exemplified with a village, with some meadow land held in common. Villagers graze their cattle on the common land. One villager buys more cattle, grazes them there, and makes more profit for himself. Another villager tries the same thing, and another. Soon the pasture is overgrazed, and all the cattle are starving. No one profits; everyone suffers.

General systems theory, with its networks of subsystems, inputs, outputs, and feedback loops, have the capacity to exhibit all the characteristics of nonlinear systems. These characteristics are stability, amplification of fluctuations, oscillations, the butterfly effect, and even chaos. Effective control does not lie in old-fashioned mechanical causality paradigm of top-down commands, but rather in analyzing an organization into the various subsystems and then determining the range and character of the organization's dynamic behavior.

Science Terminology - Explicate and Implicate Order

According to the physicist David Bohm, the world we see around us is only a shadow of a deeper reality called the implicate order. Classical physics reality was clear and unambiguous. Material objects have specific boundaries and locations in space and time was an absolute. The universe and everything in it was a mechanical clock perfect in every way. Physical properties were well defined and existed independently of any observation. This picture of physics is referred to as the explicate order and points out how deeply ingrained this paradigm (worldview) has become in everyone's thinking.

In today's world the most fundamental scientific description of the world is quantum theory, which happens to be at odds with the language of explicit order and classical physics. Quantum entities are not well defined in space but are delocalized and interpenetrating. Bohm proposes that quantum theory reveals an implicate order. This implicate order is difficult to measure in terms of absolutes. We see this with many of our organizations. Employee evaluations as well as aptitude tests, measure the explicate order and not the implicate order. The implicate order sustains the explicate order. When we measure aptitude or evaluate an employee, managers rarely give credit to a person's customer service skills. This would be too difficult for the manager to measure. It would require the manager to be more involved in the field. What does the manager do? Well, he determines who the productive employees are based on the timely submission of the weekly report. An employee can build the best customer service relations, but if that report is late, no increase in pay.

A simple example for considering implicate and explicate order is watching and observing a duck on the pond. Just as a duck is on the water, we measure the activity that is available to our obvious view of his world. The duck seems to glide on the water effortlessly. But something is being unobserved and unmeasured in this process. Underneath the water the duck is paddling and a great deal of energy is being expended in the process. This goes unnoticed by the observer. Just like the duck, many activities within our enterprise systems are not measured and identified but are a very intricate part of the company's success. This is the implicate order of the organization. It is important that we apply the new sciences to explore these hidden attributes that play a very important role in the organization.

Science Terminology - Open Systems

For more than 200 years science had treated nature as if every system was a closed box. Because of the laws of thermodynamics, entropy in a closed system will increase and run down toward featureless equilibrium. However, entropy is a statistical law, not an absolute law. Entropy only applies to irreversible processes and science has realized that most natural and social systems are open systems, capable of self-organizing, self-regulating, and structuring. We all know what happens when we do not put the time and energy into cleaning the house. It becomes disorganized. This appears to be entropy at work. But when we put effort into organizing the house once again (negative entropy), we bring back structure and order to the system.

In the world around us, we can see for ourselves the complex structures such as cities, plants, nature, businesses, and societies. These all appear to defy entropy and continue to sustain high degrees of order. They are all open systems in which matter and/or energy are free to enter and to leave. In other words, open systems provide the freedom to interact in the environment.

Science Terminology - Self Organizing Systems - Chaos?

The scientist Ilya Prigogine introduced the term dissipative structures to describe systems that spontaneously come to order. Self-organizing systems are open systems, as opposed to isolated closed systems that allow entropy (increasing disorder) to move the system toward a featureless state. In the science of physics, chaos is considered a specific kind of process that has its own kind of loose order. Chaos is not the same thing as complete disorder, randomness, complexity, or unfathomability. Chaos is different because there exists within this specific process attractors that seem to decrease entropy.

What is Science Management?

Science management is essentially the application of the aforementioned principles of science to business practices. Science management explores both the explicate and the implicate order of an organization. When identification becomes difficult and exploration unrevealing (example: probing the invisible world of the atom), then do as the quantum scientist do. The application of the principle of inclusion and complimentaries will resolve conflicts and rival explanations to reveal the invisible world.

PART ONE: SYSTEMS THINKING

Science management is the practice of these principles to probe into the invisible mechanics of the work force. How do we know atoms exist? There are scientific principles that promote the accurate description, but provide no practical mechanical model, only a mathematical one. Just as Einstein proved with time in his theory of relativity, time alterations lie outside the scope of mechanical explanation. Probing to model (paradigm) the explicate order and the implicate order will guide the process. If a process cannot be flowcharted, building the mathematical model and system diagrams will approach a more accurate description of the implicate and explicate order of the organization.

Celestial navigation is still used today by ships and airplanes, even though it is based on the Earth being the center of our universe. A science manager will test a model (paradigm) for its usefulness. Systems-thinking models serve as illuminators of the processes at work in an organization. A science manager skills test these illuminators for their usefulness to determine how well does the model construct a strong understanding of the system for the purpose of implementing effective change. A science manager (Hero) does not set out to prove that a model is 100 percent true, but tests it to find which parts are not useful reflections of the system.

Conceptualizing with school of thought and movement cannot accurately describe processes completely nor are they a test to determine usefulness. Science management starts with a curiosity to become a learning organization. Heroes always participate in the learning organization and have over come the disease of the hierarchy. As Peter Senge pointed out in his book *The Fifth Discipline* (page 181), "In the traditional authoritarian organization, the dogma was managing, organizing, and controlling. In the learning organization the new dogma will be vision, values, and mental models." The three models presented in this book provide a scope and boundaries to guide system thinking. With these models, thinking skills will improve in the organization and people will discover the relationships necessary to create a systems thinking model that is useful for any enterprise organization.

Heroes are also validation thinkers. Validation thinking is the nonsystems-thinking counterpart to systems thinking. Validation thinkers seek exact matches between the data the model generates and the data from the system itself. Heroes are first concerned with usefulness of the models generated with systems thinking. Heroes, with respect to people, will validate truth of information by detecting fallacies and deception. With respect to processes of the organization, heroes find truth in numbers. Heroes do the math (statistics).

PART TWO:
VALIDATION THINKING

COMMUNICATION & INFORMATION ANXIETY

Information will be the downfall of any organization unless we distinguish between what information is important and what information is just interesting or trivial. Information can be important, interesting, or trivial. Interesting information as well as trivial information is usually harmless, important information can be controlling and intimidating because of its increased value. If we need to know something and it affects the future of our needs, then the information is important. Each of us has an information base filled with important information, interesting information and trivial information. If the important information is outside your information base then it is also outside our comfort zone. When important information is outside our information base, information anxiety begins to grow in the organization.

Information anxiety is also the result of inaccuracy or acting on unreliable information. An example would be a computer software application training manual for a new computer program install. If we read the instructions to install a new computer program and these instructions contained unreliable information, the installation will be unsuccessful. When we participate in the installation process and steps to the installation procedure have been left out, then we have an unexpected outcome that breaks our entire computer system. The same is for any training programs in our organizations. Students in training will read the manuals for important information and will test important information for its reliability. When the student graduates from training and begins operating in the real world, situations with their customer will authenticate the information. If information provided in the manual says "Warning - Never touch the exposed wires on the computer power supply when the protective cover has been removed!" Then all we have to do is touch the wires, get shocked, and we have authenticated the information. Think of all the times you read information on the internet only to find that it caused you to make a wrong decision. This is information anxiety.

Many organizations have failed to train employees to be better information evaluators. In general, many are too lazy to learn and build a better knowledge base. As a result, they become skeptical about listening to others and trust is out the window. They become skeptical about statements that are not in their information base. They have no concept of the new ideas (paradigm shifts) and they have little knowledge of ideas that are old. New logical notions are needed. A bit of information becomes common knowledge among a group of people in an organization if everyone shares that knowledge and knows everyone else knows it. Then this knowledge is common knowledge that is equally distributed to all people participating in the organization. A creative person is one who can process in new ways the information directly at hand. Heroes have the ability to take the data that is available to all and intuitively see possibilities for transforming ordinary data into a new creation. Heroes understand the differences between the two processes of gathering data and transforming data creatively.

Information anxiety occurs when zeroes stifle important data. What is important is that we are diligently looking and it only becomes urgent that we are looking for something in particular. The scientist Alexander Graham Bell urgently looked for something specific, the hearing aid; but the act of diligently looking for a specific brought about something different, the telephone. Bell transformed the data in a new and creative way. Heroes may start with researching something in particular, but discover facts that differentiate important information from interesting or trivial information. Heroes are armed with the tools to identify important information and how this information fosters development for the organization. Information can be either helpful or harmful to any organization. Organizations spend a tremendous amount of time and money in gathering information, but very few people understand how to evaluate information for its real value to increase better customer service, economic growth, and increase market share.

EVALUATING INFORMATION: TRUTH, DECEPTION, & FALLACIES

How do we transform information to bring meaning to our organizations and foster development? When a fellow worker presents an idea, it is generally presented as information in some form or media. How do heroes determine truth, deception, and fallacy? How does one determine if the information is fact, opinion, or testimony?

Important information provides the evidence to support a point or prove the worthiness of an idea. Information anxiety occurs when information is disguised as important information, when in reality it is only used for the self-interests of the person bidding for power. People who are promoted present powerful convincing information as evidence why they should be promoted over others who are more qualified. There are three forms of information evidence, facts, opinions, and testimonies.

<u>Facts as Evidence:</u> A fact is a statement, which can be verified. When we conceptualize with science, truth and fallacy can distinguish the difference.

Validation Thinking: Three Methods Used to Verify Facts

1) By definition
2) Historically
3) By experiment and/or observation

<u>Fact verses Opinion</u>: Opinions are statements of personal belief, which are open to questions. Generally, when people conceptualize with school of thought, they are

trying to get support with espoused theories rather than theories that are in practice. Effective important information must be supported by facts (conceptualizing with science and the use of an objective measure) and not by opinions. Opinions generate rival explanations.

> Rule 1) Select only relevant facts to support the organization's goals.
> Rule 2) Prioritize relevant information in their order of importance with stakeholders of the organization.
> Rule 3) Eliminate information that is urgent, inappropriate, and unimportant. This strengthens the organization's vision and mission.

Interpretation of information is the act of using factual data, or facts themselves to support an idea or point of view. Why do organizations make bad decisions? Generally it is a result of miss-interpretation of information as well as an inability to validate a fact.

Three major reasons why Interpretation of Factual Information Goes Wrong

1) Interpretation is often done on the basis of too few facts and not enough information.
2) Interpretation is often done on the basis of wrong or irrelevant facts and information.
3) Interpretation often overlooks or ignores one or more facts of information, which are pertinent.

In the previous paragraphs it may seem that opinions should be eliminated all together. Opinions can be important information and bring value to the organization. However, when we prioritize information, facts are more important than opinion. But heroes understand that opinions can be beneficial to an organization if the opinion has a high level of credibility. Credibility refers to the reliability or believability of the information. Heroes also practice the art of listening to others opinions but never immediately act on the opinion. Opinions generate questions, but this can be a good thing or a bad thing for the organization. Managing opinion information can be difficult and convoluted. Heroes use four (4) tests to determine the credibility of an opinion.

> Test 1) Is there a high possibility of disagreement? (if so-lower credibility)
> Test 2) Could there be a deliberate intent to deceive? (if so-lower credibility)
> Test 3) Is the opinion a reasonable interpretation of the facts? (if so-higher credibility)
> Test 4) Is the source free of bias? (if so-higher credibility)

Test for Credibility #1) Is there a high possibility of disagreement?

Example: A child has a bad cold, a fever, and his skin is covered with small red spots. A medical doctor offers the opinion that the child has the measles. Does a disagreement exist in this opinion? Is this a good indicator of measles? The higher the possibility of disagreement over an opinion, the lower the probability that the opinion is credible. The source of the opinion is often the deciding factor in evaluating an opinion. In general, family doctors are a very good source or why would we go to them for an opinion? We go to doctors because we agree that we can rely on their opinion. In the example, the statement has credibility and a low possibility of disagreement.

Test for Credibility #2) Could there be a deliberate intent to deceive?

Example: A salesman selling only red polka dotted pink suits says it looks great! Obviously the person selling is more interested to sell suits than he is interested in pleasing the buyer.

Test for Credibility #3) Is the opinion a reasonable interpretation of the facts?

Reasonable interpretation is the test based on sound judgment, intelligence, and most of all our personal experience in the area of an opinion.

Test for Credibility #4) Is the source free of bias?

Bias implies a lack of rationality, objectivity, or open-mindedness. What causes bias? General two reasons cause bias.

1) Conflict of Interest - refers to a person's inability to express a fair and objective opinion because that person has a special interest in the matter at question.
2) Prejudgment (or prejudice) refers to an opinion or a judgment which is expressed before one has examined all the relevant facts. Jumping to a conclusion.

Example: Lester Nerd firmly believes that anyone who wears a beard may be a revolutionary who is out to overthrow the United States government. That evening Lester Nerd's daughter brings home a date who is sporting a big bushy beard. Does an association exist between this person's preference to grow a beard and his desire to overthrow the United States government? It is obvious that Mr. Nerd was guilty of bias due to prejudgment.

<u>Testimony as Evidence and Information</u>: Testimony is a form of evidence used to support a point or prove that an idea is worthy of consideration. Testimonies may be

either written or spoken information. It is important to understand and have the ability to test credibility of information of all types. Heroes have the ability to define and understand the various forms of testimony. Heroes also can determine the credibility of testimony offered as evidential information. In today's computer information age, we are inundated with voice mail and email. The focus of this section is to assist one to evaluate testimony both written and spoken. Heroes generally have the following five (5) tests for credibility to evaluate testimony of other people when reading email, office memorandums, voice mail messages, and co-worker spoken words. It is one thing to be a good listener, but it is even better when we have tools that validate what we have heard.

The Five Tests

Testimony I – Credibility of the Author (the person originating the information)
Testimony II – Credibility of the Document (written word)
Testimony III – Credibility of Subject Matter
Testimony IV – Credibility of Primary Sources
Testimony V – Credibility of Secondary Sources

Testimony I – Credibility of the Author (the person originating the information)

The credibility of a person giving testimony is determined by their expertise, their objectivity, and their past record of accuracy. Expertise refers to the extent of a person's specialized knowledge or skill in a particular field of interest. Their objectivity refers to a person's ability to present testimony, which is free of emotional bias and personal prejudice. Their previous record of accuracy refers to the correctness or exactness of their testimony. Does their walk talk loader than their talk talks? Historically, has the person previously contributed knowledge to the organization that fostered development and efficiency?

Testimony II – Credibility of the Document (written word)

Guidelines used to determine the credibility of a document (email, memo, etc.) offered as evidence are 1) presumed authenticity, 2) internal consistency, 3) the care used in generalization, and 4) the willingness to include opposing testimony. Presumed authenticity refers to the assumption that the document is original in thought. Are the words contained in the office memo the words of the person writing, or were ideas forged and stolen from others that understand the true meaning of the content. Internal consistency refers to the degree of uniformity or agreement of the information contained in the document. There should be no contradictions. The care used in generalization refers to the caution and reasonableness by which conclusions are arrived at within the document. The conclusion is even more meaningful when the person originating the document is willing to include the opposing testimony.

Willingness to include opposing testimony refers to the degree to which other ideas (even though detrimental and damaging) are included in the document. The greater the presumed authenticity and internal consistency of the content of a document along with the care used in generalizations with the willingness to include opposing ideas, the greater is the credibility of the document offered as evidence.

Testimony III – Credibility of Subject Matter

Guidelines used to determine the credibility of subject matter are the degree of tension over the subject, availability of the subject matter, and the freedom to present the information as everyone sees it.

The degree of tension over the subject matter refers to the pressure or controversy concerning an event or subject. If the information lowers the controversy between people's interpretation, the higher the credibility and we all avoid rival explanations. If the information is too controversial, then people will begin to bid for power and conceptualize with schools of thought or start a movement.

Example: Is there a high degree of controversy over the price of spinach? NO
Was there (and is there still) a high degree of controversy concerning Vietnam? YES

Availability of the subject matter refers to the accessibility of information concerning the subject matter and information.

Example: Much of the useful information concerning certain periods of world history were lost when Julius Caesar ordered Cleopatra's Great Library in Alexandria (Egypt) to be set aflame. Information was burned and now will never be available. The destroyed records affected the credibility of historical accounts. As a result of reduced availability, we can only speculate about certain events. We are missing information. The greater the availability, the higher the credibility.

Freedom of the person originating information refers to the degree of liberty one has to report the evidence as one sees it. An example of this is Galileo Galilei. This 17th century astronomer studied planets and moons in our solar system and provided data that the sun was the middle of our solar system (not the earth). The authorities at the time refused him to publish his findings. Galileo's lack of freedom to publish hindered mankind's knowledge of our solar system. If a person does not have the freedom to present information and others are not allowed to evaluate the finding, then there exists a low degree of credibility. When information is hidden from others, this form of censorship may be interpreted as hiding truth to perpetuate the lie.

PART TWO: VALIDATION THINKING

Testimony IV – Credibility of Primary Sources

The guidelines used to determine the credibility of primary sources or eyewitness authorities are the degree of the personal observation and the time elapsed since the event. The degree of personal observation refers to the completeness of the information given. When people conveniently leave out important information, the credibility gap between true and false is widened. An example of incomplete information would be a dentist telling you he has to remove your tooth. You ask why? The dentist then says, "Because I feel like it." Wouldn't you like to have more information before agreeing to have the tooth removed? Wouldn't additional information be of value in order to make the best decision?

The time elapsed since the event refers to the period of time that has passed between the event and the information given concerning an event or circumstance. As time passes, we tend to forget the details unless we write it down in a journal or diary. So the greater the degree of personal observation along with a short elapsed time since the event, the greater the credibility of the information.

Testimony V – Credibility of Secondary Sources

Guidelines used to determine the credibility of secondary sources are the originator's choice of primary or eyewitness sources and the originator's accuracy in quoting a primary source. Sometime we are unable to obtain information from a primary source. As a result, we ask others to research the primary sources of where the information originated. It is important that we understand the accuracy in which a secondary source has selected accurate and reliable information as evidence. The secondary source accuracy is also determined in how well the quoting of primary sources was done concerning carefulness and fairness with primary information. The wiser the choice of primary sources and the more accurate the quotations from primary sources, the higher the information credibility will be.

Deception & Fallacies

Deception has been with mankind from the beginning of history. It has been recorded and handed down generation after generation. You would think that we have all learned our lesson that deception just doesn't pay. Throughout history, there have been periods of the ever-increasing deception as well as periods where the practice of deception declined. People deceive other people and there are people who seem to actually enjoy lying most of the time. A lie is often the truth in masquerade. Lies often contain an element of truth. That is why so many people believe in lies. Heroes advocate a no tolerance for deception. Heroes are armed with the tools to stop deceptive practices. Heroes recognize fallacies and stop them before deception destroys the character ethic of the organization as well as the organization information integrity.

The word fallacy comes from the Latin word fallere, "to deceive." A fallacy may not necessarily be intended to deceive; it may just simply result from an error in thinking. So there is a difference in the technical definition and the general definition. The technical definition that a logician would use would be that a fallacy is a failure to follow the rules of logic, resulting in an invalid argument. Invalid argument is a faulty chain of reasoning, which allows a false conclusion to be drawn from true premises.

A general definition for fallacy is a mistaken idea, or error in reasoning. Fallacies result in ideas or concepts that seem to prove something but in reality does not. As a result, people become suspicious that something is wrong. Here are some examples of fallacy statements.

1) Every time I wash my car it rains. Therefore, washing my car makes it rain.

This is an example fallacy called jumping to a conclusion. The fact that it rains every time the car is washed doesn't necessarily establish a cause and effect relationship nor does it establish a pattern of behavior for stimulus and response.

2) Anyone who violates the law should be put in jail. Writing fallacies is breaking the law of logic reasoning. Therefore, anyone who writes a fallacy should be put in jail.

The word law has a double meaning and the definition of the word law shifts its meaning in the statement. Just because a person breaks a mathematical law in college doesn't mean they have broken a civil law that should be enforced by jail sentience. Fallacious writing is against the laws of logic and reasoning, but not against civil law.

3) Senator Powerhungry is in favor of the Energy Bill. This Energy Bill is obviously worthless. It is known that special interest groups are paying Senator Powerhungry. It is obvious that only special interest will benefit if the bill were passed.

The senator's personal motivations, however, had nothing to do with the Energy Bill. This statement is typical of what newspapers often report. The writers rarely offer all the facts. The statement lacks a persuasive description.

We all encounter thousands of fallacies in our daily lives. Many people and organizations persuade others using arguments that appear to be sound, but the information content is not descriptive. Heroes usually recognize unsound reasoning when they hear it or see it. Heroes learn to think critically about what they hear and see.

PART TWO: VALIDATION THINKING

I. Fallacies of Faulty Inference

When we think we have all the facts, we stop looking for more facts. The fictitious stories of Sherlock Holmes are all about an individual who never stops looking for the facts. Holmes' ever-persistent curiosity to bring closure to the most difficult cases is an example we should emulate. I have always said, "Isn't it a pity that ignorance is not painful." There is a difference in being stupid and being ignorant. When we don't look for the facts, we become ignorant. Ignorance can be cured with learning, but if a person is stupid, they stay stupid. Stupid people are unwilling to learn and these are the people who just don't get it. There are four fallacies of faulty inference that will be discussed in this section. They are:

1) Preconceived Opinion (accepting belief for facts)
2) Hasty Generalization (insufficient data or lack of needed information)
3) Oversimplified Generalization (forgetting the exceptions)
4) Post Hoc (false cause and effect)

1) Preconceived Opinion

Preconceived opinion is a fallacy of substituting belief for facts. Any sound, persuasive argument must be built on a foundation of provable facts. In the past, many believed that a flying machine was possible, but only facts turned the belief into reality. Never let preconceived opinion substitute for facts. Heroes do not allow it. Heroes put the facts in front of their beliefs. Nothing wrong with having a belief, but if the belief is preconceived, then you are hurting yourself as well as others.

Example: The heavier a thing is, the faster it falls to the ground. Therefore, if a five pound rock and a ten-pound rock are dropped at the same time, the heavier one will hit the ground first.

People knew from experience that a heavy weight placed in the hand of an outstretched arm would jerk the arm faster downward than a lightweight rock. This is the way people thought before Galileo's famous demonstration (history now tells us that someone else may have actually done the demonstration - *The Nature of Science* [page 3] by James Trefil). Galileo was said to have dropped objects of various weights from the top of the Leaning Tower of Pisa and compared their falls. Contrary to Aristotle's assertion (and the statement of this example), Galileo found that a stone twice as heavy as another did not fall twice as fast. Galileo's experiment found new facts concerning objects of various weights. He discovered they fell together. It has been written that many observers of this demonstration witnessed the objects hitting the ground at the same time scoffed at the young Galileo and continued to hold fast to the Aristotelian school of thought.

Example: My mind is made up; don't confuse me with the facts.

We think we have the facts, so we stop looking for additional facts. Remember that this is referred to as a preconceived opinion.

Example: Ladies and Gentlemen of the jury, my client could never have committed this terrible murder. You have heard the testimony of those who know him. They agree that he is a kind man, a man who loves children and small animals, and attends church regularly. He could never have done such a thing.

This lawyer presents evidence that this person is a nice guy. He is not on trial to prove he is a nice guy. The issue is not if he is nice or not, the issue is did he commit a murder. The lawyer presented no evidence that his client could not commit the crime based on facts. These facts would be a physical impairment that proves he cannot shoot a gun or that he was not even in town during the murder. The lawyer is arguing a different case other than the murder case.

Example: Germans are great musicians. Just look at Beethoven, Bach, and Wagner. Hans is German. He must be a great musician.

A simple test can prove that not all Germans are good musicians. Without additional information and having Hans audition in the presence of musical experts, we cannot prove Hans is a good musician. It is of no consequence that Hans is German. Chopin was Polish, not German, and he was both a composer and a musician.

Example: Nothing is better than peace of mind, but a ham sandwich is better than nothing. Therefore a ham sandwich is better than true peace of mind.

A word with double meaning "nothing" has slipped into the argument and then shifted in meaning.

Preconceived opinions tend to be self-supporting because we see what we expect to see. We hold to our original belief as a self-evident true and expect the facts to only support that belief.

Example: I have always thought that airplanes were too dangerous. Just the other day I read about a terrible airplane crash last week. I am very sure that I will never travel in one of those flying coffins.

The person making this statement is noticing only the one fact that will support their own argument of their preconceived opinion. The belief becomes self-supporting because the person making the statement has not included other evidence that is contrary.

PART TWO: VALIDATION THINKING

A very **common form** of preconceived opinion is the **substitution of interpretation** for fact. Substitution of interpretation occurs in all kinds of religious organizations, schools, colleges, in the newspapers, and during radio and television talk shows. Why don't people call it for what it is and not what they think it is. If a person is staggering down the street, just say they are staggering down the street. So often people will remark, "That person is drunk, they are staggering." Another may guess, "That person has a nervous disorder." We really don't know until we get to know the person. The fact is that we have only seen someone stagger.

Example: In a courtroom.

Witness - "Then the defendant tried to hide his face by turning up his coat collar.

Defense Attorney – "I object your honor."

The defense attorney objected because the witness couldn't have known that the defendant turned the coat collar up for only one reason and one reason only (to hide his face). There exist several other possibilities why this person turned up the coat collar. Maybe his neck was cold. Maybe the defendant has made it a habit to turn up the coat collar. The witness was trying to substitute interpretation for fact. See how we can all be deceived by preconceived opinions. Be aware of the danger of substituting interpretation for facts.

Example: A Student talking to another student says: "They're up to no good, I am sure of it. I saw them scheming together in the cafeteria. I couldn't hear them, but I could see them laughing about what they were going to do. In fact, one of them looked at me and smiled, just to let me know they were talking about me."

The observable facts are – First, they were talking and laughing together in the cafeteria. Second, one of them smiled at the student. The rest is interpretation. The error is that we see what we want to see or expect to see.

2) Hasty Generalization

Hasty generalization is based on insufficient or unrepresentative data. A valid generalization must be based on a large number of representative cases. As you remember generalizations occur when we take our observation of specific cases and extend them to all cases.

Example: Insufficient Data

Student talking: "In order to project the results of tomorrow's student election, we stopped the first seven students out of 2,371 students who walked by the newspaper office. Three were for Walker and four were for Evans. Therefore, we predict that Evans will beat Walker."

This is obviously an inappropriate method for sampling a population for statistical significance. The number of students polled is not large enough to escape the effects of chance (coincidence).

Example: Unrepresentative Data

A reliable bar tender talking: "Listen, just about everyone thinks the laws against drunk driving are too strict. I've asked every person who's come into this bar for the last two months, and almost all of them said that the penalties should be lowered."

This study was not documented. Without the use of a questionnaire, we cannot determine if the questions asked by the reliable bar tender made it difficult for respondents to declare his/her support for the opposition. Also we are unable to duplicate the study without the proper documentation in a research report. What were the research hypothesis and the research methodology used? Where are the charts and data to test statistical significance?

3) Oversimplified Generalization

Oversimplified generalizations are often expressed as absolute rules, but in reality these generalizations are almost always exceptions to the rules. One way to commit this fallacy is to make, or accept, overboard sweeping generalizations.

Example: Sweeping Generalization - "All cigarette smokers die of lung cancer."

Some cigarette smokers die of heart attacks or other causes. Also, it has been noted that non-smokers die of lung cancer. There are exceptions to the sweeping generalization. To link cancer to smoking requires compelling data.

Other forms of the fallacy of oversimplified generalization occur when a general rule is applied to a case for which it was not intended.

Example: In the United States of America, everyone has the RIGHT to vote. Therefore, a person who is confined to the state hospital for the criminally insane has a right to vote!

The general rule was never intended to apply to children, criminals, aliens, and the insane.

Example: All statements are lies including this one!

Have some fun with your friends with this last generalization.

PART TWO: VALIDATION THINKING

The most common issue with generalizations is that they spawn more questions. Stating a problem with a generalization only creates more time and effort by others to focus on the real issues. Generalizations never state the real problem. Heroes rarely use generalizations when communicating specifics to other people. Zeroes communicate with generalizations. Zeroes use generalization to initiate turmoil to hide information that may be incriminating.

4) Post Hoc

Post Hoc (false cause) has to do with cause and effect. Post Hoc, Latin – *ergo proptes hoc* means after this, therefore because of this. Post hoc is the fallacy of assuming that because one event follows another, the first event is the cause of the second event. Many people structure their reasoning to look for causes and effects. Many people in the world perceive all systems as cause and effect. Known to science as causality, many people hold to the interpretation that nature as well as business organizations can be explained in terms of cause and effect relationships. This is because nothing seems to appear out of nowhere without a trace and nothing appears to arise out of nothing. The notion that effects have causes is fundamental to common knowledge, science, and technology. Immanuel Kant described causality as one of the basic categories of human understanding. We can't imagine a world without it.

We all need to watch out for post hoc reasoning and be aware of it. I do not necessarily agree with Kant that everything is accurately described in terms of causality. All systems do not operate in a cause and effect manner. There exist contingency systems as well as quantum systems where effects precede causes. This will be discussed in more detail in the math and statistics section.

Many organizations' primary paradigm is viewing everything in terms of causality. Effects must be preceded by a cause. Cause and effect relationships are the most commonly studied relationships. People who are investigating organization processes seek to determine the effect (outcomes) that is a result of an effort put forth by people and a process (cause). Let us understand that there are several systems that can be explained in terms of cause and effect. As a result, we need to understand the fallacy of these relationships. Many of these common false cause and effect relations present itself in one of these forms.

Superstition – A belief that an action taken or circumstance is truly related to a non-related course of events. When we spill salt on the table, many people take some of the salt and throw it over their left shoulder to prevent bad luck. This does not prevent bad luck or cause good luck.

Example: "Never walk under a ladder. It is bad luck. Last week I walked under a ladder by mistake, and that same day I got a parking ticket."

This is another superstition and is post hoc because there exist no connection between the ladder and a parking ticket. Ladders don't cause parking tickets to happen, people do. It is a fallacy when a particular event (getting a ticket) is held to be the result of a prior one, rather than an independent or coincidental event (a policemen writing tickets that day).

Example: "That new cold medicine is great for getting rid of colds. I used it last time and my cold was gone within two weeks."

Most colds are gone within two weeks. There is no reason to connect the medication and the cure, so no cause and effect relationship. In order to establish a true cause and effect relationship, we would need to experimentally test this medication with a control group and determine if a strong association exists. For all we know the new medicine is a sugar pill (just a placebo). Personal testimony is considered anecdotal.

The **fallacy** of the **anecdote**: The anecdote is one of the strongest influences on persuading people's opinions and behavior but is a statistical error of great magnitude. An **anecdote** is a story based on a person's experience or situation. Anecdotes make the individual appear to be participating in something sensational, but sensational stories are outliers from the norm of our life experiences.

[Before and After Post Hoc] Another form of *post hoc* is the before and after effect. An example would be a person showing you a change in something and then telling you that they were the powerful influence to bring about this change that is fostering positive outcomes. This type of post hoc (before and after) dominates conversations during political elections.

Example: "Under Governor TaxNoMore, wages in this state have risen 32% in the last four years. Vote for prosperity! Re-elect Governor TaxNoMore!"

What is the most likely factor that is causing a rise in wages? There are several other variables involved outside the Governor's action. Inflation could be a cause of wage increases. We need more information concerning how the Governor caused the effect. What were his plans to increase wages? What legislation was passed during his tenure? Did the administration attack the state's economy by focusing on supply or demand? Post hoc is one of the most deceiving methods of exercising the power to influence and persuade people that present processes are producing results. We must always investigate how exactly does the cause produce the effect.

PART TWO: VALIDATION THINKING

Remember!

- Always demand the facts and don't settle for beliefs and superstitions.
- Always examine the facts and determine if they are free of fallacies and bias.
- Always examine the rule to determine if generalizations are hasty and oversimplified.
- Always examine the cause. Many times only natural probabilities are at work.

II. Fallacies of Confusion

Fallacies of confusion are errors caused by confusing one thing with another thing because they appear similar. These similarities create the illusion that the communications between people are assumed to be understood by the listeners. When information is communicated to others, information is either common knowledge or mutual knowledge. If we have all of the information communicated accurately and without errors, we have common knowledge shared among the group. Information is distributed homogeneously. When we exclude information, then receivers of this information act on a mistaken idea and the information is only mutual to the person who originated the data and shared with selected others the entire information.

Information that was thought to be communicated in entirety but causes confusion because of resemblance errors are information errors that are devastating to the organization. They are devastating because we think we have made knowledge common to everyone in the organization, but in reality people act on mistaken ideas. This is also the fallacy of "common sense." Common sense ain't so common. We need to make sure that common knowledge is understood and shared by everyone in our organization.

Equivocation – is the fallacy of confusing one meaning of a word or phrase with another meaning of the same word or phrase. How does this confusion work to create a fallacy?

Example: It is our duty to do what is right. We all have the right to make mistakes. Therefore, it is our duty to make mistakes.

What one should do is to re-write the example. Try replacing the equivocal word or phase with its meanings. If the argument falls apart, it is an equivocation. This is how to detect equivocal words, simply replace the word or phrase with its meaning.

Rewritten Statement: It is our duty to do what is proper and correct. We are all free to make mistakes. Therefore, it is our duty to make mistakes.

The rewritten version couldn't fool anyone.

<u>Composition</u> – is the fallacy of confusing what is true about things taken individually with what is true about things taken as a collected whole (composite). This fallacy argues from the parts of information taken from the whole information.

Example: Every player on the all-star team is the best there is. Therefore, the all star team is the best there is.

Not necessarily true. The excellence of a team is usually determined on how well the teammates play together and not how good they are individually. So we cannot reason logically with the individual excellence of the individual players to the collective excellence of the team. So this is the fallacy of composition.

<u>Division</u> – is the fallacy of confusing what is true about something as a whole with what is true about its individual parts (division). So the fallacy of Division is totally different from the fallacy of composition, because this is an inverse of fallacy of composition.

Example: The championship team is the best there is. Therefore, every player on the team is the best there is.

The error is obvious. Just because the team is the best, doesn't mean that everyone on the team is the best players in the league. Always remember that the error of composition is reasoning fallaciously from the parts to the whole and the error of division is reasoning fallaciously from whole to parts.

<u>False Analogy</u> – is the fallacy of confusing what is true in one case with what is true in a similar case. Fallacies happen sometimes when we try to compare two things favorably.

Example: The moon is very much like the earth. Both are heavenly bodies. Both are nearly spherical in shape. Both receive light from the sun. Therefore, since the earth has intelligent life, the moon does to.

This reasoning is assuming that the moon and earth are identical in everyway. The more important the differences are between two cases, the worse the fallacy becomes. The moon and the earth are not identical when we examine all the things that are needed to support life. The word "like" in the example statement means similarities exist in more than a few aspects. So we probe deeper into the important differences (the inverse of similarities) to determine if a fallacy exists. Ask, what is the important differences between the earth and the moon as far as life is concerned? The moon has no air or water. This is where the analogy is broken down.

Metaphors and Similes are Kinds of Analogies

Not all analogies are fallacies or used incorrectly. There are many good uses of analogies. There is nothing wrong with using metaphors, they serve to illustrate, describe, or suggest what one is saying when illustrating a point of view or construct. They shouldn't be used to prove something to be true. When this is done the analogy becomes fallacious.

Longfellow metaphorically uses this analogy in *The Building of the Ship*:

> Thou, too, sail on, O ship of State!
> Sail on, O Union, strong and great!

In this example, Longfellow compares a ship with the Union (USA) and there is nothing wrong with this statement, we understand that it is a metaphoric comparison. However, take a look at the next example.

"A democracy is like a ship, with the citizens pulling together like members of the crew. Thus, we owe our total allegiance to our government, just as the crew owes allegiance to a captain and officers. There is no room on board this ship for those who cannot pull their own weight such as people on welfare."

Again, this person is suggesting that people on welfare have no allegiance to our government. This analogy attempted to prove an opinion by suggesting that allegiance to the United States of America is similar to the allegiance a crew gives to the officers of a ship. Analogies can be used to illustrate, describe, explain, or suggest; but should never be used to prove a point.

III. Fallacies of Irrelevance

<u>Ignoratio Elenchi</u> – is the fallacy of irrelevant argument. In its pure form, ignoratio elenchi consists of simply ignoring the issue under discussion.

Example: (From a television commercial) "We've coated this micro-scope slide with staff-germs, the same kind that are found in your throat. Now we will treat this sample on the microscope slide with a concentrated solution of Gargle-X. Under this microscope, you can see that Gargle-X kills germs on contact! Think what it can do for your throat!"

Staff-Germs have nothing to do with a sore throat, ignoratio elenchi.

Here is another Issue: "We should increase student activity fees to increase the quality of the movies shown for entertainment on campus.

Which of these replies is relevant to the issue under discussion?

1) They don't make movies like they use to.
2) The increase in movie quality would be too small to justify the increase in fees.

Note: State the issue, then we see that number one ignores what is relevant.

Special forms of Ignoratio Elienchi (irrelevant argument)

1) Ad Hominum (getting personal)
2) Ad Verecundiam (misplaced authority)
3) Ad Populum (appeal to the crowd)
4) Emotional and Physical Appeals
5) Tu Quoque (you're another)
6) Strawman (false position)

1) Ad Hominum (getting personal)

Ad hominum is a fallacy of attacking a person's character or motives instead of what the person is saying. A person who is a Zero often makes others look like a looser to feel like a winner. This attack of a person's character is manifested when Zeroes are desperate to win an argument.

Example: "My opponent claims that we should cut back on defense spending. My opponent is a fuzzy-headed idealist!"

The question is defense spending. The other candidate is attacking the character and looks of the person who suggested a budget for defense spending.

Example: "You shouldn't pay any attention to what Senator Jackson has to say in support of subsidies to bean farmers. The Senator owns the biggest bean farm operation in the state."

The speaker claims that the Senator's position is a result of bean farming and that this was the motive. The argument is not relevant until we have more information concerning this special interest. But if a personal attack is relevant and we have facts concerning the motive, then it is not a fallacy.

Ad Verecundiam (misplaced authority)

Ad verecundiam is the irrelevant appeal to our respect for an authority, person, or thing. People who misplace authority to appeal to others use a tactic to make others feel ignorant for not understanding their misconception. Zeroes act discussed and attack the other's lack of conventional wisdom and common sense. The appeal is to go along with the misplaced authority (often ambiguous), so others will not question their source of authority. Often the misplaced authority is questioned by others and they are made to think that they lack the knowledge to think at a higher level.

Example: "Don't be silly. Informed sources and everyone knows you cannot do that. It is common sense."

Note the irrelevant appeal to conventional wisdom. Many people do not want to question this statement because it might be an admission to being uninformed as well as not being willing to join with others and their common sense.

Familier pharases of ad verecundium are:

> Those who know............................
> Everyone knows............................
> Scientists say...............................
> Figures prove...............................
> Informed sources say.......................
> It says here.................................
> A government study........................
> It says in the Bible..........................
> According to this book.....................
> It has been proved with mathematics......

Example: A famous actor Mark Handsome says, "I drink Old Label Bourbon. It is the best there is!"

This is an irrelevant endorsement. Mark Handsome has brought himself into our respect by being a famous actor and not by being a bourbon expert. So we have a misplaced authority. We would want his opinion concerning the acting business, but his knowledge concerning bourbons is a misplaced authority.

Arguments from authority occur when we rely on experts for our facts. The arguments from authority are never completely certain. When we argue from authority, we place our trust in experts and they could be wrong.

Ad Populum (appeal to the crowd)

Ad populum is a fallacy that occurs when we appeal to people. There are several types of ad populum; glittering generalities, name-calling, soft-soap, snob appeal, plain folks, bandwagon, them verses us, and waving the bloody shirt.

Glittering Generalities – An appeal for approval.

Example: Political Candidate Mr.Goodperson stands for truth, justice, progress, fiscal responsibility, full employment, and wants to put an end to cancer.

It is unlikely that many are against truth, justice, etc. I certainly don't know anyone who is for getting cancer. All these generalities meet our approval, but we need more detail. Everything sounds positive in the example, but not necessarily practiced.

Name-calling – This is an appeal to disapproval by using denigration.

Example: "My opponent is a tool of vested interests, a representative of the forces of reaction, decay, and government interference.

Soft-soap – This is an appeal to pride.

Example: "People of Puritan heritage have contributed to the greatness of our country out of all proportion to their numbers. Puritan Americans like yourself are the backbone of our nation. Your neighborhood is beautiful and your food is the best I have ever eaten. Vote for me next November."

Snob appeal – This is an appeal to status.

Example: (From a magazine advertisement) A picture of a richly dressed, elegant man and woman sitting in an expensively furnished room having a drink together, with this caption, "Only the best people drink Old Label Bourbon. Its got class!"

Plain folks – This is an appeal to identification (a lower status) toward what people are in general.

Examples: (starting with)
- My fellow Americans….
- A man of the people, just like you………
- The average college student loves UltraSonic sound systems

PART TWO: VALIDATION THINKING

Bandwagon – This is an appeal to popularity.

Examples: (starting with)
- I am voting for Mr. Rat, he is going to win anyway.
- Smoke Richmond cigarettes, the nation's number one selling.
- Everyone plays the piano, why don't you?

Them versus us – This is an appeal to our fears.

Example: "Our nation's enemies are growing stronger day by day. Their intentions grow clear with every passing moment. Soon the enemy will be on our very doorsteps. We must devote our full resources to the manufacturing of weapons before it is too late."

Waving the bloody shirt – This is an appeal to sorrow and revenge. Symbols of an event are used that demand that we take revenge.

Examples:
- Slogans – Remember the Alamo!
- Objects – POW bracelets.
- Horror Stories – They are murdering and torturing people.

Note: It is not a fallacy to want to be prepared, the fallacy occurs when thoughtful preparedness is replaced by mindless fears. This is when we conceptualize with movement rather than science.

Emotional and Physical Appeals

Emotional and physical appeals are irrelevant appeals to our feelings and our physical well-being. There are several appeals toward pity, our humor, hunger, fatigue, etc.

Appeal to pity ("sob story" ad miscricordiam)

Example: An attorney says, "Ladies and gentlemen of the jury, my client has four children and an elderly mother. What will become of them if you send him to prison?"

Appeal to humor (laughing it off)

We are all familiar with this approach when people laugh at a remark or answer a question by responding with an irrelevant laugh.

Appeal to force (ad baculum)

There are two kinds of force used, direct and indirect. When direct force is used it is in a form of physical violence. Direct force people will choose a weapon to physically injure a person. Indirect force is when we bare false witness against others (slander).

Appeal to hunger, fatigue, pain, sex, etc.

We all have witnessed advertisements appealing to our hunger, fatigue, and other emotional and physical senses.

Example: Are you hungry? Then eat at Great Food Restaurant!

Tu Quoque (you're another)

Example: Two people talking.

First Person: "You are a liar!"
Second Person: "You're another!"

We have heard children do this from time to time, but adults in our organizations have Tu Quoqued. Tu Quoque is the fallacy of irrelevant counter attack. It consists of throwing an argument back at the person proposing it. The fallacy that "Two wrongs make a right" is a kind of Tu Quoque.

Here is a relevant Tu Quoque that is not a fallacy.

Example: Two people talking.

Sally: "Divorce is wrong under any circumstances."
Tom: "You're just saying that because you were brought up to believe that."
Sally: "According to that logic, you're just saying that divorce is permissible because you were brought up to believe that."

Strawman (false position)

Strawman is a fallacy of disapproving an irrelevant contrary position. In other words, it is misrepresenting an opponent's point of view for the purpose of disproving it.

Example: A political Candidate speaking.

"My opponent calls himself a moderate! All this means is he cannot make up his mind how others will benefit from change. We all understand the economic consequences of taking the middle position."

IV. Fallacies of Assumptions

Assumptions are things we take for granted without offering any proof. We cannot always prove everything that is used in a complex argument. Assumptions are proper if they are openly in agreement with others and if proof is available. However, the fallacy of assumptions occur when something false or unproved is assumed, or taken for granted.

Special Forms of Faulty Assumptions

1) Assumed Premise
   a) Assumed Rule
   b) Complex Question
   c) False Dilemma
2) Assumed Conclusion
   a) Begging the Question
3) Assumed Proof
   a) Shifting the Burden of Proof
   b) Self-Evident Truths

1) The fallacy of Assumed Premise

a) Assumed Rule

Assumed rule is the fallacy of taking for granted an unproven general rule.

Example: How do I know she is a good student? She always comes to class.

In this example the assumed rule is "people who always come to class are good students." This is not necessarily true and as a result is the fallacy of an assumed rule.

b) Complex Question

Now we will examine how a fallacy of assumption can be hidden in a question. Complex Question is a fallacy of asking a question that contains a hidden assumption.

Example: "Have you stopped beating your wife?"

The assumptions are that you have a wife and that you have been beating her regularly. If a person answers the question (yes or no), they are admitting to the assumption of beating their wife. This is a form of entrapment.

c) False Dilemma

False dilemma is the fallacy of making a hidden assumption about choices.

Example: "We must have total freedom to do whatever we please, or we must submit to slavery."

The speaker is assuming only two alternatives exists and are the only two choices available. Freedom is much more complex than what the statement makes freedom to be.

2) Assumed Conclusion

a) Begging the Question

Begging the question is the fallacy of assuming the thing to be proved.

Example: Two people talking.

Tom: "All Christians are highly moral people."
Sally: "What about George? He is a Christian and he stole Ms. Goodness money and was put in prison for three weeks last month. He also stole his parent's car and drove it to Florida last summer. These are only a few of the immoral things he does toward other people. If you are a Christian, shouldn't you honor your mother and father?"
Tom: "If George does immoral things then he must not be a real Christian."

In the example of Tom and Sally having a conversation, Tom is trying to prove his statement. When he is contradicted by the facts, Tom chooses to hold dear to his definition and assumes George could not possibly be a Christian.

Another form of begging the question consists of giving the conclusion as evidence by changing the wording.

Example: Alcohol causes <u>drunkenness</u> because it is <u>intoxicating</u>.

Drunkenness and intoxicating means the same thing. So we have an assumed conclusion presented as evidence.

When begging the question takes place in several steps, it is called arguing in a circle.

Example: Circular Argument

The Reverend Falseprophet: "You can believe what I say because I am God's true prophet on earth."
The people: "How do we know that you are God's true prophet on earth?"
The Reverend Falseprophet: "Because this book I wrote is a divine revelation from God that says I am God's true prophet."
The people: "How do we know we can rely on the book you wrote?"
The Reverend Falseprophet: "Because God says you can and you can believe whatever I tell you."

So the person who says he is a true prophet of God never proved he was, but he assumes that everyone should believe him because he says so.

Begging the question can also happen in a single word. Such a word is called a question-begging epithet. An epithet is a noun that is a phrase or word used adjectivally to express some quality or attribute.

Example: "Ladies and gentlemen of the jury, how can you let this <u>murderer</u> go free of the awful crime of killing his grandmother!"

The jury has not made a decision to call the defendant a murderer. They are there to listen to the facts of the case and make a decision if the person is a murderer or not. It has not been proven that he is a murderer yet, it is only an assumption.

Heroes always ask themselves, what is the question and what is the evidence.

2) Assumed Proof

a) Shifting the Burden of Proof

The fallacy of shifting the burden of proof has two closely related forms, they are assuming a failure to disprove is proof and assuming a failure to prove is disproof.

Example: Shifting the Burden

Person 1: "It is true!"
Person 2: "Prove it."
Person 1: "I don't have to prove it, let's see if you can disprove it."

Sometime this fallacy appears with what is known as "super tasking" your opponent. Here is an example of super tasking.

Example: Provide a simple definition based on partial deferential equations of the Universe, and then provide three examples of a Universe. You have two minutes to complete this task.

This statement is exaggerated, but it illustrates the point. When all else fails, people will lower themselves to presenting questions that are far from anyone's conceptualizations. Super task questions create an immediate failure in the thought processes of many people and humiliates the respondent by manifesting their inability to manage a task destine for failure. To answer such a question is irrelevant to proving or disproving the facts that have been presented. Zeroes create the illusion that they are intelligent and knowledgeable people by responding to disputes with a super task question. Always boasting with a statement like, "See! They cannot even give three examples of the Universe. How stupid they are!" But the zero using super task questioning as a tactic can never answer the super task question either. It is only used to make others look like losers to feel like a winner.

b) Self-Evident Truths

The fallacy of "self-evident" truths consists of making unsupported assumptions and calling them "self-evident" or obvious truth.

Example: "It is obvious that the earth we live on is flat."

This is a preconceived opinion that is an unsupported assumption with the word "obvious" in the front of the statement. When a person states that something is obviously true or necessarily true, they are in effect simply refusing to give any evidence for their statement by claiming their statement is universally accepted as the truth. The statement becomes a self-referenced self-proclamation. Obvious means clearly seen and understood by everyone. Heroes are never afraid to ask for the evidence. They demand proof.

When we are Given Rules: A statement is said to be necessarily true if it is logically unlikely to be false. A necessarily true statement is one, which requires no evidence to establish its truth. In general, there are only three kinds of statements that are necessarily true. When we are given rules that are generally accepted by the majority of people, then rules are essential to what we need to prove.

Example: Rules of Logic, Math and Grammar.

Logic: If all A is B and all B is C, then all A is C.
Math: If $x + 2 = 4$; then x must equal 2 to complete the equation.
Grammar: The verb always agrees in number with its subject.

PART TWO: VALIDATION THINKING

Just as it is with rules of a basketball game or any other sport, participants that have provincial agreement accept them. Rules will be changed and modified from time to time, but these rules of the game require little evidence only cooperation of the participant.

Definitions

Defining words can set out to do a number of different things. A good definition of a word provides guidance, unification, and universally understood meaning. Dictionaries frequently employ *usage-context* indicators such as "slang," "nonstandard," or "regional." Dictionaries are a valuable resource to answer questions about how a language is used today, especially with regard to dubious or controversial locutions. In order to avoid equivocation, we need to accurately define what we mean with our words and phrases.

Example: "That person is a **bad** dude!"

This statement contains the word BAD. We need to ask what are the usage - context indicators or are there context clues that accurately describe this person. The word "bad" could be slang that describes this person as one who has elevated their "cool" behavior beyond their piers. So we have a nonstandard use of the word. It could also mean the person is in need of discipline and their behavior is unacceptable to others. We need to ask the originator of the statement to explain their definition of the word **bad** if the information is of an important matter.

Example: "A triangle is a closed figure having three straight sides."

This is a definition from Euclidean geometry. It is often accepted by mathematicians as a good definition that is used to differentiate this geometric object from other geometric objects. It is important to the understanding of geometry that we establish rules and agree to the nomenclature of many geometric objects and have a good definition that distinguishes the various shapes.

Tautologies

Tautologies are often perceived as needless repetition of the same sense in different words. It is redundancy. However, in logic it is a statement composed of similar words and/or phrases in a fashion that makes it true whether the simpler words and/or phrases are true or false. The word tautology comes from the Latin word *tautologia* and from the Greek word *tautologos* meaning to repeat the same thing.

Example: "It will either rain tomorrow or it will not rain tomorrow."
       "All bachelors are not married."

We can see that these necessarily true statements say nothing about the facts. It carries no information and tells us nothing we don't already know. But, tautologies can be used to re-emphasize ideas communicated to others. So we can use tautologies to emphasize abstract rules and information.

Example: "Three strikes and you're out." (rule of the game-baseball)

Ad Hoc - with respect to this particular thing.

This is not necessarily a fallacy, but because it is used in many organizations with respect to information, I feel that we need to discuss ad hoc. Ad hoc is Latin meaning toward this, for a specific purpose, case, or situation. The phrase ad hoc means that the need for a specific set of information could not have been anticipated. Many organizations purchase an information reporting system that informs managers about the general well being of their departments, but it is often not helpful when a manager must make a specific decision. So a manager must turn to a decision support system (computer programs or using their brains) which allows him or her to produce management reports in an ad hoc fashion.

Often people are required to make a decision in an ad hoc manner. This is when we must make a decision in the absence of information and become victims of unforeseen unanticipated outcomes. An event comes that requires our immediate attention and we have to stop and ask the question, "What went wrong?"

Post Hoc is false cause and effect. Ad Hoc is the aftermath of unforeseen consequences. Ad Hoc is the process of understanding what the opportunities are as well as the threats before they occur in our organizations. Ad Hoc will be discussed further in the section of business statistics and risk management.

Conclusion

This section needs to be understood by everyone in an information age. In today's business world we are asked to document everything. We document medication administration, customer service calls, and log many of our daily activities in all types of business reports. Heroes evaluate and authenticate the written and spoken word with these tests and credibility checks. Zeroes believe everything they read the first time and never look for the context clues and usage context indicators that would reveal the fallacies as well as the self-intent of the person originating the information. Heroes understand that integrity of information is the first step to reduce conflict and to make better decisions. It is important that these errors in reasoning and communication are identified. Heroes look for relevance of information and respond to questions with real answers.

PART TWO: VALIDATION THINKING

Since communications is such a commonplace activity, it would seem that most of us have a good understanding what communications is. Even though there are entire volumes that have been written on the physical, theoretical, and psychological aspects of communication; heroes find it quite sufficient to understand the basic fundamentals of the subject. Communication is the transfer of meaningful information from one person (or system) to another person or a group of people (or systems). This definition is a basic one that only requires that the term information be defined. Information is a physical pattern that has been assigned a commonly understood meaning. A drawing of a horse or the name horse spelled in a language understood by other people would communicate the concept of a horse to a person. The communication might still not be complete or meaningful unless the writer and the reader both agree that seeing the symbol or the name horse meant some complete idea. The meaning of the words we read and pictures we see must be unique using an objective measure. Heroes think before they speak. They are careful not to send information that contain fallacies or errors that will confuse listeners.

Unlike management, heroes understand that leadership does not require formal recognition of authority. However, it does place other requirements when assuming the leadership role. Before people will follow (follower readiness), a need to be reassured that the leader is deserving of both trust and confidence. Good relationships that share values are paramount. Heroes understand that communication is the prime tool for building those relationships. Removing deception and fallacies will ensure that objectives are agreed upon, understood, and achieved. Heroes know how to guide team members to achieve organizational objectives and demonstrate the trustworthiness of the position. To do this a leader must communicate who they *are*, what they *know*, and what they *do*.

Heroes communicate who they are with their actions and words. People mistrust leaders that are self-serving or unethical. Heroes love people and use things. Heroes understand that the people in an organization have follower readiness levels and will participate in the leader's actions if the follower is willing to share values with the leader. When leaders communicate and demonstrate honesty and integrity, followers will begin to show their readiness levels to share these values. Heroes resist the temptation to sidestep the truth by being evasive. Heroes avoid unethical actions and decisions. Heroes remind themselves that any sign of dishonesty will damage the organization's credibility.

Heroes share information and communicate what they know to be truthful and accurate. Followers have no confidence in leaders who are incompetent or who lack essential knowledge. It is necessary to communicate what is known. Heroes demonstrate their knowledge of their own job, team members' jobs, and the organization. Heroes know what is expected of themselves and their followers. Heroes ensure that the team has the skills and abilities to perform competently.

Heroes do not make others look like losers to feel like a winner. Heroes are interceding (not interfering) by being personally involved in the training and coaching of followers in the organization, never micro-managing. Heroes know the organization's policies, procedures, products, and services. Heroes share this knowledge with team members to help everyone meet team objectives.

Heroes communicate to followers what they *do*. Heroes visibly participate to attain organizational goals. It is difficult to inspire a person to follow a leader who apparently does nothing. Heroes give practical support by providing workable processes, well thought out plans, and solutions, as well as assisting with implementation. People who are supported in this way have confidence in their leaders and their organizations to achieve self-esteem that motivates higher morale. Heroes recognize the benefits of reducing the errors in communication by removing deception and fallacies. Heroes effectively communicate strategies with both their actions and their words. Heroes never let their talk, talk loader then their walk talks.

STATISTICAL THINKING

Business Statistics & Business Math-What to do in the Absence of Information

In the absence of information, we need to do the math. One way of judging the future is by examining the past. Usually a little experience upsets a lot of theory founded in school of thought. Statistics can help any organization make a decision to practice a process with precision and effectiveness. During the 1800s several hospitals in the United States practiced cleanliness next to Godliness in their delivery wards. Even though these medical professionals lacked information concerning bacteria (before Pasture) they tracked results of a lower birth death compared to other birthing wards in other hospitals that did not consider cleanliness to be an issue because there was no proof, just results. As a result of the practice without empirical purpose, babies had a higher survival rate due to a process practiced of killing germs even though germs were not known to exist or to be harmful.   Statistics is one of the most important parts of science management. The food and drug industry would be a lost business without it. Without the use of statistics, we would not know which drugs, foods, and liquids are safe for consumption or which ones are harmful.

This section's focus is a continuation to test information (inferences) for meaning. Inference is when we take one piece of data (information) and draw conclusions about another piece of data (information). This section will discuss why we all need to be statistical thinkers to be better systems thinkers. Most of all, it is important to understand how to be statistical thinkers when we communicate risk as well as have a statistical understanding to never **tamper** with system processes in our organizations.

THE RED BEAD EXPERIEMENT

Heroes Avoid Tampering With Processes-The Fundamental Principal of Business and Relationships

In demonstrations and seminars that I have conducted throughout the years, I always make use of a simple experiment that Edward Deming introduced to the business world. Dr. Rondy Smith first demonstrated the Red Bead Experiment to me while I was completing my master degree in business. Dr. Smith developed a curriculum master's degree program centered on the Total Quality Management practices and the Deming philosophy of science management. This demonstration is referred to as the Red Bead Experiment. It is a simple model used to demonstrate that it is all too easy to blame workers for faults that belong to system processes. I have been a participant as well as a person who guided the demonstration on several occasions. Other lessons have also revealed themselves from this experimental exercise.

The experiment starts with the selection of ten volunteers from the audience. These ten people come forward. Six of these selected will act as apprentice workers. Two others are appointed as inspectors, another as a chief inspector, and the tenth person is the recorder. The person leading and conducting the demonstration acts as the foreman.

There is an open box that contains a total of 3750 wooden beads. Of the 3750 wooden beads, 3000 are white beads and 750 are red beads. A paddle is available for scooping out beads from the box. This paddle has 50 beveled depressions (10 x 5); one scoop with the paddle pulls up 50 beads.

The conductor of this experiment (the person presenting the Red Bead Experiment) acts as the foreman. The foreman explains that we are a manufacturing company and we make white beads for our customers. Our customers only accept white beads and not red beads. The foreman also strongly states that the company has work standards. The work standard is each worker must produce 50 bead items per day, good and bad combined. The company goal, "No more than one red bead per day for anyone on the job."

After a brief demonstration by the foreman, all the people on the job agree that they understand what to do. They take the paddle, scoop up beads from the box containing red and white beads, and present their work to the inspectors. Each worker begins to follow the process. After scooping the beads the inspectors count the number of red beads and white beads. These results are written down to prepare a statistic. The worker (using the paddle loaded with 50 beads) then carefully puts the beads back into the box for the next worker to take a scoop. After recording the results of everyone's first turn, the foreman acts angry concerning the results. It is rare that anyone gets a scoop of only one read bead. It is even rarer to see a paddle of white beads only. Usually the results show 3 to 9 red beads on the paddle. The foreman pretends to be disappointed with the workers. Only one of the workers on the first day had only 4 red beads. Everyone else had more. But the foreman encourages the workers by isolating one of the workers and praising the one for the almost good results. Why can't the rest of you workers do as well as this one? This process continues for three more turns by each participant.

At the end of the experiment, the foreman reviews the data and informs the workers that even though they have tried hard, their best was not good enough. No worker has met the goal of one red bead. Shouldn't this goal be a reasonable goal? The company never expected perfection of only 50 white beads. The procedures were fixed and we included a margin of error for the workers. There should have been no variation. Why is one lot different from the other? The workers produced a low yield and this constitutes closing the company due to unexpected production outcomes.

PART TWO: VALIDATION THINKING

Flow Chart of the Process

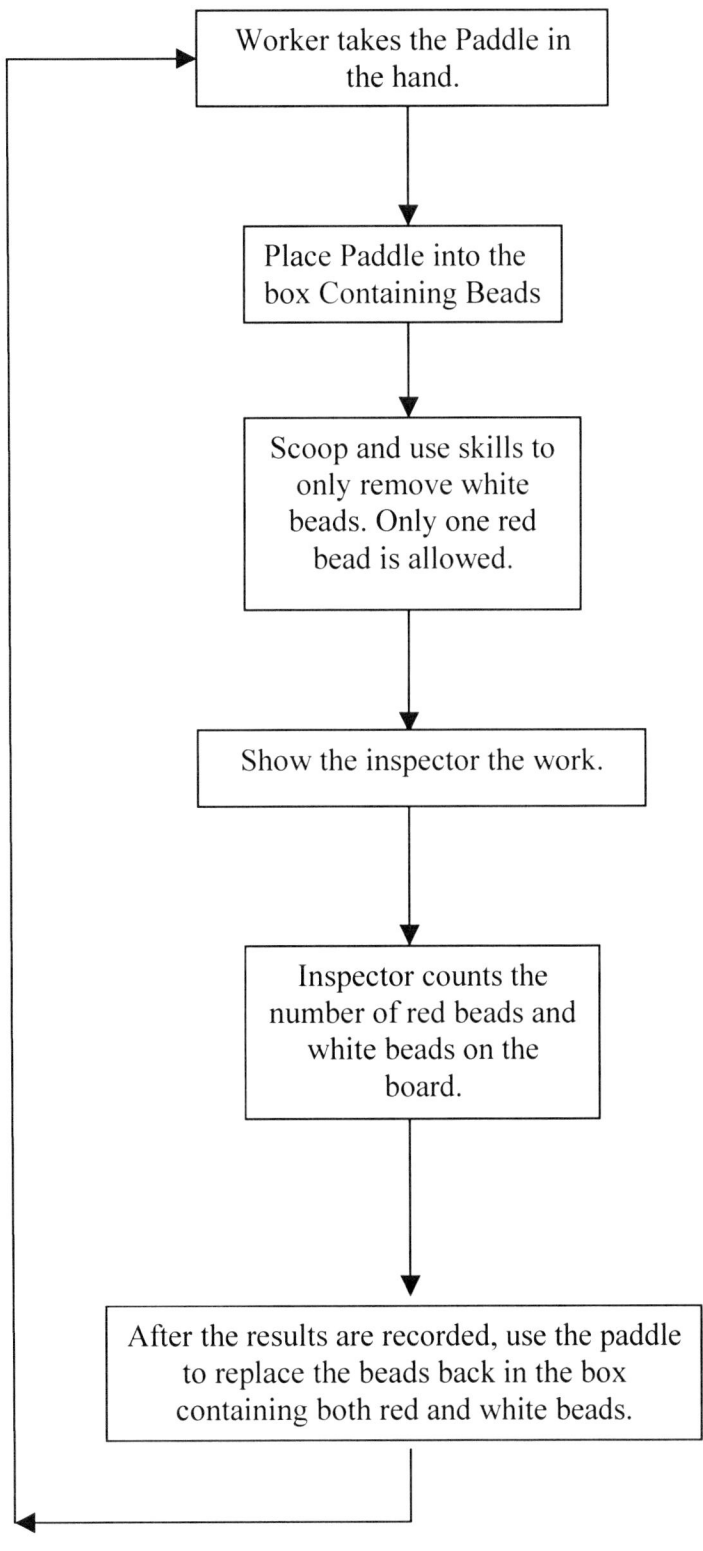

Here are the results of the Red Bead Experiment we conducted while I was attending graduate school.

	Day 1 Red Beads	Day 2 Red Beads	Day 3 Red Beads	Day 4 Red Beads	
Worker 1	6	10	6	6	28
Worker 2	4	11	13	13	41
Worker 3	8	9	7	6	30
Worker 4	9	10	3	10	32
Worker 5	6	12	6	13	37
Worker 6	9	6	11	3	29
Totals	42	58	46	51	197

These are the Total Number of Red Beads or occurrences of defects recorded from the paddle. So, 197 red beads (defects) were identified for six workers during 4-day period. The four working days, represents the four turns those apprentice workers took. We are modeling a process to illustrate what occurs when we tamper with processes. The chart below shows the number of defects plotted per worker per day for a total of twenty-four recorded values.

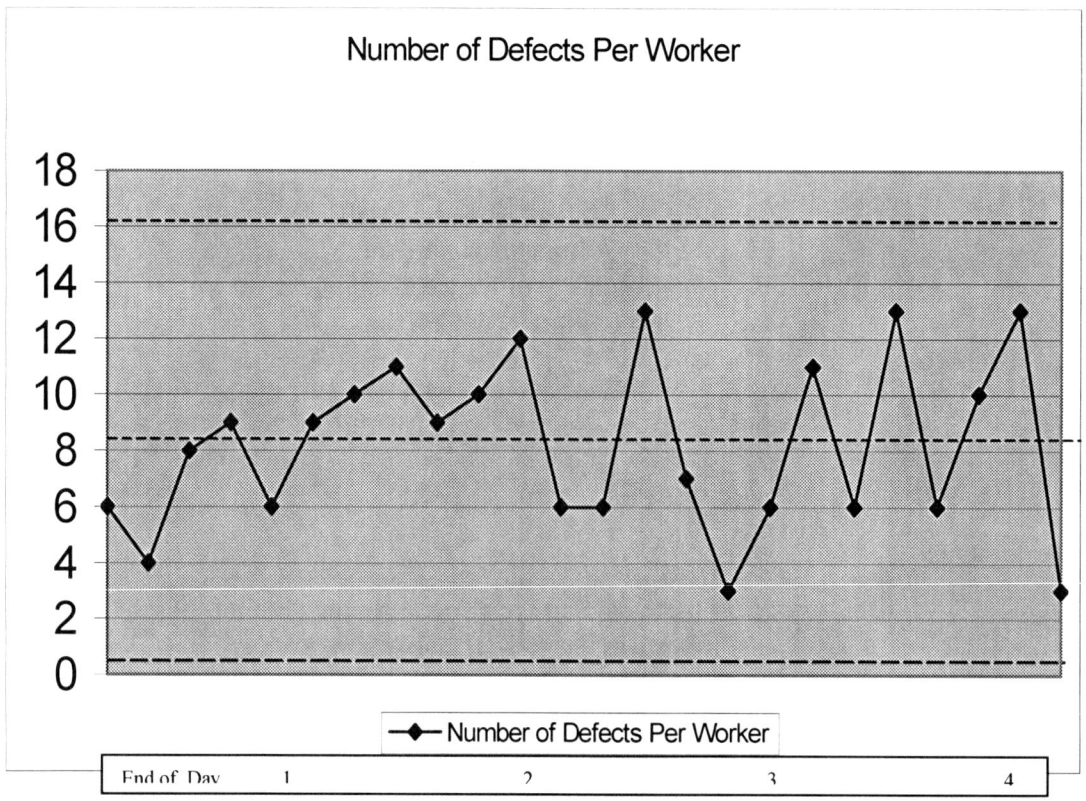

PART TWO: VALIDATION THINKING

In order for our run chart to become a control chart, we must calculate the upper control limit, the average, and lower control limit. We will need to do the math to understand what these values mean and why their calculations are important. I have already drawn the dash lines for the values of the average, lower and upper control limits. Here is how we do the math to calculate the upper and lower control limits.
1) First, calculate the daily average:

There are 6 workers taking 4 turns (days) with the paddle. Total defects are 197.

So the average = $\bar{x} = \dfrac{197}{(6 \times 4)} = 8.21$ this is the central tendency of this process.

2) Now that we have the average daily occurrences, let us calculate the upper and lower control limits for this process:

Let $\bar{p}$ represent the average proportion or ratio of red beads to total beads drawn from the box using the paddle that holds 50 beads of both red and white.

$\bar{p} = \dfrac{197}{(6 \times 4 \times 50)} = .16$ rounded to two digits

6 = the number of workers, 4 = the number of turns taken by each worker, there are 50 wholes on the paddle that have a possibility of taking on any number of white and red beads, and 197 is the total number of red beads observed during this process.

So the limits for this process are $x \pm 3\sqrt{x(1-p)}$ Note: the number 3 stands for three standard deviations on either side of the mean.

The upper limit is = $x + 3\sqrt{x(1-p)}$

$\qquad$ Upper Limit = $8.21 + 3\sqrt{8.21(1-.16)} = 16.08$

The lower limit is = $x - 3\sqrt{x(1-p)}$

$\qquad$ Lower Limit = $8.21 - 3\sqrt{8.21(1-.16)} = 1.13$

The upper limit, the lower limit, and the mean are represented in the chart with dotted lines. When we begin an interpretation of the chart, one might conclude that the process is in statistical control. No points fall above or below the control limits. For purposes of managing the organization, management would conclude that it would be wise to proceed and focus the workers to gravitate to the goal of only one red bead permitted (maximum) for 50. If the process is stable, then it would be futile to try to discover why a particular worker had 3 red bead errors on one day and then on another day made 11 red bead errors. We would like to think that any point on the chart is discrete and is self explaining. Others will insist that every point on the chart must be explained. We have a process that is in statistical control, yet there exists variation in this process. A hero will always view these variations and all the other variations in the table and the chart as data that came from the system, not necessarily from the workers themselves.

It is important to understand what it means to be in statistical control and why processes should be reviewed first before blaming people. When people are targeted as the blame, we are committing an availability error. Our experiment was simple, but it makes a point. Once a person has participated in the red bead experiment they begin to find red beads (sources of trouble) all over their organizations.

What does it mean to be in statistical control? In order to answer this question, we will examine the experimental red bead process. This means understanding accuracy and consistency. Quality equals accuracy plus consistency. The control chart is a specialized time chart that displays the values of the data in the order in which they were collected over time. In our chart, the person who went first was plotted on the chart and we continued to add data over time. Even though the goal was to allow one red bead per person per turn, the actual value for this process was 8.21 red beads on the average. So our chart focuses on red beads (errors) because the goal was to only have one red bead (error) per person per one scoop of the paddle.

To use statistics to monitor quality, you first have to figure out a way to define and measure accuracy and consistency. It is okay to begin with a hypothetical value of only one error out of fifty. However, once the process began the data showed that our consistency was eight errors on the average. Statistically speaking, we are consistent if the standard deviation is small. It is obvious that even though we are within control limits, our process is not meeting our goal. It may be that one error in fifty is incapable of achievement if workers continue to follow this process. The beautiful thing about this control chart is that we have a true picture to better understand what the process is capable of producing. The data is accurate if it does not contain any bias. Bias is a word we hear quite often and most people consider it a bad word. But bias is a systematic favoritism that is present in the data collection process that results in lopsided, misleading results.

There are several lessons we can learn from our experiment. One lesson is that variation is part of any process. We also learn that workers will be average, some above average, and some below average. But workers performance will vary over time, because worker performance is part of this process. Average workers become above average and vise versa. Many managers set goals and hold workers to these goals even though the goals may not be achievable without changing the process. Workers are often punished or rewarded for performance over which they have no control. The most important lesson we learn is that only management can change a system or empower employees to change it. But we should never make a change unless there is an understanding of the difference in common cause variation and special cause variation. Making a change without identifying these two types of variation would be tampering with a process.

The collection of the aspects of the process that affect every occurrence and their interaction is often referred to as common cause variation. Common cause variation is produced by the interaction of aspects of a process that affects every occurrence. The control chart we produced diagrams the variation due to the process that was flow- charted. Once we have done the charts and calculations, we have a model of the common cause variation of a process. However, variation in a process that does not affect every occurrence but arises because of special circumstances is special cause variation.

An example of "common cause" and "special cause" variation in a process, let us consider a baseball pitcher. If the pitcher has good control, most of the pitches are going to be where the pitcher wants them. There will be some variation, but not too much. If the pitcher is a "wild" pitcher, the pitches aren't going to be in the strike zone; there's more variation. There may not be any special causes - no wind, no physical change in the baseball itself - just more "common cause" variation. The result: more walks are issued, and there are unintended fast pitches out over the plate where batters cannot hit them. In baseball, control wins ball games. Likewise, in most processes, reducing common cause variation saves money. Happily, there are easy-to-use charts, which make it easy to see both special and common cause variations in a process just as the one produced with the red bead experiment. These control charts are also known sometimes as Shewhart charts, after their inventor, Walter Shewhart, of Bell Labs. There are many different subspecies of control charts, which can be applied to the different types of process data, which are typically available. When a person (manager or worker) takes action without taking into account the difference between special and common cause variation, that person is **tampering**.

An example of tampering with processes can be illustrated with the following exercise. This is also known as Shewhart's Lesson. If we take a group of people numbering from 10 to 100 people, we give this group a simple exercise (process) to accomplish. First we ask who are left hand dominant and right hand dominant, as well as ambidextrous. We then ask participants to take pencil and paper and begin writing down the letter "a." Sometime I have asked people to draw a three dimensional box. We continue drawing or writing with the predominate hand, then the group is asked to switch hands and continue to write or draw. Here are some of the results.

The cursive letter "a" was written with the dominant right hand (starting from left to right) four times. Then the person was asked to use the left hand to write the next three letters. Another person who was left-handed drew boxes. When asked to change to the other hand, note the difference. Think about this lesson on a larger scale every time you think about variation. Assignable causes of variation may be found and eliminated. In this lesson, a manager brought about change in a process. These managers who just don't get it, end up whipping the horse when in actuality it is the rider that is at fault.

Another example of common cause variation would be writing your name ten times, your signatures would all be similar, but no two signatures will be exactly alike. There is an inherent variation, but it varies between predictable limits. If, as you are signing your name, someone bumps your elbow, you get an unusual variation due to what is called a "special cause". If you are cutting diamonds, and someone bumps your elbow, the special cause variation can be expensive. For many processes, it is important to notice special causes of variation as soon as they occur.

With respect to the red bead experiment, I have personally added both special cause and common cause variation to the experiment. By assigning causes of variation to the process, the experiment changed dynamically with respect to form and degree. One part of the process that I would change is the output. Instead of having the workers empty the beads back into the same box, they would have to separate the red and white beads into two separate boxes. The original process was to have the workers empty their paddle of red beads and white beads back into the box that they took beads from. When we put beads back into the box we took them from, we are statistically performing replacement. We are not removing red and white beads from the system. Instead we have a feedback loop that has been created and every worker has an equal chance of scooping red and white beads. The recorded results are quite different when we put red and white beads in other containers not making the beads drawn previously available for the next person.

One could suggest that if we didn't replace beads back into the box, then eventually we would remove all the errors. The interesting thing about the red bead exercise is that we are not giving credit to the workers for removing errors (red beads) we are punishing them for committing errors. If we were able to invert this process and note a different perspective, assignable causes of variation may be found and eliminated. Our process does not say to remove the red beads from the system, only to count them and return them back to the container. So instead of rewarding workers for removing errors, we punish them by recording errors committed and feeding the error (red beads) back into the system due to the process design.

Most of us have heard the expression, "that child's behavior is out of control." Until we do the control chart, we really do not know. We have to have a measurement, a metric. We have to agree to what it is we are measuring and what the initial conditions of the system are. Then we must monitor and document a statistic to understand what are the control limits of our process. It is very much like traveling faster than the speed of sound. It starts with rival explanations and espoused theories predicting what could or will happen at such speeds. Braking across any barrier in life is this way. Getting to the goal seems very chaotic and out of control. Many experts theorized that a jet plane breaking the sound barrier would cause any designed aircraft to brake apart. Air Force Captain Charles "Chuck" Yeager broke this barrier on October 14, 1947. Pushing an aircraft to go over the barrier was an out of control experience. But once we brake over the barrier, new and wonderful things begin to happen and a different set of control values takes over the process. We recalculate our information with the new applied theories.

Summary and Interpretation of the Chart - Deming -TQM

According to Dr. Deming, continuous improvement means growth through quality. This concept of continuous improvement can be applied to all aspects of our personal life as well as organizations. Dr. Deming's quality principles in the context of education, business, and other enterprises are providing new inspiration to organizations seeking to create a culture of constant learning. Total Quality Management (TQM) is an integrated management system for creating and implementing a continuous quality improvement process. An established continuous quality improvement process eventually produces results that exceed expectations. The control chart is the heart of Total Quality Management in monitoring any process.

All control charts have three basic components:

- a centerline, usually the mathematical average of all the samples plotted.
- upper and lower statistical control limits that define the constraints of common cause variations.
- performance data plotted over time.

There are things to look for and a point to making control charts. The point of making control charts is to look at variation, seeking special causes and tracking common causes. Special causes can be spotted using several tests:

- 1 data point falling outside the control limits
- 6 or more points in a row steadily increasing or decreasing
- 8 or more points in a row on one side of the centerline
- 14 or more points alternating up and down

During chart analysis that pairs two charts together, it is important to review both charts for anomalies. The simplest interpretation of the control chart is to use only the first test listed. The others may indeed be useful (and there are more not listed here), but be mindful that, as you apply more tests, your chances of making Type I errors (false positives), will rise significantly.

There are several types of errors that can occur when evaluating control charts. Control limits on a control chart are commonly drawn at 3-sigma (3 standard deviations above the center line and 3 standard deviations below the center line) from the center line because 3-sigma limits are a good balance point between two types of errors:

➢ Type I (one) or alpha errors occur when a point falls outside the control limits even though no special cause is operating. The result is a witch-hunt for special causes and adjustment of things here and there. The tampering usually distorts a stable process as well as wasting time and energy. This is where most zero managers go wrong. I have also noticed this with Six-Sigma programs. Zero managers turn everything into a six-sigma project. Making coffee in the morning for workers in the office is a preference (how strong or not strong) not a six-sigma project.

➢ Type II (two) or beta errors occur when you miss a special cause because the chart isn't sensitive enough to detect it. In this case, you will go along unaware that the problem exists and thus unable to root it out.

All process control is vulnerable to these two types of errors. The reason that 3-sigma control limits balance the risk of error is that, for normally distributed data, data points will fall inside 3-sigma limits 99.7% of the time when a process is in control. This makes the "witch hunts" infrequent but still makes it likely that unusual causes of variation will be detected. Detecting causation in a process requires clear thinking. So, how should one respond to special cause variation that is picked up by your control chart? If your process is in control, is that good enough? Most will say "No." You have to start by removing special causes, so that you have a stable process to work with. But then comes the real fun, and often the most substantial benefits: it is time to improve the process, so that even common cause variation is reduced. How to do that?

Stability involves achieving consistent and, ultimately, higher process yields through the application of an improvement methodology. Does a process need to be stable in order for an organization to improve it? Try educating a child when he/she is having fits of joy and emotional distress at the same time (as many youngsters do!). The child's emotional state is out of statistical control. Process stability (also known as variation reduction) is important to understand. Building widgets to be within customer specifications or tolerances demonstrate variation. Some variation is inherent in the process, but the variation may not be wider than the specifications allow, otherwise the widget may not fit or function properly. Changing the oil in your car is important every 3000 miles (or now even longer): Adding too much or too little oil may damage the engine.

We can evaluate any process and monitor whether the process is under statistical control. Blood pressure or the sugar in our body, if it is to low or to high then medication is administered to control the high blood pressure or solve the diabetic problems. Heartbeat should be at a certain rate, if too high or too low, you die. Banks look at loan to deposit ratios to be in control. Again, variation is inherent, but the specifications of high or low must be met. So, how does one define process stability and or process control? Managers must agree on some given amount of process shifting, maybe 1.5 sigma or perhaps we can agree that a stable process is where its sigma is 1.67. Perhaps some combination of these or other events need to take place such as three consecutive samples over 1.67. Until we can define what a stable process is for our organizations, we are doomed to argue forever. This is why control charts are so important. They provide the objective measure (remember the example of the thermometer), a picture, that acts as a tool to reduce rival explanations. Stabilizing a process or system means that we are in control of the system rather than the system controlling us. A stable process means understanding and identifying as many of the causes of variation that govern the system so our output of the process is more often predictable (trying for 99.7% of the time) than not predictable.

So what does this have to do with improving our educational system, student achievement tests, business systems, or any other system for that matter? When we recognized Total Quality Management as a tool for improvement, it becomes apparent that any organization moves from a philosophical (school of thought) process to a more scientific process. I find it interesting that the philosophical movements (such as the Progressive movement) in education were strong at times in America's education. Philosophical thought seemed to guide much of the educational climate as well as our businesses. Each group of thinkers champions the cause, which to its supporters appears to contain the greatest degree of truth without reference to science. We need to understand how people learn from a scientific approach. The question to ask is what is the science of learning, not what will be our philosophy of teaching.

So where are we now? The issues that may arise within systems that fail to produce results, is that we are looking at a third order problem with first and second order thinking. There are obviously different ways to convince people of what process stability is depending upon many different types of situations. We need a universally acceptable solution supported by respectable organizations or some other more obvious third order solution (via breakthrough) that fits all types of situations. Are the goals of our system within control limits and are the processes we have given to worker/employee capable? The Capability Coefficients of the control chart are statistics that measure short and long term capability. I think that if these two measures of capability are not significantly different for a certain period of time, then we can conclude that the process was also stable during that period of time or will never work to produce outcomes. The purpose of any control chart is to help one understand any process well enough to take the right action. This degree of understanding is only possible when the control limits appropriately reflect the expected behavior of the process. When the control limits no longer represent the expected behavior, you have lost your ability to take the right action. This state of cycling between the brink of chaos and the state of chaos can be broken. Process improvement evaluates the efforts at improvement and then the cycling is between the threshold state and the ideal state. Every process will naturally migrate toward a state of chaos. With the knowledge and the continual recalculation of control charts, the repairs to any organization's process are fairly easy to make. Without the use of control charts, how can anyone determine whether any system is in the state of chaos or in an ideal state? There are instances of a system manifesting a chaotic state, but it works well as an ideal state.

Management Actions to take when Process Variation is due to Both Special and Common Causes

- ➢ Immediately try to understand why a special cause occurred. Measure first, then fix.
- ➢ Determine what was different when the special cause occurred.
- ➢ Identify ways to prevent the special cause from reoccurring, if undesirable.
- ➢ Do not make fundamental changes in the process (never tamper).

The goal is to be in statistical control. This means stability. When a special cause is identified, it must be eliminated.

Management Actions to take when Process Variation is due to Common Causes Only

- ➢ Understand that any process has an inherent capability, which will not change unless the process is changed.
- ➢ Identify aspects of the process that affects all occurrences and look at process variables to improve the result.
- ➢ Determine which aspect of the process to change in order to reduce variation and /or shift the mean value. Note: Our red bead experiment, the target mean was to be one red bead. Could it be possible to lower the actual mean value of our experiment?
- ➢ Do not try to interpret individual occurrences of the process or theorize the differences between occurrences that are above and below the mean on the control chart.

Errors in Interpretation of the Statistic

"There are lies, damn lies and statistics." This familiar quote has been given credit to several famous people to include Mark Twain, Will Rogers and Prime Minister Benjamin D'Israili. However, statistics do not tell lies, only people do. If we avoid the errors and some of the pit-falls of statistical interpretation, statistics actually assists in approaching the truth about people, products and processes. It is generally people who misinterpret a statistic and that particular person tell the lies. The issue is that most people have an innumeracy problem and as a result these people have low familiarity with statistical probability assessment.

PART TWO: VALIDATION THINKING

I have stressed the importance of statistical measurement using the control chart to monitor processes over time. It is important to understand statistical thinking to reduce the many selection possibilities that are inappropriate actions for improvement. Heroes rarely take inappropriate action. Many of our organizations (education & business) fail to find special causes. Because people are not trained to distinguish common cause variation from special cause variation, it becomes inevitable that inappropriate action is taken only to create the illusion of improvement. Zero (manager/leaders) just don't get it. The first rule in statistical thinking is to avoid tampering a process. Processes can be identified as a thought process, a procedure for building computers, or any process implemented in our organizations. Heroes identify these processes and understand that the best decisions for any organization or relationships are driven by data. In all aspects of our lives, and importantly in the business context, an amazing diversity of data is available for inspection and analytical insight. Heroes have learned to apply statistical thinking and justify their decisions based on the data. Heroes understand the importance of statistical based decision support. Heroes understand and recognize the statistical skills that enable organizations to intelligently collect, analyze, and interpret data relevant to their decision-making processes. Statistical concepts and statistical thinking enable organizations to:

- ➢ focus on special cause problems in a diversity of contexts.
- ➢ add evidence and substance to decisions.
- ➢ reduce risk and guesswork.

Statistical thinking is a data driven method for decision making based primarily on an understanding of process variation leading to process improvement. It results in wise management actions which contribute to the continuous improvement of quality. The key points are:

1) Conceptualize the thought process with science rather than conceptualizing with school of thought or movement. Identify the objective measure.
2) Data should be used to guide the improvement process, not dictate or generate a new process. Never implement a new process unless verified results of the old process have been recognized and accounted for.
3) Variation in a process is assignable to special and/or common causes.
4) The common cause system must be studied to improve a process affected only by common cause variation.
5) Tampering with a process only makes things worse.
6) In order to extract meaning from data, the data should be collected over long time sequences as they occur.
7) Predictions cannot be made about a process affected by special causes. This means if a process is unstable it makes it very difficult to make predictions about the future behavior of this particular system.

8) Look for evidence of special cause variations.
9) Statistical thinking means having knowledge transfer of people and the process studied.

The above are some of the principles that heroes apply in statistical thinking. The following are some examples that heroes try to understand and to avoid.

The Hawthorne Effect

At the Western Electric Hawthorne Company in Cicero, Illinois (a suburb of Chicago) experiments were conducted from 1927 to 1932. Professor Elton Mayo conducted studies and examined productivity and work conditions at the plant. These experiments started by examining the physical and environmental influences of the workplace such as brightness of lights, humidity, etc. Later psychological aspects such as rest breaks, group pressure, working hours, and managerial leadership were studied.

The studies grew out of preliminary experiments at the Hawthorne plant from 1924 to 1927 to determine what the effect of lighting had on worker productivity. Those experiments showed no clear connection between productivity and the amount of light illumination in the plant, but researchers began to wonder what kind of changes would influence output. Specifically, Mayo wanted to find out what effect fatigue and daily routines had on job productivity and how to control them through such variables as rest breaks, work hours, temperature and humidity. In the process, he stumbled upon a principle of human motivation that would help to revolutionize the theory and practice of management.

Mayo selected two women, and had those two select an additional four from the assembly line, segregated them from the rest of the factory and put them under the eye of a supervisor who was more a friendly observer than disciplinarian. Mayo made frequent changes in their working conditions, always discussing and explaining the changes in advance. The group was employed in assembling telephone relays - a relay being a small but intricate mechanism composed of about forty separate parts which had to be assembled by the workers seated at a long bench and dropped into a chute when completed.

The relays were mechanically counted as they slipped down the chute. The intent was to measure the basic rate of production before making any environmental changes. Then, as changes were introduced, the impact to effectiveness would be measured by increased or decreased production of the relays. Throughout the series of experiments, an observer sat with the workers in the workshop noting all that went on, keeping them informed about the experiment, asking for advice or information, and listening to their complaints.

PART TWO: VALIDATION THINKING

The experiment began by introducing various changes, each of which was continued for a test period of four to twelve weeks. The results of these changes were 2,400 relays were produced by these women, under normal conditions with a forty-eight hour week, including Saturdays, and no rest pauses. They were then put on piecework for eight weeks. The output increased. They were then given two five-minute breaks, one in the morning, and one in the afternoon, for a period of five weeks. Output increased, yet again. The breaks were each lengthened to ten minutes. Output rose sharply. Six five-minute breaks were introduced. The girls complained that their work rhythm was broken by the frequent pauses. Output fell only slightly. Then the original two breaks were reinstated, this time, with a complimentary hot meal provided during the morning break. Output increased further still. The workday was then shortened to end at 4.30 p.m. instead of 5.00 p.m. Output increased. The workday was then shortened to end at 4.00 p.m. Output leveled off. Finally, all the improvements were taken away, and the original conditions before the experiment were reinstated. They were monitored in this state for 12 more weeks. Output was the highest ever recorded - averaging 3000 relays a week.

Elton Mayo came to the following conclusions as a result of the Hawthorne study. He determined that the aptitudes of individuals are imperfect predictors of job performance. Although they give some indication of the physical and mental potential of the individual, the amount produced is strongly influenced by social factors. The Hawthorne researchers discovered a group culture among the workers. The studies also showed that the relations that supervisors develop with workers tend to influence the manner in which the workers carry out directives. The Hawthorne researchers were not the first to recognize that work groups tend to arrive at norms of what is "a fair day's work." However, they provided the best systematic description and interpretation of this phenomenon. The Hawthorne researchers came to view the workplace as a social system made up of interdependent parts. The worker is a person whose attitudes and effectiveness are conditioned by social demands from both inside and outside the work plant. Informal group within the work plant exercise strong social controls over the work habits and attitudes of the individual worker. The need for recognition, security and sense of belonging is more important in determining workers' morale and productivity than the physical conditions under which they work. The major finding of the study was that almost regardless of the experimental manipulation, worker production seemed to continually improve. One reasonable conclusion is that the workers were happy to receive attention from the researchers who expressed an interest in them. Originally, the study was expected to last one year, but since the findings were inexplicable when the researchers tried to relate the worker's efficiency to manipulated physical conditions, the project was incrementally extended to five years.

It becomes clear that the improvement in working conditions did not improve performance. The results must have been related to the research process itself. In essence, the Hawthorne Effect can be summarized as "Individual behaviors may be altered because they know they are being studied." In the Hawthorne experiments, an increase in worker productivity was produced by the psychological stimulus of being singled out, involved, and made to feel important. Additionally, the act of measurement, itself, **tampers** with the results of the measurement. Just as dipping a thermometer into a vial of liquid can affect the temperature of the liquid being measured, the act of collecting data, where none was collected before creates a situation that didn't exist before, thereby affecting the results. This type of accidental tampering is known as the Hawthorne Effect. I use the Deming terminology "tampering" because during Dr. Deming's outstanding career, he was once employed as an engineer at the Hawthorne Plant. Elton Mayo had made an interesting discovery concerning measurement that was already previously discovered by modern physicists, that the very act of the measurement procedure in quantum mechanics introduces uncertainty into the data collection. This is known as the uncertainty principle. Often researchers come to experiments with expectations. If their expectations are numerous and extremely varied, no bias will result. This was an excellent study because the unexpected results of the experiment were made known rather than concluding that light illumination produced the expected results of increased productivity.

So what can we learn from the Hawthorne experiment? When researchers took an interest in the people, the process improved. Changes to the environment did not improve the process. As stated earlier, love people and using things are the mark of good heroes. During the research, the researchers focused on things and were unaware that their interest in people (not things) is what improved the workers production.

Beware of Lurking Variables

Many times answers to system problems become paradoxical. This means that several solutions exist that are counter to what our intuition tells us. Here is another example where intuition (common sense) fails concerning a case of discrimination. To illustrate, let us review data given by an attorney concerning a University's lawsuit over the admissions practices for both men and women. The initial data showed that there was no discrimination against women who had applied for the college of business and the school of Law. The initial data tells that there is no discrimination. By percentages more women were admitted to the Business College of this University and the law school also admitted more women.

PART TWO: VALIDATION THINKING

Business College

120 men applied	18 men accepted	15%
120 women applied	24 women accepted	20%

Law School

240 men applied	180 men accepted	75%
80 women applied	64 women accepted	80%

So now a question of causation arises. Percentage-wise, it appeared obvious to everyone on the jury that more women were being accepted for admissions than men were. Was there favoritism toward the men or the women? The jury had to decide. A statistician was asked to evaluate this data. It was necessary to investigate further to determine if there really existed a strong association with regard to discrimination. The women involved in this lawsuit insisted that the University discriminates, but the data told a different story. So, it was necessary to go beyond common sense and investigate the data several times to find lurking variables not identified by the original study. Statisticians used defendant's data to prove a point by adding a new category called TOTALS.

Here is the result of a simple calculation.

Simpson's Paradox

	Business	*Law*	*Totals*
Men	$\frac{18}{120}$	$\frac{180}{240}$	$\frac{198}{360} = 55\%$
Women	$\frac{24}{120}$	$\frac{64}{80}$	$\frac{88}{200} = 44\%$

When a statistician was asked to combine the data of the two separate categories, a different answer emerged. This answer was counter-intuitive to the original data that had been considered mutually exclusive data by the defense attorney's analysis team. The answer displayed in the category identified as "Totals," is a paradox. In statistics this is known as Simpson's Paradox. The initial data showed that there was absolutely no association with gender, but further investigation gave us a different answer, women were being discriminated against. This is to illustrate why analysis of information is so important and why everyone must investigate all possibilities. Many times answers to system problems become paradoxical. This means that several solutions exist that are counter to what our initial intuition tells us.

The Space Shuttle Challenger

In January 1986 when the Space Shuttle Challenger took off on a routine flight, less than 2 minutes after take off, the space shuttle exploded. This was due to a miscalculation of risk to the lives of the people that were on board the shuttle. Due to a misunderstanding of calculating an event probability, the true risk value of a safe and successful flight was mis-communicated. Where statistics could have provided truth of the real risks involved with the "O-Ring" failure, engineers made assumptions founded essentially on common sense. NASA tested a single O-Ring to be 97.7% reliable. Common sense informed engineers that the total risk of 6 failures would only be equivalent to the risk of the one. Statisticians later determined that 6 O-rings should have been considered as 6 independent events. As a result, the true risk was $(97.7)^6$ = 87.6% reliability for the system

An automobile is not safe without four tires aligned and balanced around the car. Engineers can test each tire independently, but without the accuracy of all four tires tested as a whole, the automobile could end in a fatal failure. Statistics plays a very important role and again should be essential in evaluation and decision making practices concerning risk. Instead of using statistics for accuracy, we choose to use common sense, which has proven to be ineffective in many incidents. Common sense alone cannot always determine risks and probabilities. We must put all possibilities to a statistical test. It was proven during the shuttle investigation that treating six o-rings as one independent event is like playing Russian roulette. The improper application of statistics can cause outcomes to be chaotic and destructive.

<u>Drug Testing & Bayes' Rule</u>

Assuming that a new test has been proposed to test potential illegal drug users by a company. Clinical trials have been done for the test using a controlled environment. These trials have produced the following estimates: if a person is an illegal drug user the test is 99% successful in identifying it, but if a person is not an illegal drug user then the test says so 99.5% of the time. The proponents of the test are claiming that these numbers show that the test is highly effective. Is the test reliable enough to terminate a worker's employment for those people who test positive on the first test for illegal drugs?

In effect, we are asking for the probability that a person actually is an illegal drug user given that the test says so. Let us say that if this probability is close to 1 (say at least .99 or 99%) the test is a reliable indicator of the presents of illegal drugs.

PART TWO: VALIDATION THINKING

Now let E1 be the event that a person is an illegal drug user, while E2 is the event that a person is NOT an illegal drug user. Let E be the event that the test is positive. Suppose it is estimated that one person of 250 people in our organization is a regular illegal drug user. If this person or several other people test positive, how reliable is the drug test?

To answer this question in this example we will want to compute P(E1|E). In order to compute P(E1|E) we will need to have an understanding of Bayes' Rule when revising estimates. The statement P(E1|E) we call it the conditional probability that event E1 will occur, given that event E has already occurred (the test shows positive). So the statement P(E1|E) is said "the probability of event E1 given E. This is a statement of revising our estimate. Let us use the example of dice to show this relationship.

This is the sample space for a pair of dice. One dice is white and the other one black, this is so we can tell them apart. This sample space has 36 elements or outcomes if we roll the dice together. When we roll two dice there are 36 equally likely outcomes, so the probability of these unbiased dice (these dice are not rigged) each is 1/36. This probability is to say that if anyone were to roll the dice a very large number of times (looking for the number 3 to appear on the first dice rolled and then a 6 on the next dice), in the long run this outcome of (3, then 6) would be expected (if unbiased) to occur 1/36 of the time if the order is three first six second.

In order to talk about an event, we need to introduce a new idea. When we look at the table of dice, if we describe an event to be "dice that add to 3" then the probability of this event is the sum of the probabilities of the elementary outcomes in the set.

Dice Add to 3: {(1,2), (2,1) so the probability P (Event)=2/36 or 1/18

So we have two (2) occurrences in our sample space that add up to the number 3. Because we have placed a condition on our sample space, we have placed a restriction on the possible outcomes. Suppose now we alter our experiment again. In the example of dice adding up to 3, we calculated the probability before the dice were thrown. Now suppose one of the dice is thrown first and it is revealed to be a one (1).

Now we have an observed event that we will call event (B). What is the probability of the next dice being a two to add up to three (3)? We will call this unobserved event (A). This is what is referred to as conditional probability. The condition that event B is observed to have already occurred, what is the probability of event A occurring? In statistics it is referred to as the probability of A given B P(A|B). Remember, before any dice were thrown, the sample space was 36 outcomes. Now we have observed an outcome of event B to be 100% certainty to be a one (1). Now we need to diagram the reduced sample space as a result of event B.

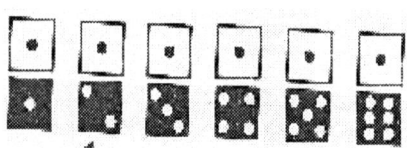

In the reduced sample space of six elements, only one element will add to make the number three (3). The conditional probability is now 1/6. In general, to find the conditional probability of two events (A|B), we must evaluate the two events as part of the reduced sample space B. This is a demonstration of how heroes revise their estimates the proper way.

Conditional probability is an essential concept in statistics that will help us understand drug testing and Bayes' Rule. Returning to our original issue with drug testing and the 250 employees:

P(E1) = 1/250, event that one tests positive   P(E2) = 249/250 event that 249 do not test positive for illegal drug use. Note, the lab people told us that the test is 99% accurate in successfully identifying drug users and if a person is not a user the test is accurate to 99.5% of the time. This means that 0.5% of our group will indicate that a person does illegal drugs, but in actuality they are not an illegal drug user. These people are the false positive testers.

P(E|E1) = .99, P(E|E2) = .005 which says that the test will indicate positive but is negative

Using Bayes' Rule:

$$P(E1|E) = \frac{P(E|E1)P(E1)}{P(E|E1)P(E1) + P(E|E2)P(E2)}$$

Substituting the numbers = $\frac{.99(1/250)}{.99(1/250) + .005(249/250)}$ = $\frac{.00396}{(.00396) + (.00498)}$

therefore $\frac{.00396}{.00894}$ = .4429530 or 44.29%   this is the probability of being an illegal drug user given a positive result.

Interesting, after doing the math, there is only a 44% chance that a person actually is an illegal drug user when tested positive. This seems too small to be taken as a reliable indicator. Despite the high accuracy of the test, less than 44% of those testing positive actually are illegal drug users. This is called the ***false positive paradox***. The word paradox comes from the Greek word *paradoxos*. *Para* meaning beyond and *doxa* meaning opinion. Earlier in the book I mentioned what can happen when things go beyond our concept horizon and things conflict with an expectation founded in schools of thought and movement conceptualization. Without an objective measure (statistics), we commit the availability error. A seemingly contradictory statement challenges our errored beliefs. Bayes' rule probes statements and processes that are seemingly contradictory to opinion, but nonetheless become true. Reversing an opinion to test for truth is rarely considered by zeroes. Zeroes hold dearly to the availability error and trust their first opinion. Statistics is an excellent tool to test our intuitive logic with an objective measure. Statistics assists us in identifying paradoxical actions, situations, and opinion.

Concerning Randomness - Birth Dates and The 1970 Draft

A mistake concerning randomness was made concerning the Vietnam draft lottery in 1970. Accusations that the draft was unfair became a political issue. Many United States citizens complained that the draft boards were only selecting people on the lower income brackets and selection avoided the privileged upper income groups. So in order to make everything fair, Congress changed the selection process to be a random selection based on birth date. Random means that a clear pattern is generally not apparent and free of bias. So due to claims of unfair selection, in 1970 the draft board turned draft selection for Vietnam into a lottery to make the selection process fair. Or did they?

In 1970 the selection board took the birthdays of age eligible young men, printed these numbers on balls, and then put the birthday labeled balls in a big bin. A person was assigned to remove the balls one by one and assign a draft selection number. The first ball removed from the bin would be assigned the selection number 1, the second ball removed assigned the selection number 2, etc. This meant that young men who had a birth date that had a low selection number would be called to go to war in Vietnam. Sounds like a pretty fair process.

Let us take a look at a graphic display used in statistics called a scatter plot. When two variables are quantitative, these numerical values are typically organized in a graph, a scatterplot. A scatterplot has two dimensions the horizontal axes and the vertical axes. Each of these axes corresponds to variables collected for the vertical axes category and variables collected for the horizontal category. In the example provided, the two variables are fluoride levels used in city water and the number of tooth decay documented by dentist located in these cities. This provides a visual display of possible associations or relationships between two variables.

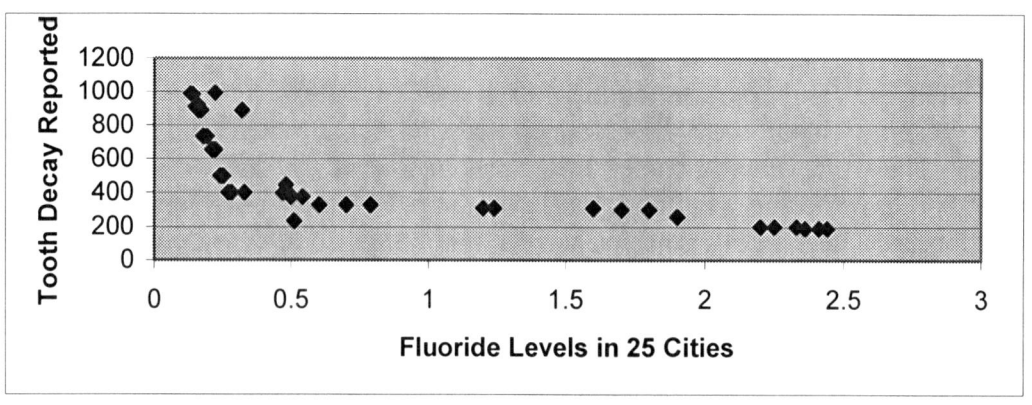

It appears that an increase in the use of fluoride reduces tooth decay. Remember that this data only came from an observational study, not by experimentation. To prove cause and effect, we need to do experimentation. However, a pattern has emerged as we read our graph from left to right. There appears to be a trend. Even though the points on the graph are not perfectly positioned in places, it becomes obvious that the data is not random compared to the graph displayed concerning birth dates and draft selection numbers.

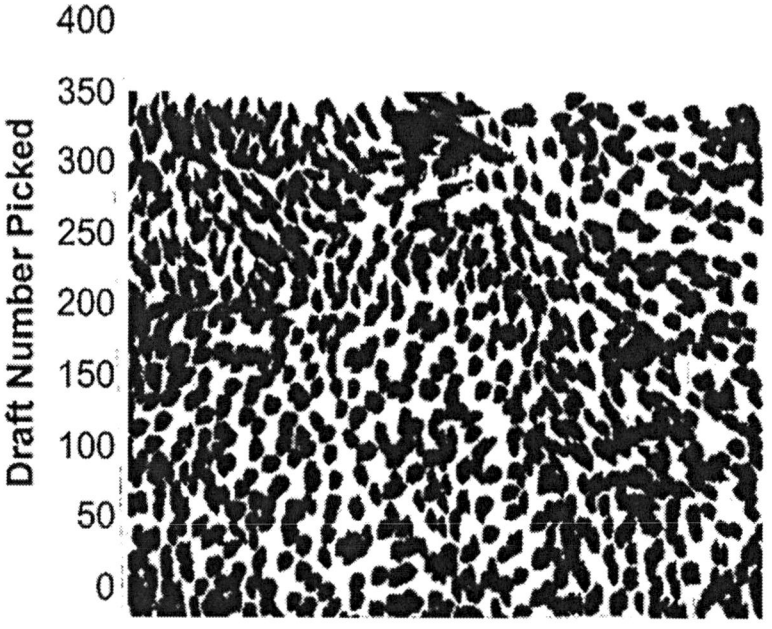

This is an interesting chart. There appears to be no patterns and the variables are random. It seems difficult to show any possible associations or relationships between these two variables. However, people complained that it appeared that the draft picks were not fair. People born in the month of December complained that their month was selected more often for selective service than the birth dates in the other months. But looking at the chart, it appears to be a random process of selection and no patterns displayed that would indicate a bias toward one month over another. Bias means a systematic favoritism that is present in the data collection process. This is a bad thing when our processes need to be a truly random chance process like a lottery. It is just the opposite with quality control and control charts. We add bias into the process to target and produce a favored quality in the products we produce. Do we need to continue testing this data to determine if our initial data is misleading? Yes.

Here is how it is done. We need to use an additional tool in statistics know as box plots. Box plots are especially good for showing the differences between groups. With respect to the draft lottery, we have 12 groups, the people born in the month of January through December. So we will demonstrate that there is more than one way to measure a spread (in statistics a spread is called a range). We want to determine the range for each month and then compare them to each other. So a second generation of the data will be graphed on a box plot. Box plots not only provides additional information on the distribution, but it can let one know more about some of the statistical properties of the sample population the data came from. Here is how we do a box plot to discover the truth about the randomness of this lottery procedure.

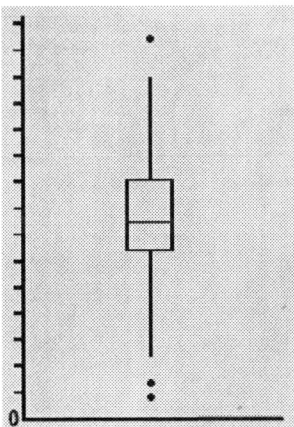

The box plot, as shown in the diagram, has several graphic elements that will assist in the analysis of what may or may not be random data. The lower and upper lines of the "box" are the 25th and 75th percentiles of the sample. The distance between the top and bottom of the box is the interquartile range. The range is sometimes referred to as the "spread." The line in the middle of the box is the sample median, as opposed to the mean value. The median is the numerical data point at which there are an equal number of values above and below the median value. So we are using a value that is truly the middle of our data set. If the median is not centered in the box, that is an indication of skewness. The "whiskers" are lines extending above and below the box. They show the extent of the rest of the sample (unless there are outliers). Assuming no outliers, the maximum of the sample is the top of the upper whisker. The minimum of the sample is the bottom of the lower whisker. By default, an outlier is a value that is more than 1.5 times the interquartile range away from the top or bottom of the box. An outlier is indicated by the dot in the diagram. The outlier may be the result of a data entry error, a poor measurement or a change in the system that generated the data.

Here are some examples of bar graphs and sideways box plots. The following examples show some of the different ways data may occur on a bar graph and how the box plot provides the diagram to show the relationships between different types of bar graphs.

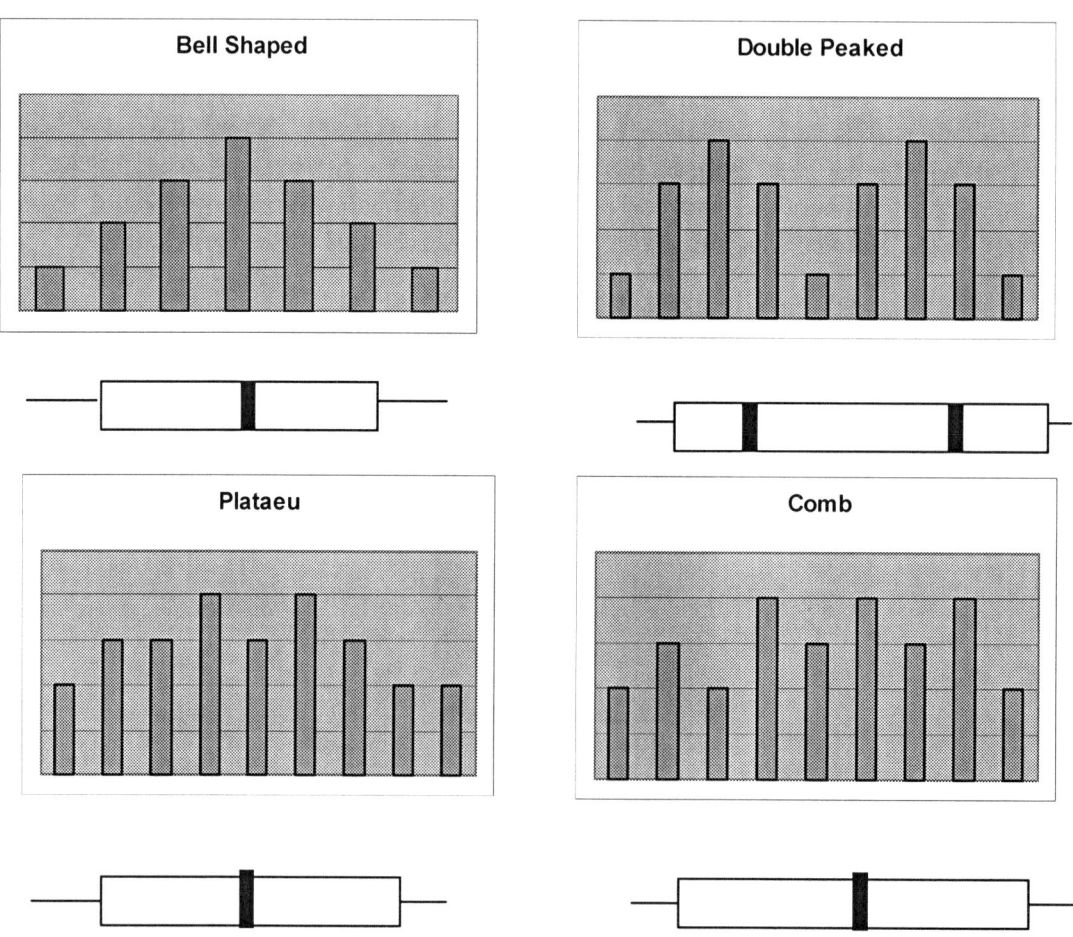

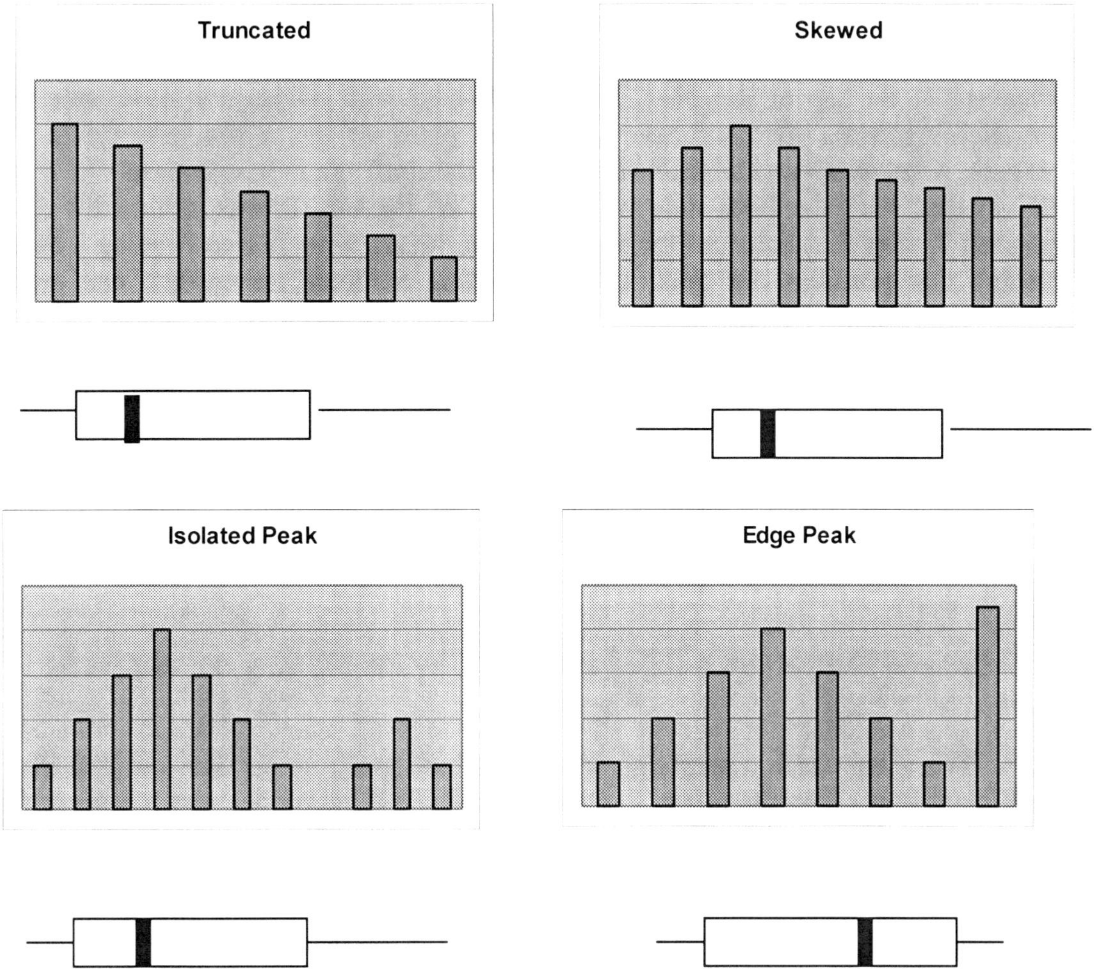

PART TWO: VALIDATION THINKING

Now we need to use the box plot to determine if the 1970 draft lottery was a fair draw of the numbers. We are investigating to determine if the process created a random result. We will use the box plot to determine if a trend exists.

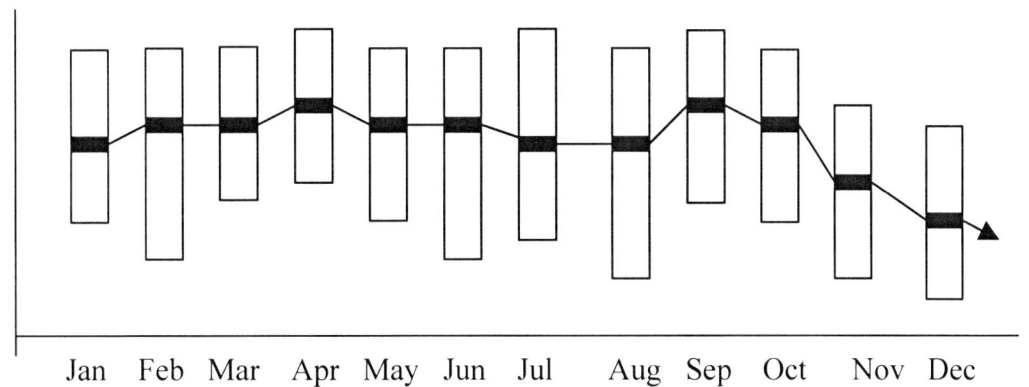

It starts to become obvious that the capsules with birth dates were not thoroughly mixed. There is a downward trend toward the end of the year. After the real investigation conducted in 1970-1971, it was determined that the December dates remained at the top of the bin. The balls labeled with month and day, were not thoroughly mixed. We now have discovered some of the errors inherent in the process. Also, there was additional bias with the draft number selection. When the ball labeled with the birth date was taken from the bin, it was assigned a draft number. First picked balls got the low numbers. It was now time to develop a better process that practices our goal, to pick random numbers rather than one group receiving a disproportionate share of the lower numbers. The process was changed to have a barrel containing balls labeled with birth dates and another barrel with balls labeled with draft numbers. These barrels were turned over and over again to thoroughly mix the balls. When a ball labeled with a birth date was taken out of the turning barrel, it was then matched with a random draft number taken from the barrel containing draft numbers. This created a more random process of selection. At first glance, everything looked good, but we were not truly picking numbers at random. Heroes will take the extra steps to insure fairness.

Statistics and Illustrations of Life Fairness - Why People May not always be Fair

When we watch a sports game such as basketball, notice that one basketball goal is not lower than the other. The playing field is dimensioned and measured for fairness. The distance from the center of the court is equal to both goals. The goals have been measured to equal ten feet and boundaries have been established as well as the rules of the game. As the players interact on the court, decisions are being made during the game.

Bad Calls - What are bad calls?

A bad call resorts when officials on the court (the referee), a coach, or player tampers with the process of teamwork. A referee may be in the way of a player executing a play and as a result, the play being executed is broken up. The referee may call a foul during a critical time in the game that gives the other team a turnover and the conversion resulting in an unfair advantage. A coach may send in a play that causes confusion to the players or a player may make the decision to do it their way and not execute the play according to the training drills of practice. This disregard toward others and the lack of taking responsibilities causes a process to go bad. These are all examples of BAD CALLS.

There is a difference in team players and team workers. People who don't understand processes inevitably tamper with the expected outcome to end up with results that appear to be chaotic and out of control. This is why we need to understand zero sum gaming theory. A zero game is when the winner takes all. The process is statistically designed to create and perpetuate loses by tampering with the other systems process. This tampering effectively removes the management techniques and structure that monitors common cause variation.

Just as it is with the alcoholic, there does not exist a cure; however, we learn techniques that assist in managing the problem. This is different then thinking we are defeated to accept our condition. We must manage to keep all of our character within a statistical control limit.

How do we determine if it is Fair

Avoid Adding Random Variables / Is the Process Capable?

Let us define the process. Here is a simple gambling game involving a coin toss. Once we have calculated and determine the mean and variance of a random variable, what can we do with the information? Let us examine the fair toss of a coin. Let x=1 if the coin comes up heads and 0 if it comes up tails. Let the probability of either heads or tails be P(x)=percentage.

	$x°$	x
x	0	1
P(x)	.5	.5

or 50% One event, two outcomes.

Looks very fair according to our calculations. Both players have equal chances of their preferred outcomes (electing to take heads or tails). Potential for expected outcomes are 50%. So 50 outcomes are expected providing 100 fair events take place. Let us find the mean for this process:

Expected Outcomes for x=heads or tails are: $E(x)=x°(p(x))$ and also $E(x)=x((p(x))$
$x°$=not heads (tails)

So the **mean** for this process is $\mu = 0(.5) + 1(.5) = .5$ So both players have a 50% chance of receiving the preferred outcome of choice (heads or tails).

Let us now find the variance of the process about the mean value.

And the **variance** for this process $\sigma^2 = (0-.5)^2 * p(0) + (1-.5)^2 * p(1) = .25$ Both players have equal opportunity to vary from the mean by 25%.

Still fair!

Now let us look at what happens when I add a new variable to the process. Let us make the process more interesting by you ante up $6.00 to play against me. I will flip the coin and you win $10.00 if the coin comes up heads and you win zero dollars if it comes up tails. So the equation for this process involves dollars

Win − 10x 6

Wow!!! I have an opportunity to make $4.00 for every $6.00 placement. It appears to be a 40% return on the placement of $6.00. But wait, we now have a new random variable!

What are the mean and variance?

	x°	x
x	0	1
W	-6	+4
P(x)	.5	.5

Here we have added the additional variable to our original table.

So E(W) = E(10x – 6) which works out to 10(0.5) – 6 = -1

Your expected winnings are a loss!

On an average you will lose $1.00. One definition of probability is the relative frequency of the event in the long run. This applies to our example. The only two possible outcomes are –$6.00 or $4.00. What has occurred is that the variance of W(wins) must be greater than the variance of x (failures or successes of a binomial event). So before we played for money our mean (expected value) was greater before we added a new variable that gives our value x a coefficient of 10.

$$\text{Variance} = [P(x)]^2 * (10)^2 * (x)$$

$$\sigma^2 = (.5)^2 * (100)(1) = .25 * 100 = 25$$

$$\sigma = \sqrt{25} = 5$$

This increase in variance has a result in a decrease of our relative frequency of the expected mean.

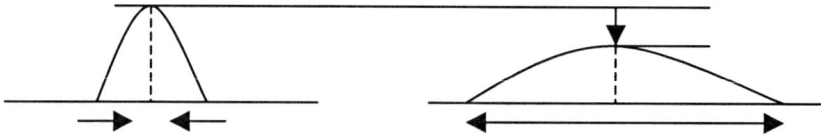

See, we must look for what change has occurred in our process. Were new variables introduced that have caused a change in our expected mean and standard deviation? Let us summarize the experiment. If we flip a coin one thousand times in succession we obtain a sequence of heads and tails. Incidentally, make sure you do the experiment by flipping and not spinning the coin. Spinning the coin results in heads only about 30% of the time, not the 50% that results from unbiased flipping.

PART TWO: VALIDATION THINKING

Tracking the Proportion Heads Exceeds Tails

Now we are going to do a new experiment with our coin. Let us say we want to track the proportion of the time that the number of heads exceeded the number of tails, you might be surprised to discover that it is rarely close to 50% or ½. We can relate this to the Dow Jones Industrial Averages. Here is how our experiment goes.

Picture two players, Dumb and Dumber, who flip a coin once a day and then bet on heads and tails, respectively. Dumb is ahead at any given time if there have been more heads up until that time, while Dumber is ahead if there have been more tails. Although Dumb and Dumber are each equally likely to be in the lead at any given time, it can be proved that one of them will probably be ahead almost the whole time. Thus, if there have been one thousand coin flips, the chances are considerably greater that Dumb (or Dumber) has been ahead more than 90 percent of the time than that he has been ahead between 45 and 55 percent of the time! Likewise, it is considerably more likely that Dumb (or Dumber) has been in the lead more than 98 percent of the time, say, than that he has been ahead between 49 and 51 percent of the time.

This result is counterintuitive because we tend to think of deviations from the mean as being somehow bound by a rubber band: the greater the deviation, the greater the restoring force toward the mean. But even if the coin landed heads 525 times and tails 475 times, for example, the difference between the total number of heads and the total number of tails tossed is just as likely to grow as to shrink with further flips. This is true despite the fact that the proportion of heads does approach ½ as the number of flips increases.

Note: The gambler's fallacy and this more subtle consequence should be distinguished from another phenomenon, regression to the mean, which is valid. If the coin were flipped one thousand more times, it is more probable than not that the number of heads on the second thousand flips would be smaller than 525.

If even fair coins behave so oddly, one should expect that some stock pickers will come to be known as losers and others as winners without there being any real difference between them other than luck. If Dumb and Dumber have won respectively, 525 and 475 trials, Dumb will likely be profiled in the business pages as a visionary and Dumber disdained as a plodder. Winners and losers are often just people who get stuck on the right (or wrong) side of an event. It can sometimes take a very long time for the lead to switch hands.

Now we have introduced yet another issue, the rate at which Dumb and Dumber arrived at their average. The counterintuitive aspect of the coin flipping concerns the surprising number of consecutive runs of heads or tails of various lengths. If anyone continues to flip a coin every day to determine who pays for the

Wall Street Journal, then it is more likely than not that at some time within about nine weeks, Dumb will have won five papers in a row, as will have Dumber. And at some period within about five to six years, it is likely that each will have won ten papers in a row.

Random events can frequently seem quite ordered. The following diagram is a computer printout of a random sequence of 260 flips of heads and tails (52 groups of 5), each letter appearing with the probability of 50%. Note the number of runs and the way there seem to be clusters and other patterns. If you feel compelled to account for these, you will have to invent explanations that will of necessity be quite false.

```
THHHT   HHTTH   HHHTT   HTTHH   THTTH   TTHTT   THTHH
TTTHH   TTHTH   HHHHH   HHHTH   HHTHT   HHHHT   HTTHH
HTTTH   HHHHT   THHTT   THHTT   TTTHH   TTHHH   HHHTH
HHHTT   HHHHT   THTTH   HTTHH   THTHH   THHHT   HHTHH
HHTHH   HTHHT   HHHHH   HHHHT   HHHHH   TTTTT   HTTHH
HTTHH   HHTTH   TTHTH   HHTHH   HHTTT   THTHT   HHTHH
HTTHH   TTTTH   HHHHT   TTTHH   HHTHH   TTHHH   HHHTH
HTTTT   TTTHT   HHHHH
```

The Case of Chuck E. Cheese

(Always a Winner / Making You Look Like the Loser)

My grandson had his third birthday party at Chuck E. Cheese located in Franklin, Tennessee. This is a pizza restaurant for children that include games of skill for the children to play and win prizes. I noticed that as children cashed in their winnings (tickets) they were angry and disappointed. I watched as parents struggled to correct their children's disappointment on the gift return for their winnings. Children immediately saw the flaws and unfairness.

Here are the calculations:

A token is 25¢. It takes two tokens to play one game: .25 * 2 = 50¢

If you win one time, 100% success, you receive eight tickets.

You need 1,028 tickets to win a Barbie doll: 1,028 / 8 = 257 * .50 = $128.50

This is referred to as the odds are in their favor.

If a child were skilled enough to win 100% of the time, they would have to pay $128.50 in tokens to win a Barbie doll. Yes, it is possible to win the Barbie doll; however, will our resources (money & time) and ability of replenishment (add more money) run out prior to obtaining the targeted goal. The cost of the effort exceeds the reward and is therefore unreasonable to pursue the target (unless you continue at any cost and have timeless replenishment). You would be better off buying the gifts and having the children hand tickets to you personally and you give out the gifts for tickets after the party. As it is with business, trial and error is very costly.

In a real market, prices are negotiable. If you have ever been to India or other countries throughout the world, their products are not priced. Unlike our markets in the United States where most businesses set a price and it is non-negotiable. This is my price love it or leave it. This is what happens when children create rules as the game continues. Every time we add a new ruling prior to the football season, we are adding a new variable to the system. As a result, we all have to play out the season to determine if the outcomes were fair based on the new rules.

Luck is when preparation meets opportunity. You will always reduce risk when you are continuously preparing for a large number of random opportunities. It is a numbers game. But, you will not win unless you are preparing to meet an opportunity that arises. Heroes broaden their skills to include a wide variety of future opportunities.

Always be aware of percentages.

If I was given $100.00 to do a job and my manager increased my pay by 25%, I would then have $125.00. Later he comes to me and says, "I can no longer pay you the 25% increase. I will need to reduce your pay by 20%. You are still ahead by 5%. Is that okay with you?"

20% of $125.00 is $25.00

$125.00 – $25.00 = $100.00 you are right back where you started from.

What is with this 5% difference?

Therefore, we must recognize that there is a difference in being right, being correct, pursuing a low risk solution, and having a preference. Most people have a preference conceptualized in a particular school of thought or movement strategy. But the illustrations provided demonstrate some of the pitfalls that can occur when we use our common sense only. Often our common sense deceives us into choosing our preferences (availability error) and to stop the investigation of other possibilities.

While I was serving as Vice President of systems development for a company, I commented about what a positive motivational speaker said concerning abilities. The speaker said, "Any one can accomplish and do anything if they only put their mind to it." I commented that this statement needed further clarification. If we can do anything just by putting our minds to it, then can a person knock down the Empire State building using a feather? Immediately one of the other officers of the company said, "YES, if you hit the building in the right place." I am not dismissing the importance of mental attitude, but it is obvious that more is required than just thinking positive. Inventors such as Thomas Edison understood that the prepared mind and inspiration was part of it, but perspiration (hard work) with persistence is a very important part. Planning, engineering, testing, and additional hard work is mandatory to complete an idea such as sending a person to the moon. But when we hold to a preference and mandate the ideology to be factual only to win the argument, we are committing an error in the reasoning and planning process. Part of committing the availability error is defending a personal preference as an absolute truth, when in actuality truth becomes statistical with respect to our reality.

The statistical examples were to demonstrate that there is a difference in being certain of a fact (single event) and the reliability of the certainty over a period of time. Upon first investigation we can say with 99% certainty that this drug test will identify illegal drug users, but on the average how reliable is our certainty with respect to time and performing a process more than once. Introducing the random drug testing scenario is a demonstration of being certain yet we are not reliable when processes are repeated time after time. Variation will enter into the process if we do not monitor that process for statistical stability.

The red bead experiment and the Hawthorne effect teaches all of us that taking measurements during research studies cannot be precisely measured without making quantifiable sacrifices. Before the advent of quantum mechanics, it was believed by most research scientist that better and better accuracy in measurement could be obtained by simply improving measuring instruments. This has been true to an extent, but perfect accuracy cannot be achieved no matter how fine the measuring instrument. There exits some uncertainty in every measurement we make because of the unavoidable interaction between the observer and the observed. This was true for the study conducted at the Hawthorne Plant. Something is lost for every measurement that is gained. If we test a material (wood, metal, etc.) for its buoyancy features to build a boat, we cannot simultaneously test how good the property of the substance is for making houses. Heroes take no issue with people that read and believe in false positives (like the Enquirer magazine-enquiring minds need to know), but Heroes never exercise power over others to force them to believe in false positives.

The correspondence principle states, "If a new theory is valid, it must account for the verified results of the old theory." The new theory and the old theory must overlap and agree in the region where the results of the old theory have been fully verified. Heroes never make a change to a process until they research to reveal the genuine features of the process. Heroes never make a change to a system without an understanding of the verified results of the processes that integrate to become the organization.

How do Heroes combine all of the observations, experiences, and intuition to fix issues? They first form a hypothesis of the cause(s) and contingences of the problem and then research to prove or disprove it. If you cannot guess a cause and/or contingency, try to reverse the approach by inverting the statement (as done in the previous section). Form a hypothesis and then work backwards to prove or disprove it. The next step is to test the hypothesis. Just as it is with the red bead experiment, the world is designed to cooperate and work to be in homeostasis statistical control. It has gone unnoticed in many of our organizations the many brave and willing people who make this process of self-organizing work in our enterprising businesses.

In a world of change, new technologies develop rapidly; the nature of work is changing. These changes need to be documented statistically to determine the variation boundaries that are in constant flux. It is important for organizations to be specifically and statistically designed for adaptation to change. Even systems theory can be too rigid an approach if the boundaries around subsystems are rigidly fixed or inapplicable. Heroes monitor systems to determine the capability for people and processes in the enterprise to be self-organizing.

BUSINESS ETHICS & LEADERSHIP

Those who really deserve praise are the people who, while human enough to enjoy power nevertheless pay more attention to justice than they are compelled to do by their situation.

Heroes of the organization do not advocate or believe in the concepts of situational ethics; however, they do recognize the power that a situation has over people's decisions. Ethics is about doing the right thing first so we choose justice (the things that benefit all of us) even though we are compelled to let the power of the situation control the organization. To prevent this controlling effect, we must be conscience of the application of core values and principles that two or more people must agree upon to *over power* situations that become controlling of the organization. This is why I also oppose the school of thought concerning situational leadership and situational ethics. Why are people willing to let the situation dictate and control an outcome when we ourselves could take control? Heroes never let the situation control people, people should control the situation. Heroes believe that we could do anything, but stop to ask should.

An interesting example of ethics where a CEO of a company did not allow the situation to dictate an inappropriate outcome was the 1982 Tylenol crisis. In the year 1982, Johnson & Johnson experienced a major crisis when it was discovered that numerous bottles of its Extra-Strength Tylenol capsules had been laced with cyanide. Seven people had died. The way in which Johnson and Johnson dealt with this situation set a new precedent for crisis management. Rather than think about protecting financial losses and what will happen to the lost market share, CEO James Burke immediately turned to the company's Credo. The credo was written by Robert Johnson in 1943, the document defined the focus of the company service and dedication was toward its customers. With this as its inspiration, J&J used the media to promptly begin alerting people of the potential dangers of the product. It dispatched scientists to determine the source of tampering. This was an additional expense to the company. The company was lauded for its quick decisions and sincere concern for its consumers. The company ordered a massive recall of more than 31 million bottles at a cost of more than $100 million. It also temporarily ceased all production of capsules and replaced them with more tamper-resistant caplets. This type of drastic response had never been attempted, which prompted much criticism by some stackholders of the organization. Despite initial losses, Johnson and Johnson regained and exceeded its previous market share within months of the incident, because they did the right thing first. The company's willingness to be open with the public and communicate with the media helped the company maintain a high level of credibility and customer trust throughout the incident. If James Burke did not share values with Robert Johnson, then there existed the potential risk of death to the consumers and damage to the company.

Another interesting example of people before profit was Walt Disney. The Davy Crockett phenomenon has survived much longer than the two television series that Walt Disney launched in 1954 and 1955. Starring Fess Parker (played-Davy Crocket) and Buddy Ebsen (played-George Russel). The Davy Crockett shows are a fascinating example of a talented, savvy, and adventurous Walt Disney striking out in new entertainment directions. 1954 had to be a pretty busy time for the master entertainer; besides producing one of the biggest shows on television and continuing with his animated classics. The Davy Crockett shows are nicely produced by utilizing top Hollywood talent and clearly shepherded by Disney himself and often on location working with the production crew. His animation writers and art directors got a chance to move into live-action, and Peter Ellenshaw had more opportunity to do great work.

The program scripts for the Crocket series were simple and efficient. They made great use of the American conceptualization of heroism. This was to make your hero beloved and associating the hero with a friend that is a doting sidekick. Buddy Ebsen was an excellent choice to play along side the straight man Fess Parker. The Crocket series was very profitable. The sales of raccoon skin caps and the sells of the Davy Crocket ballad were proof of the success of the series. Following this successful season, the second series made in 1955, was a marked improvement overall from the 1954 season. More emphasis placed on scripting and character. Two programs that were produced in this year were <u>Davy Crockett's Keelboat Race</u> and <u>Davy Crockett & the River Pirates</u>. In one of the scenes, writers had written a part for Buddy Ebsen (character George Russel) to be drunk as part of a comedy portion to the script. Walt Disney, always being involved, objected with the scene. Walt Disney did not want a beloved character to be portrayed as an intoxicated fool. Disney felt this was an inappropriate display for children and families. It would not make for wholesome entertainment. The writers disagreed and insisted that the scene would be appropriate and insisted it be added to the comedy and made for better entertainment. The writers felt that Walt Disney was over reacting to the situation but needed his approval to have the scene remain in this program. Walt Disney took everything under consideration and stopped production at a high cost to the company. Walt Disney finally agreed to show the scene of George Russel acting drunk in a bar, but in order to keep this scene an additional scene would be written that had Davy Crocket correcting and rebuking his sidekick George Russel for behaving irresponsibly. The compromise worked. Walt Disney understood the value of showing children that we must repent, promise not to repeat, and repair. The ethics of Walt Disney will live forever in these classic series as well as many of the other high quality wholesome production made by the Disney Company. Walt Disney is a hero because he put people before profit in his convictions. This is what ethics is all about. Just as with the model, "Love people and use things" or "Are we using people for the love of things?" Both Walt Disney and James Burke are heroes. Intuitively they followed model #3. Without a second thought they put people before profit (things).

The decision to bring a positive contribution to others is what customer service is all about. If it does not foster moral development, then it is not ethical. Just because we have availability to commit an unlawful or immoral act, does not mean we should let the situation overwhelm us to the degree that the situation forces a decision. Nobody has to participate. Ethics helps us realize we can control the outcome. When we do the right thing first, we are being proactive to control the situation rather than the situation controlling us. This is what ethics is all about. We manage the situation with our values and principles. These values and principles if practiced, will unify our organizations to be proactive when the power of a situation tries to control and drive the business plan. I have often asked myself when someone has committed an unethical act, "What was the thought process of this person?" Why did the situation take control even though we were compelled not to, during other unethical encounters of similar situations?

In order for organizations to control the situation, people participating in the organization must share values. It is value management by prioritization. Remember what was mentioned earlier in the book, even if a married couple both do drugs and never take care of the children, they would stay together because they share values. However, parents that demonstrate these types of values are removing themselves from the responsibilities and obligations toward others to take control of a situation that is controlling them. This is a failure to manage and control a situation that is not fostering development. Whether we agree to be moral or immoral, if we share values, relationships with co-workers will continue. Heroes align their values to promote a better relationship that fosters development. Heroes have respect for others and reject the myths concerning ethics.

Heroes understand that some of these myths arise from general confusion about the notion of ethics. Other myths arise from narrow or simplistic views of ethical dilemmas. Altering people's values or souls is not the aim of an organization's ethics program. This would be tampering. Others in the organization react that codes of ethics, or lists of ethical values to which the organization aspires, are rather superfluous because they represent values to which everyone should naturally aspire. It seems obvious to many that all people should be honest. However, if an organization is struggling with continuing occasions of deceit in the workplace, a priority on honesty is very timely and honesty should be listed in that organization's code of ethics. Note that a code of ethics is an organic instrument that changes with the needs of the organization. Another myth that seems generally accepted by Zeroes is that ethics cannot be managed.

Heroes develop ethics programs to identify preferred values and ensure that organizational behaviors are aligned with those values. This effort includes recording the values, developing policies and procedures to align behaviors with preferred values, and then training all personnel about the policies and procedures. This overall effort is very useful for several other programs in the workplace that require behaviors to be aligned with values, including quality management, strategic planning and diversity management. Total Quality Management includes high priority on certain operating values, such as trust among stakeholders, performance, reliability, measurement, and feedback. Attention to ethics promotes strong public relations that build more market share with people the company can share values with.

Admittedly, managing ethics should not be done primarily for reasons of public relations. But the fact that an organization regularly gives attention to its ethics can portray a strong positive to the public, as did the situation controlled and managed properly by Walt Disney and James Burke. People see those organizations as valuing people more than profit. During my doctorate research, it was interesting to discover how aligning behavior with values is critical to effective marketing and public relations programs. Again consider how Johnson and Johnson handled the Tylenol crisis versus how Exxon handled the oil spill in Alaska. Bob Dunn, President and CEO of San Francisco-based Business for Social Responsibility, puts it best: "Ethical values, consistently applied, are the cornerstones in building a commercially successful and socially responsible business." Our heroes are the people like James Burke and the people with Johnson and Johnson.

Heroes develop and document a procedure for dealing with ethical dilemmas as they arise. Ideally, ethical dilemmas should be resolved by a group within the organization, such as an ethics committee comprised of top leaders/managers and/or members of the board. Consider having staff members on the committee, as well. The following three methods can be used to address ethical dilemmas. Heroes understand that people are a crucial factor in ensuring ethical management. Unethical actions account for a far greater degree of economic loss than all other sources combined. Of such losses, the actions of an organization's insiders normally cause far more harm than the actions of outsiders. The major causes of loss due to an organization's own employees are: errors and omissions, fraud, and actions by disgruntled employees. One principal purpose of ethical awareness, training, and education is to reduce errors and omissions. However, it can also reduce fraud and unauthorized activity by disgruntled employees by increasing employees' knowledge of their accountability and the penalties associated with such actions.

Management sets the example for behavior within an organization. If employees know that management does not care about ethics (only profit), then followers will change their follower readiness (model #2) to the value level of the leader. This "tone from the top" has myriad effects an organization's ethics program. Heroes work with their workers so that everyone undergoes regular ethics awareness training. This training should be a requirement for managers, designers, developers, maintainers, operators, and users. You will find that sources of training material for ethics programs and briefings abound on the internet and at the local library. Heroes understand that ethics starts with a belief in something greater than they are. While I was an employee at Federal Express for over four years, it was magical the many heroes that shared values and have outstanding character ethic as a result of excellent ethics programs. It was the same for the Pyxis Corporation when I was an employee during the time Ron Taylor was President of the company. These organizations elevated the quality of ethical leadership and practices by desire and living the example, not by the use of fear.

I hope that you will enjoy the case studies of heroes and zeroes in the following sections. I have had the privilege to be employed by several great organizations such as Federal Express as well as other prominent ones such as MediClaim Incorporated and The Pyxis Corporation. The concepts developed in these sections of the book are for the reader to use as a tool to develop who your heroes and zeroes are. While reading the cases, understand that heroes are those who really deserve praise. Heroes put people first and while human enough to enjoy power nevertheless pay more attention to justice than they are compelled to do by their situation. Heroes refuse to let the situation drive the decision.

CASE STUDIES

Case #1: The Educational System

The creative educator is one who can process in new ways the information directly at hand. The ordinary sensory data available to all of us is presented in many good and bad textbooks, but hero educators seem to intuitively see possibilities for transforming ordinary data into a new creation that transcends over the mere raw materials used in our education system. There is a difference between the two processes of gathering data and transforming data creatively and teaching it as vital information needed to grow successfully in a capitalistic society. The good teachers we remember remove self interest and the bid for power from the process of educating others. My educational experience showed me that selfishness lowers the commitment to a teacher student relationship; therefore we must remove it (both the student and the teacher). As a result of the removal of selfishness, excellence in integrated education becomes a habit not just an act.

Education consistently ranks among the top issues facing our nation (past present and future). When it comes to public opinion polls and political issues, education is a top concern of the American people. When a politician favors improving education, then that candidate has the ear of the American people. Even though many debate the decline of curriculum and values over time, others discuss how well the education system measures with respect to international standards. Many advocates will argue that more money needs to be spent on education. Others will insist that hiring more teachers to reduce student-teacher ratios is a problem. Some educators will say that raising teacher salaries to levels comparable to other professions would make improvements. Other issues that are argued is that educational resources should be distributed more evenly so both economically deprived school districts are not left behind to more financially fairing school districts. However, there is less concern generally expressed about America's colleges and universities. They are widely regarded as among the best in the world. But, the issue with the college and university education has become the cost of education.

The financial budget for our educational organization is not only astounding, but could be considered a reflection of where the United States places their priority. At the end of the year (2001), it is reported that 371.9 billion dollars was spent for public school education grades K-12 (does not include spending for private school education). Our education organizations have a tremendous operating budget and is about one-third of our sub-national government spending. When we include universities, colleges, vocational schools, private schools, special education schools, music schools, etc; it becomes apparent that people in the United States spend trillions of dollars on education. This spending would include video tapes, books, and other forms of learning. Revenue resources for these spending levels come from students raising money with candy sales, car washes, and other fund-raising efforts. Private schools, colleges, universities, and nonprofit organizations have been busy raising billions of dollars each year from corporations, foundations, the government, and private citizens. Fund-raising for our American education is big business. The American Association of Fundraising Counsel reported that charitable giving in the United States surpassed $190 billion as the 20th century came to a close. Corporations gave more than $11 billion annually to worthy causes; foundations gave more than $19 billion; and individuals gave by far the largest amount at $143 billion, including an additional $15 billion in bequests. Of the total amount contributed, more than $27 billion was given to public and private education, which ranks second only to religious organizations as a recipient of grants and gifts. In addition, the federal government continues to give significant dollars to the schools in competitive and noncompetitive grants. In the year 2002, schools received grants totaling more than $40 billion from the U.S. Department of Education, the Department of Health and Human Services, the Department of Agriculture, the Department of Energy, the Department of the Interior, and the Department of Defense. No doubt about it, education is a big **business** and we are a society that emphasizes education and will pay the cost.

Yes, we do live in an educational society. The United States emphasizes education and provides many schools and universities, but with all this education why have we not become a learning culture. A society that learns, takes in information; but a learning culture will embrace learning, researching, and test implementing new ideas. If it were imbedded into people as part of our culture, then people would not just be content to take in information. We should be embracing and celebrating the people who are part of a learning culture (our heroes).

There is a difference in a society and a culture. A society is made of a group of people who have opinions and convictions. These are the people that talk, but rarely walk the talk. A culture are people who demonstrate with action that which is important in their lives. If ignorance were painful, then nobody would be ignorant and then everyone would join the learning culture. To illustrate the idea of society's verses cultures, let me explain using Albert Einstein as an example (Educators always get the illustration concerning Einstein and learning wrong). I have heard many times by educators in elementary school, high school, and college; that Albert Einstein failed math tests. This is so far from the truth that it is ludicrous that anyone should ever say it again. The failed test that educators try to reference is Albert Einstein's entrance exam to the Swiss Polytechnical Institute in Zurich. When he applied to college he was sixteen (16) years of age. This was two years prior to the age when students would normally apply. Einstein's scores on the entrance exam were way above excellent. The professors noted and praised him on his over achieving scores in math and science. Why was Einstein not admitted? He failed the languages portion of the exam. Educators felt that Einstein would not be a successful student due to his low scores in this area. Einstein was disappointed, but not defeated. Einstein always enjoyed learning and taught himself Latin and other languages during the summer. Einstein took the test again and passed the languages portion of the test with scores higher than many of the other students applying that year. In 1905, the University of

Bern rejected Einstein's Ph.D. dissertation, saying that it was irrelevant and too fanciful. Albert Einstein was again disappointed, but not defeated. Most know the rest of this story (photo electric effect & relativity).

What should this tell us about learning and education? Albert Einstein was a member of a learning culture. The people, who examined his aptitude in Zurich and reviewed his Ph.D. dissertation in Bern, were members of an educational society. A society that prides themselves in all the progress made in managing structure, but fails to move students toward a learning culture, to embrace learning, researching, and the implementation of new ideas. Apparently, educational organizations fail to see that they have put us in a learning era and refuse to move students to be members of the learning culture. There were no creativity experts or creativity programs during Einstein's education. As with the true story of Albert Einstein and his educational experiences, learning is not how much we have committed to memory, rather it is our commitment to learning. It is being able to differentiate between what we do know by authentication of theories and what we need to learn to improve holistically. It is knowing where to go to find what we need to know; and it is knowing how to use the information we get. The best education in the world is that which individuals obtain by struggling and persevering. Nothing is more astonishing as the amount of ignorance many institutions accumulate in the form of inert facts. We will all be victorious if we have not forgotten how we learn and the science of learning.

How do we measure teacher performance and student performance? How should everyone in this enterprise be held accountable? The reason why teachers do not want testing as part of their evaluation to teach is because teachers often know that these tests do not have an objective measure. But these teachers are told to test students without the use of an objective measure. Administrators and parents want teachers to have a measure of how well they perform or not perform. This argument will go on forever because administrators continue to solve problems conceptualizing with "schools of thought" and a philosophy of education rather than understanding learning by science. My personal experience with learning and dealing with many educators is that the excellent educators understand the science of learning. The vast majority of those that teach can and do an excellent job. When we apply the rules, an objective measure must be identified and incorporated in the measurement process. An axiomatic system that classes problems is worthless in authentication of results without an objective measure.

My personal experience is that the education system gets blamed for many poor outcomes that are not their responsibility. Often radio talk shows, newspapers, and other reporting media, have misrepresented issues and inaccurately presented the statistics. A radio talk show host in Nashville, Tennessee told his audience that Tennessee was rated 49th in the country in education. The truth is that at this particular time Tennessee teachers salaries were 49th in the nation and student testing was 26th in the nation for standardized tests. This means that Tennessee teachers should be praised for doing more with less, not criticized for being 49th in the nation.

Teachers have no control over their salaries. An educational issue was identified over the radio and callers began to tell all of the negative stories about the education system, when in reality the issue was misrepresented.

Often this is the case. Most educators are above par. But there continues to be created issues that haunt our educational system that just are not founded in facts. One of the many issues at the forefront is accountability. This issue is one of many brought about by public demand. This demand is spawned by television shows that interview a very small number of professional athletes that complain they cannot read or write. During the interview, the educational system is criticized for passing athletes that did not make the grades. I never understood how this was a tragedy. Why doesn't the professional ball play who is making millions of dollars a year, simply pay to have a teacher (on a low salary) tutor them? Certainly, any low paid educator would welcome the professional athlete into their home and would not only enjoy the company of a professional athlete, but could use the extra money. The educational system has not failed; the student never took initiative to join a learning culture. But this is never the issue. The teacher and parents are blamed. This blame is passed around and around and identifying the true problem is like trying to hit a fast moving target. It requires an expert. On a similar note, a local middle Tennessee newspaper gave credit to one of our politicians for increasing teachers pay by 2%. This was only the county supplemental pay that only amounted to a little over $300.00 a year. Sounds like this politician is for education?

How should we approach public demands for accountability in education? What about the other issues? During the 1980s, the nation's governors gave a proposal to the educators in public schools. They would provide more flexibility in how schools operated, if educators would agree to be held more accountable for student achievement. In practice, the push for accountability has encountered some problems. No consensus has been reached on how to design a strong accountability system that educators and the public perceive as fair and legitimate to this day. In many places, accountability has focused almost exclusively on raising scores on state-mandated tests. States are increasingly holding students accountable for performance. In the year 2000, 18 states required students to pass a test in order to graduate from high school. Three states tie student promotion to test scores and four others are planning to do so. Some states and districts are also attempting to tie teacher evaluations and pay to students' scores on state tests. But many educators and teachers' unions contend that too many factors contributing to student performance are outside their control.

Many critics also argue that the focus on "high-stakes testing" will narrow and impoverish the curriculum, encourage cheating, and fall most heavily on poor and minority students, who traditionally have done least well on standardized exams. Opponents of such testing also complain that states have rushed to hold students accountable before they've put in place the curriculum, instruction, teacher training, and other resources that would enable young people to meet the higher standards. In some places, concerns about the results of high-stakes testing have produced a backlash. In California, Massachusetts, Michigan, Ohio, and other states, grassroots opposition campaigns are encouraging parents to keep their children home on test days. All these issues continue to go on and on.

I could continue with listing all the common issues that many people think are problems and issues, but they are not an issue or a problem. The things I read on the internet, newspapers, or other media are generally in the form of an "availability error." People are complaining about their education, their children's education, and everyone has an idea of what they think the agenda should be. I would like to stop and address an area of education that is being neglected and that issue is ***tampering***. Before we change curriculum, define and hold teachers to accountability, or list other issues; we need to understand tampering with processes. I will present two examples where the decision makers of two educational institutions tampered with the educational process. These examples relate the issue of tampering that has not been identified as an issue officially, but has been discussed by many educators.

University of Tennessee Medical Units

During my doctorate studies, students were asked to do a curriculum specialist interview for one of our assignments. I decided to interview my father, Dr. Richard Paul White. He was an early investigator in the field of neuropharmacology and his research experiences are summarized in the book *The Rise of Psychopharmacology* (Eds: T. A. Ban, D. Healy, and E. Short, Animula, 1998). He performed research at the Psychiatric Research Hospital in Illinois for two years (1954-1956), spent in 1968 a Sabbatical at the Neuropharmacology Institute of Birmingham, England, and from 1959 to 1969 was a recipient of the Career Development Award of the National Institutes of Health. His love of teaching is evident by receiving four Teaching Excellent Awards from medical students and two from pharmacy students at the University of Tennessee Medical Center, Memphis, as well as commendations from neurosurgery residents and the University of Hirosaki, Japan. He began teaching medical students in 1949 while earning his Ph.D. at the University of Kansas. At that time medical schools used the stepwise Flexner program of learning where each subject, like anatomy, was taught largely independent of other courses. The best medical textbooks and the great medical advances made before and especially after WWII were the work of physicians trained under the traditional Flexner medical curriculum. Before 1960 hardly any administrator thought of tampering with the traditional Flexner medical curriculum. By 1970 it became fashionable for the deans of medical colleges to develop their own singular methods of education.

In the 1970s a new dean of the medical school at U.T. was hired to improve education. He and two cronies established their version of the modular system where new students would learn anatomy from plastic models (students might later in their senior year learn from dissection if they wished to be surgeons). Also, students would be exposed to a core curriculum for about six weeks to learn the basics of the likes of physiology, biochemistry, and pharmacology. Most of the so-called basic sciences would be homogenized as modules, thus a section on the heart may be taught by anatomist, physiologist, pharmacologist, biochemists, pathologists, cardiologists and others. A subject such as osteoarthritis was now referred to as degenerative joint disease and was taught by rheumatologist, biochemists and others. Many objected to the new curriculum and expressed concern that there was no evidence that it was as good as traditional training and required an inordinate adjustment to teach the new curriculum. To facilitate learning, the students would organize their class notes along the traditional lines such as anatomy and pathology similar to the Flexner program. The modular curriculum lasted from 1974 through 1977 when the students expressed their dissatisfaction and clinical faculty declared that the program had failed. The medical curriculum must adjust to the remarkable growth of information, but changes by administrative edict, without proof of value, is unmitigated **tampering**. Some conclusions were made after the demise of the modular curriculum.

- The best students learn well under any circumstances. Medical students were organizing their module material under the old Flexner method and integrating their learning on their own. It was absurd to fragment the teaching and instruction.
- New curriculum begins with an idea or a hypothesis-tuition. Hypothesis-tuition in the original Latin means a guardianship to teach and protect with a watchful eye as in careful observance.
- Student Disapproval of Curriculum caused a rebellion. The students wanted Gross Anatomy because it made learning together more like a "boot camp" remembrance of the medical experience. This united students to work together and brought students closer to the real medical situation.

The reader may be wondering if any real significant improvements were made to the curriculum. It became apparent that making a change from the Flexner method to the Modular method was tampering with a process that was working well. Verified results should never be changed, only accounted for. Measure first and fix later. Then improvements should be tested. Often when administrators make a drastic change (example: teaching the new math in schools), the educators have to do at least two jobs, the job task given by the new administrator that is not working for everyone and the job that educators know they need to do to foster development. This administrator did not seek to understand first, his concern was first to be understood. After going back to the Flexner method, here is a list of **additions** (not changes) that promoted improvement to the Flexner process.

New Additions to the Curriculum
- One major addition to the curriculum was making TLC (Tender Loving Care) a requirement in 1991. Doctors are now learning sensitivity along with their anatomy. This program was designed to improve the Physicians "bed side manner."
- National awareness in patient care became apparent after the making of the movie "The Doctor" starring William Hurt. The movie was based on

the account of a physician's own experience as a patient with cancer. When the Doctor becomes the patient, a paradigm shift occurs. This adds a new dimension dynamic that presents a new perspective to improve processes "Walking in another person's shoes."

Trevecca Nazarene University – Business College

During the 1980s, there was a criticism of higher learning with respect to the Master's of Business Administration (MBA) programs in our educational system. It was presented as a crisis. Business colleges were failing to produce high caliber and competent business managers. Articles in business journals as well as other forms of media blamed business colleges in the United States for failing to produce better business managers.

Rondy Smith had completed a master's degree and was interested in working on a doctorate degree. She decided to attend Peabody College, Vanderbilt University's college of education and human development. She was accepted into the Ed.D program and informed her advisors that she wanted to improve the MBA program. With all of the negative publicity concerning the MBA program in our Universities and the fact that businesses across the country were complaining about MBA graduates failing to produce results, this was an excellent idea to review the MBA curriculum to determine the validity of the negative accusations.

After completing her doctorate degree, Dr. Rondy Smith determined that the MBA programs core curriculum was solid but, there needed to be added improvement. The MBA program lacked the Edward Deming science of Total Quality Management. If the MBA programs approached management as a science of evaluating processes using statistics and remove the schools of thought concerning situational leadership, the curriculum would indeed produce a higher quality of business administrators. While researching to find these results, she was also required by this doctorate program to produce a curriculum. This was action oriented research. It involved both quantitative as well as qualitative research. So her dissertation produced a master's curriculum for Organizational Managers.

The curriculum she developed was outstanding and very promising, much better than the present MBA programs that were being offered for students. Trevecca Nazarene University made a decision to implement this master's program at their school. When other Universities continued to create MBA programs, TNU had Dr. Rondy Smith implement her curriculum for a Master's degree in Organizational Management. While traveling in my car and listening to the radio, I heard an advertisement about this unique program. I wanted to work on a master's degree in business. As a result, I enrolled in the program. This was one of the best decisions I had made in my life. We received the entire curriculum that an MBA program had to offer, but students were not subjected to "schools of thought" (model #1) and philosophies of educators that have never been in the real business environment. We were learning the science of management. I truly benefited from this program

After completion of my master's degree, I was contemplating on beginning a doctorate program. I had made inquires into several programs. However, I was frustrated to find that none of these doctorate programs provided the core concepts of science administration. So I went to talk to Dr. Rondy Smith. She was my professor during my master's degree as well as a highly respected administrator and a friend. I explained to her that I wanted to work on a doctorate degree, but I have not found a program that can compare to the Organizational Master's program that she had designed. I shared my frustrations and told her I may not even work on a doctorate degree. The entire doctorate programs in the area were to expensive and offered nothing as it relates to my master's degree. I just was not willing to spend money if there was no benefit.

Then came the good news. Dr. Smith informed me that the master's program she had designed was very successful. So successful that the college of education (TNU) was developing a doctorate program. She was selected to be the person to teach the business leadership courses included in the doctorate program. This doctorate degree program had several components; education courses, technology, and leadership studies. The dissertation research included both qualitative and quantitative research. This research was to be action oriented, which meant designing a program that put ideas into action. I signed immediately.

During my doctorate studies, a new person was employed as a new administrator at the University. This person presented a new idea. The Organizational Management Masters degree was not bringing new students into the program. It was failing to meet the market demands. Supposedly, marketing research showed that other Universities had lured more new students by offering a MBA. But didn't studies already determine that United States businesses were disappointed in MBA graduates? Yes it did. But administrators get recognition for programs that bring revenue to the Universities. This new administrator sold the University on the concept that more students would rather have a MBA, falsely claming that the business community did not understand what an Organizational Management degree was. The study also "supposedly" determined that graduates of a MBA were more marketable because anyone in a business organization understands what a MBA degree is. These studies should not have merited the attention of other administrators. It sounded good, but was not necessarily true. Students who were graduates of the Organizational Management program became better managers with increased salaries that came from new jobs or being promoted at their present companies.

An interesting perspective about MBA programs, while Fred Smith (President of Federal Express) presented his business thesis for his completion of a MBA at the Harvard University Business College, his thesis was evaluated as below average and was considered to be a business plan that was unreal and not practical.

This new administrator was hired to change the Organizational Management degree into a MBA program. Sad but true, they killed the goose that laid the golden

CASE STUDIES

egg. The program that promoted total quality management conceptualized in *science*, had been reduced to a meaningless curriculum for managers. The program that taught students to never tamper with a process is now the process that has been tampered with.

We all have witnessed such scenarios as University of Tennessee Medical Units and Trevecca Nazarene University. Faithful workers that have been with organizations for ten to twenty years are overlooked and subjected to a high turn-around rate of new manager/administrators. These fast talking people pretending to be leaders often implement a useless program and then job hop to a promotion somewhere else. An example of a similar experience I witnessed while employed with Cardinal Health Corporation, I worked for 11 different managers within a five year period. Is this type of change and reorganization cost effective? Does it really foster development? How can a manager/administrator really make improvements if they have not been part of the organization for several years? When I heard that the University was changing Dr. Smith's program, I was appalled. Someone who researched for many pain-staking years to improve the MBA degree program, implemented the program, had worked in the real world of business, and was a long term faculty member at the University with an excellent track record; had been overlooked and replaced by the new person. By the way, the new person only resided at the University for a few years and moved on to a higher paying job at another University (went to the competitor). Where is the faithfulness of this person compared to Dr. Smith? During the interview process, these job hopping manager/administrators should be asked the question, "You don't seem to stay at an organization for very long? Why is that? Are you looking for more money? The true answer is, this is how people have been taught (by the nature of the system) to get an increase in salary. It is obvious that faithful hard working employees rarely are first in line for an increase in salary. The increase in salaries goes to the new person hiring for a job. Faithful workers in the organization are not given the opportunity to negotiate for an increase in pay. That opportunity is given to the new people being hired.

These two cases may hit home with many people. Before we have verified the results of the old system, we start to make a change. Administrators failed to measure first and then fix. When we make a change, we are tampering with a process. People who have been faithful in the process of education are told (model #2) to change the process that they do best. The act of tampering with processes kills productive people. New managers/administrators are hired to make changes to the organization. This creates the illusion of progress, but it is only one of the many different forms of the Peter Principle. Laurence F. Peter very eloquently presented examples of both how competence and incompetence exists in a variety of organizations. Even though the Peter Principle is best known for promoting people to a level of in-competency, this is only a small aspect of the principle in action. Laurence Peter has many examples of issues that involve the hierarchal structures and processes of an organization. Many of Laurence Peter's examples of his principle starts with a history of competencies at the lower level of the organizations hierarchy. Just as it is with model #2, a person who can delegate the output of an organization to others, may not necessarily be ready to participate in the input to an organization. This input to the organization involves the planning of the business. This decision belongs to the executives of the company, the administrators of educational institutions who are at the level of participating. Anytime an organization fails to recognize the follower readiness of a potential promotee, we have tampered with a statistically controlled process. Laurence Peter's book is full of examples such as these two stories where a competent person performing a process that fosters development is stopped due to tampering.

While working on my Doctorate, I conducted an experiment with two other candidates in the class. Our small team of people decided to test and implement a new curriculum (this project demonstrates how an idea can go wrong). We took members of the class and asked them to roll their tongs. Several people were able to do it and others were not (of course this is a genetic trait – people are born with the capability or not). After recording the results, we determined what group of people could follow the instruction (a simple one) and who could not. These results were recorded on a chart. Then we assigned those candidates who could roll their tong to teach the ones who could not roll their tong, how to do it. We told those that could roll their tongue that this was a test to determine if they could teach. Well it became obvious during this exercise, that this was an example of a process that was incapable rather than the instructor that was incapable. Even though everyone agreed that rolling one's tongue was a predetermined genetic trait, why was there such a unanimous disagreement to this process? The question I posed to people was, "If we try hard enough, can't we do anything?" Why are we allowing the idea of a genetic trait to be a stumbling block? Is information concerning a genetic trait vital to determining an outcome? Is it possible that a person born with the inability to roll their tongue could never learn to roll their tongue even if we continue to persevere? Even though the answers to these questions may be obvious to some, it is not obvious to others. How often have we judged people based on a certain testing criteria, only to discover later that the test itself failed to determine the true capabilities of the individual? Most often the testing criteria fails, not people.

Our learning experience is authenticated during the training process. While we are in school, we are learning. When we have completed a learning process (school of thought/theories), we become armed with the ammunition to be trained in the appropriate application of our lives. As we journey in life we train ourselves and authenticate our learning. If we learned in school a particular theory, our training process (life experiences) will test and authenticate the validity of our learning. This is why I think our education system is doing better than we give it credit for. Why are so many successful people in the United States able to train them selves to collectively be the greatest nation in the world if we did not learn something prior to our life commitment to work?

There is a difference in controlling and monitoring the progress of a plan. Controlling is generally thought of as an invasion of privacy without permission.

Generally speaking, monitoring starts with permission of the participants and then as we study the processes, we select what processes (not people) need to be controlled. You can monitor my behavior, life etc. but please ask for permission first. A question that arises in my mind when an administrator wants to change a process is, "Are our administrators doing the activity to protect the future interest of students (the paying customer) or is it only protecting the departmental empire that certain individuals benefit from such activities?"

In conclusion, the reason that schools appear not to bestow wisdom, why governments cannot maintain order, why courts do not dispense justice (you just get the law), why prosperity fails to produce happiness, why utopian plans never generate utopians is because there are no plans to protect the organization from tampering with processes that foster development. Processes that have proven to be capable and produce an output that fosters development should never be changed. Processes should be monitored to determine if the process is in statistical control. Once the control charts have been done, the process should be periodically monitored for improvement only. There must be a checks and balance system so workers have a channel to evaluate those that are evaluating them. When people are promoted to manage others, it is imperative that a process is in place to reduce the various forms of the Peter Principle. Most important is to recognize the process that fosters development and only test improvements rather than make a dynamic change. I am thankful for the education I have received over the years. Our system of education is constantly improving. Let us all agree to not tamper with our educational process and only continue on the path to improvement.

I personally have experienced a great educational system. The teachers I had in Public Schools were among the best. All the teachers I had in school were involved and made me want to learn. I took art, wood-shop, history, math, literature, and many other courses that were taught by some of the most caring and concerned people I have ever met. I have also witnessed hero administrators as well as zero administrators. When we evaluate what is wrong with a system, it has nothing to do with what educational philosophy we choose, if we research the problems it is due to people who tamper with processes that hard working people have perfected. Teachers usually understand what it is to be a hero and understand the science of learning. The educational system will always be on a path of improvement if parents and administrators quit tampering with processes. We need the leadership that can re-enforce processes that foster development. We need to remove leaders who tamper with great works in progress. The number one issue with the educational system is to identify those zeroes that continue to tamper with the processes of the many heroes that faithfully instruct students that have joined the learning culture. There will always be ups and downs in every process (this is called common cause variation). As a result of many misunderstandings, teachers are caught in the middle of political controversy and educational philosophies. Our educational system is the best and continues to give opportunity to people who would never have had an opportunity to learn if living in another society.

I would like to end with a story told to me by a teacher while working on my Doctorate of Education degree. A young lady who had graduated with honors received a Bachelors degree in education. She applied at many public schools and she finally obtained a job with a middle school. She would be instructing seventh grade girls and boys. On her first day as a teacher, she went into the principle's office to introduce herself. The principle's secretary was there and informed the new teacher that the principle was in a meeting. The new teacher then asked for her student profiles. The secretary handed her student profiles and told her she would be teaching in the area at the rear of the school property. The new teacher reviewed the student profile papers. She noticed the IQ scores at the upper right hand part of the paper. The numbers were 143, 152, 133, etc. She felt blessed because it appeared that she was given the gifted students to teach. She thought that it was only natural that an honor student as herself would be teaching the gifted students.

She began to instruct the students, but she felt that she was not making her classes challenging enough for this gifted group. As she tested these students, their test scores were very low. She felt that she had cheated her students out of receiving a better education. During the year she continued to blame herself for student failures rather than blaming the students. She continued to research better ways of improving her teaching skills. She worked and worked to get student curiosity at a higher level. She did not want to cheat these students out of the learning they deserved.

At the end of the year, the school administered a standardized test to determine if the school was improving. The teacher was worried and wondered how her students did. After several weeks, the test results were in. Her students had not done so well on the standardized tests. Then she received a note from the principle that requested her to be present in the principle's office. Fearing that she would be fired, she reluctantly went to the meeting. The principle congratulated her for having the most improved students in the state. The new teacher stopped and said, "I don't understand. I was given gifted students, but I failed to challenge them. These scores are not so good." The principle said, "These students are not the gifted student group. They are the learning disabled." You increased their aptitude scores by 30 to 40 points from last year, this is remarkable!" The principle then asked, "What made you think they were gifted children?" The new teacher responded, "I noticed their IQ scores written at the upper right hand corner of their student profile page." The principle then responded, "Those were not IQ scores, these are the children's locker numbers."

When we set goals and expectations for ourselves as well as others at a higher level, we are often surprised to see the great outcomes that occur. Because this teacher created an improvement program for herself, and was other oriented, she created a learning culture in which everyone benefited. Even though the process was founded on misinformation, she never tampered with the student's process of learning. She did not blame others; she continued to make improvements to the process of learning.

Case #2: Organized Religion – Another Human Enterprise System

I want to include a section on organized religion because all religions of the world are a part of the human enterprise and are considered by many to be **big business**. I will address personal experiences with several stories and briefly discuss many of the different faiths that people practice in the United States. One way of measuring the many heroes and zeroes of religious enterprises in the United States, is to look at what is called the *generosity index*. The generosity index is a ratio between what is taken into an organization for operational expenses and what charitable benefits are given to others in need of benefits. Charitable organizations are chartered to operate as a non-profit. This means that the organization does not profit from the revenue, but takes a portion of the money to pay for operating expenses. For example, our United States government's welfare system provides those in need of food, medical services, job placement, and many other services to those individuals and families that may not be able to afford basic needs. The generosity index is a percentage of taxpayer money collected and given to the Department of Human Services for operations and what portion of that money is received by beneficiaries that the organization is servicing. The operating budget is publicly made available for the people to review. In some state welfare systems, the generosity index is 33%. This means that 33% of the money went to the needy and 67% of the money (revenue) collected went to supporting people who operate the organization. Hero leaders have a better ratio of re-giving to those who have a need and control the operating cost of the organization. Heroes have a different generosity ratio, less money is taken for operational expenses and the personal income of the leader is set to a lower limit.

Debra Z. Basil, University of Lethbridge did one of many research studies that have theorized a hypothesis concerning charitable donations. This research hypothesizes that charitable donations are a reflection of national values. Earlier in the book it was discussed about sharing values.

In this particular research study, as it is with many people's assessment of charitable contributions; charitable donations are assumed to reflect national values. Charitable donations are generally categorized as a form of helping others. There are many factors that contribute to an individual's decision to perform the act of donating money to an organization. One factor that appears to strongly influence donations is whether the cause is congruent with the individual's values. Internalized moral values are an important element in generating feelings of obligation to perform helping behavior. When people are asked why do you donate time (volunteer work) and money to a particular charitable organization, over 91% of the people respond that they are acting upon their underlying values. But which charities do we support? Well charities that deal with issues reflecting national values generally receive the higher levels of financial support than other types of charities. I am providing a chart that shows the approximate percentages of where people share values in the United States. I use the word approximation because it is difficult to determine the amount of money given to religious organizations. Even though church bulletins often report last week's contributions, it is difficult to get real numbers for all the religious organizations. The Internal Revenue Service also publishes the totals that tax-payers report in charitable contributions, but we all know how inaccurate that can be for some people. Many will claim charitable deductions, but don't have a record of actually giving a contribution. So these percentages are accurate to a 3% margin either side of the mean. The table reflects a brake-down of allocated money for charity. An example, if a person donates 10% of their income to charity (income=$100,000.00 then 10% = $10,000.00) of this $10,000.00 donated, approximately $5,200.00 will go to religion, $1,500.00 will be donated to education, etc.

Charity	Donation $
Religion	52%
Education	15%
Other	14%
Health	10%
Social Services	9%

Simply speaking, charities that deal with issues reflecting national values generally will receive higher levels of financial support than other types of charities. There should be very little doubt in the minds of people living in the United States, that we are a very generous group of people that values religion over many other enterprises. As I mentioned in the last case study concerning the United States educational system, our education system is second to the fund raising and revenue resources of religious organizations. This information is not to be taken as a criticism of religious organizations. However, it does reflect the overwhelming generosity of people who are members of a religious organization. Here is another chart that displays member (affiliation) of some of the more popular religions.

Image from the U.S. Center for World Mission (MissionFrontiers.org)

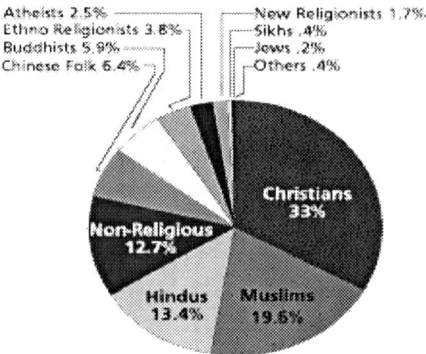

CASE STUDIES

Here is another chart that provides additional information concerning membership, place of worship, religious texts, and leadership titles.

Basic information on various religions:

Religion	Date Founded	Sacred Texts	Membership in millions	% of World Population
Christianity	30 AD	The Bible	2,039	32%
Islam	622 AD	Qur'an & Hadith	1,226	19%
Hinduism	1,500 BCE	The Veda	828	13%
No religion *	No date	None	775	12%
Chinese folk rel.	270 BCE	None	390	6%
Buddhism	523 BCE	The Tripitaka	364	6%
Tribal Religions, Shamanism, Animism	Prehistory	Oral tradition	232	4%
Atheists	No date	None	150	2%
New religions.	Various	Various	103	2%
Sikhism	1500 CE	Guru Granth Sahib	23.8	1%
Judaism	No consensus	Torah, Talmud	14.5	1%
Spiritism			12.6	1%
Baha'i Faith	1863 CE	Most Holy Book	7.4	1%
Confucianism	520 BCE	Lun Yu	6.3	1%
Jainism	570 BCE	Siddhanta, Pakrit	4.3	1%
Zoroastrianism	No consensus	Avesta	2.7	1%
Shinto	500 CE	Kojiki, Nohon Shoki	2.7	1%
Taoism	550 BCE	Tao-te-Ching	2.7	1%
Other	Various	Various	1.1	1%
Wicca	800 BCE, 1940 CE	None	0.5	1%

These membership numbers are compared to the world population numbers. Again, it is difficult to be accurate, and these numbers change from year to year. But, these numbers are more than an estimate. These numbers come from several sources such as the government census reports and membership records archived with these religious organizations.

Place of worship and Title of Religious Leader

Religion	Place of worship	Title of local leader
Christianity	Church, Cathedral, Temple, Mission	Pastor, priest, minister
Islam	Mosque	Imam
No religion *	None	None
Hinduism	Temple	Priest
Buddhism	Temple	Priest
Atheists	None	None
New Asian religion	Various	Various
Tribal Religions, Animism	In nature	Shaman
Judaism	Synagogue	Rabbi
Sikhism	Gurdwaras	Granthi (professional reader)
Shamanists	In nature	Shaman
Confucianism	Temple, Shrine, Seowon	Unknown
Baha'i Faith	House of worship	Usually a lay leader
Jainism	Temple	Priest, Pandit
Shinto	Temple	Priest
Wicca	Circle, Grove	Priestess, Priest, Wiccan
Zoroastrianism	Atash Behram, Agiyari, Prayer rooms	Mobed, Dastur

Again, this information varies due to the many denominations, factions, and branches (off shoots) of these original religions. Given that most of these faiths are based on some religious text (the Bible, the Q'uran, the Bhagavagita, etc.), religious leaders instruct their followers that a particular text or texts used are the only reliable source(s) of information. But, is it possible for a text to prove its validity by claiming its own authority? Is there any text with proven authenticity as having come from another realm, or are they all man-made creations with imaginary authenticity? Answering these questions is part of the job of the religious leaders.

I personally have read several of these texts and visited various places of worship for extended periods of time. Some religious organizations were very open to discussion, allowed me to use their library, and would participate in discussions concerning doctrine and theology. As a result, I have read the following texts from cover to cover; The Q'uran, The Book of Mormon, Bhagavagita, The Veda, The Tripitaka, The Urantia Book, The Egyptian Book of the Dead, Avesta text, Enuma Elish tablets, and other Ancient Alternative Scriptures. Alternative scriptures include the following, the Gnostic Gospels, the Dead Sea Scrolls, Christian Apocrypha, the satanic bible, and the Kabbalah. I am also a reader of The Bible (Old & New Testament / Catholic and Protestant Cannons). As a result of reading these texts, here are some interesting findings.

For instance, in the Q'uran, translated by M.H. Shakir – Tahrike Tarsile Qur'an Inc., Sarah 5-110 it states:

> *"When Allah will say: O Isa* (Jesus' Arabic Name) *son of Marium* (Mary's Arabic Name)! *Remember My favor on you and your mother, when I strengthened you with the holy Spirit, you spoke to the people in the cradle and when of old age, and when I taught you the Book and wisdom and the Taurat* (Torah) *and the Injeel* (Gospel); *and* **when you determined out of clay a thing like the form of a bird by My permission, then you breathed into it and it became a bird by My permission**, *and you healed the blind and the leprous by My permission; and when you brought forth the dead by My permission; and when I withheld the children of Israel from you when you came to them with clear arguments, but those who disbelieve among them said: This is nothing but clear enchantment."*

I have shown this quote from the Q'uran to several Christians, their comments vary. Some find it interesting that the Q'uran acknowledges miracles that Christ performed such as healing the blind and leprosy. They never knew that Jesus Christ was even mentioned in the Q'uran. In addition, many Christians recognized the part in this passage that Christ raised people from the dead, such as Lazarus (John 11:11-28). Interesting that this gospel records Jesus as saying, "Our friend Lazarus sleepeth;" (John 11:11). Many use this verse to say that Lazarus was not dead, but suffered from catalepsy. However, reading further in verse 14 Jesus said to them clearly, "Lazarus has died."

Catalepsy «KAT uh LEHP see», is a condition in which a person temporarily loses the ability to move voluntarily. A person suffering from catalepsy is not paralyzed, but simply lacks the will to move. The person will be in a complete trance-like mental detachment. The arms and legs of a cataleptic person can be placed in unusual positions. The person will maintain such positions for many minutes and sometimes for hours or days.

But many of the Christians question the part in the Q'uran that Jesus made clay figures of birds and then turned these clay figures into breathing birds. Christians would respond that there is nothing in the Bible that refers to this particular miracle. As a result, Christians reason that the Q'uran has included a false story concerning Jesus' miracles. But in actuality, this story is recorded in Thomas' gospel that was not canonized in the Christian New Testament.

I, Thomas the Israelite, announce and make known all you brethren from the Gentiles the childhood and great deeds of our Lord Jesus Christ, which he did when he was born in our country. This is the beginning.

When this Jesus was five years old, he was playing at the ford of a stream. He made pools of the rushing water and made it immediately pure; he ordered this by word alone. He made soft clay and modeled twelve sparrows from it. It was the Sabbath when He did this. There were many other children playing with Him. A certain Jew saw what Jesus did while playing on the Sabbath; he immediately went and announced to his father Joseph, "See your child is at the stream, and has taken clay and modeled twelve birds; He has profaned the Sabbath." Joseph came to the place and seeing what Jesus did cried out, "Why do you do on the Sabbath what is not lawful to do?" Jesus clapped His hands and cried to the sparrows, "Be gone." And the sparrows flew off chirping. The Jews saw this and were amazed. They went away and described to their leaders what they had seen Jesus do.

The Infancy Gospel of Thomas
<u>The Other Bible</u> - page 399

This gospel also ends with Jesus at the age of twelve in the Temple, amazing the elders and teachers with His ability to solve the problems of the Law and the parables of the prophets. This account of Jesus in the Temple at twelve years of age is also found in the gospel of Luke which is canonized in the New Testament (Luke 2: 42-49). The story of the sparrows (birds) referenced in the Q'uran, but not in the Bible may be a result of Mohammad's many travels to many countries. Even as a child he traveled with his Uncle (who was a trade merchant) to the land of Israel. The gospel of Thomas, even though not canonized in the New Testament, remained in circulation, at the time of Mohammad and even in today's literature. However, this text is in the Q'uran, translated by M.H. Shakir – Tahrike Tarsile Qur'an Inc., Sarah 5-110 is also in other Koran texts it is found in Sarah 3:49.

"I have come to you with a sign from your Lord. I make for you the shape of a bird out of clay, I breathe into it, and it becomes a bird by God's permission. I heal the blind from birth and the leper. And I bring the dead to life by God's permission. And I tell you what you eat and what you store in your houses...."

(Quran, 3:49)

I have three different copies of the Koran/Q'uran. The orders of the Sarahs are different and some are eliminated. I have asked Muslim friends and three different Imams which texts I should use. I received several different answers.

I find it interesting that even though Jews and Muslims have had their disagreements for hundreds of years; they both have one thing in common, that is they both agree that Jesus Christ is not the Messiah. The Q'uran notes that Jesus is the son of Mary and even though Muslims accept that Jesus did miracles, these miracles were done by Allah's permission. I have heard people from other faiths, non-Muslims, that Muslims hate Jews and Christians. Hate is a very strong word. A Muslim friend shared with me that this is not true. He said nowhere in any Islamic texts is it written to not be friends with other religious groups. Muslims have nothing against Jews and Christians. I then asked him about this verse.

O you who believe! Do not take the Jews and Christians for friends; they are friends of each other; and whoever amongst you takes them for a friend, then surely he is one of them; surely Allah does not guide the unjust people.
Surah 5:51
Q'uran, translated by M.H. Shakir
Tahrike Tarsile Qur'an Inc.

This is an example of how we can be caught off guard. I have found that many of our religious followers and leaders are not as familiar with their religious texts as they would like to think they are. Let me illustrate with some Christian experiences I have had. In 1976, I was a Sunday school teacher and a youth director. While providing services at a Christian summer camp, I over heard a counselor chastising a 12 year old boy because he said he had to take a piss. The counselor informed the youth that God would never use such profane language. He also said you would never find such words in the Bible. I later sat with this counselor in private and asked if I could see his Bible. He informed me that he only uses the King James Version of the Bible; this was the Bible that God told him to use. So I turned to the book of Isaiah and asked him to read 36:12.

But Rabshakeh said, Hath my master sent me to thy master and to thee to speak these words? hath he not sent me to the men that sit upon the wall, that they may eat their own dung, and drink their own piss with you?
Isaiah 36:12 - KJV

Another experience I had concerning the misconceptions of scriptures was visiting an Evangelical Independent Church. I was asked by friends to attend Sunday School and Church services. During the Sunday School Class, one of the attendees told the class that her brother was backsliding (falling into sin) because he met a girl that was a prostitute and wanted to marry her even though family members objected.

The instructor informed everyone very quickly that God would NEVER ask anyone to marry a prostitute. After the class I asked him to open his Bible to Hosea 1:2.

The beginning of the word of the LORD by Hosea. And the Lord said to Hosea, Go take unto thee a wife of whoredoms and children of whoredoms: for the land hath committed great whoredom, departing from the LORD.

Also, while visiting an adult Sunday school class at a local Southern Baptist Church, the class began a discussion about a topic one of the class members saw on television. According to this person, a lady was interviewed that is a stripper, but she wrote Bible verses on her skin (such as John 3:16). The stripper told the interviewer that she does this to be a witness for Jesus. When men come to see her strip naked, they read the Bible verses on her body. The Sunday school instructor told the class that God would **never** tell **anyone** to uncover themselves and be naked. After class, I showed this verse to the teacher.

At the same time spake the LORD by Isaiah the son of Amoz, saying, Go and loose the sackcloth from your loins, and put off thy shoe from thy foot. And he did so, walking naked and barefoot.
Isaiah 20:2 - KJV

On another occasion, friends of mine asked me to come and visit their church. They were Mormons, followers of the Church of Jesus Christ of Latter Day Saints. It was at a later time in my life that I learned that there was the Church of Jesus Christ of Latter-day Saints and the Reorganized Church of Jesus Christ of Latter Day Saints which accepts a different version of the work as scripture. I was able to obtain a book of Mormon after attending services that day. I read the book from cover to cover and began to understand many aspects of the religion. I learned that polygamy was a feature added by Brigham Young after Joseph Smith's death. Before Brigham Young it was regarded as an abomination. Here is a verse from the book of Mormon that I obtained while visiting the church and a verse concerning polygamy.

II.of the book of Jacob:

For behold, thus saith the Lord, this people begin to wax in iniquity; they understand not the Scriptures; for they seek to excuse themselves in committing whoredoms, because of the things which were written concerning David, and Solomon his son. Behold, David and Solomon truly had many wives and concubines, which thing was abominable before me, saith the Lord; wherefore, thus saith the Lord, I have led this people forth out of the land of Jerusalem, by the power of mine arm, that I might raise up unto me a righteous branch from the fruit of the loins of Joseph. Wherefore, I the Lord God, will not suffer that this people shall do like unto them of old.

This verse is from the same chapter:

> *Behold, the Lamanites your brethren, whom ye hate, because of their filthiness and the cursings which hath come upon their skins, are more righteous than you; for they have not forgotten the commandment of the Lord, which was given unto our fathers, that they should have, save it were one wife; and concubines they should have none.*

In chapter IX. of the Book of Nephi, I learned that Jesus selected other disciples.

> *And it came to pass that on the morrow, when the multitude was gathered together, behold, Nephi and his brother whom he had raised from the dead, whose name was Timothy, and also his son, whose name was Jonas, and also Mathoni, and Mathonihah, his brother, and Kumen, and Kumenenhi, and Jeremiah, and Shemnon, and Jonas, and Zedekiah, and Isaiah; now these were the names of the disciples whom Jesus had chosen.*

When reading the Book of Ether, I found that there were many interesting historical accounts of battles and sieges among people that have not been formally documented in other history sources. King Coriantumr declared war with Shared, and Lib, and Shiz, etc. in the plains of Heshlon and the valley of Gilgal, and the wilderness of Akish and the land of Moran and the plains of Agosh and Ogath, and Ramah and the land of Corihor, and the hill Comnor, by the waters of Ripliancum; that after the fighting had stopped, King Coriantumr made a calculation of his losses. These losses were calculated to have been two million men, and also their wives and their children (so the number could be even greater). Needless to say, I was unable to find this account (people, locations, and dates) in any archeological sources or other historical records. This is not to say it did not happen, but usually when 2 million people are reported dead (or more), then there is usually forensic evidence of mass killings of this magnitude. I was disappointed that additional information could not be found concerning geographical location or archeological data of this war.

While on a business trip, I happened to be at an airport where a group of people where soliciting for money and explaining their religion to weary travelers. A young lady asked me for a donation and said that she had a book she wanted to give me. She said, "You shall find in this Bhagavad-gita that the complete whole is comprised of the supreme controller, the controlled living entities, the cosmic manifestation, eternal time and karma, or activities, and all of these are explained in this text." Another person informed me "All of these taken completely from the complete whole, and the complete whole is called the Supreme Absolute Truth. The complete whole and the complete Absolute Truth are the complete Personality of Godhead, Sri Krishna. All manifestations are due to His different energies. He is the complete whole." After receiving all of this advice I obtained the book for a donation of $10.00.

After reading the Bhagavad-gita, I had many questions concerning the content. I am familiar with hermeneutics, the principles and processes of Biblical interpretation, but this was not working well to be a science of textual criticism for other religious texts. So I had several meetings with spiritual leaders and the so called experts of the Bhagavad-gita. I was informed by leaders that my copy of the Bhagavad-gita did indeed contain the complete knowledge of Vedic wisdom. All Vedic knowledge is infallible, and Hindus accept Vedic knowledge to be complete and infallible. So I asked why is any information concerning the dung of animal's consequential to purification or having a relationship with God. I was specific to mention that "if one touches the stool of an animal he has to take a bath to purify himself, but in the Vedic scriptures cow dung is considered to be a purifying agent. His answer was, "This is not a contradiction. It has been accepted because it is Vedic injunction, and indeed by accepting this, one will not commit a mistake; subsequently it has been proved by modern science that cow dung contains all antiseptic properties. So Vedic knowledge is complete because it is above all doubts and mistakes, and Bhagavad-Gita is the essence of all Vedic knowledge."

I am not trying to shock my religious friends into believing something different, nor is it the intent of this case study to defame anyone's Holy Scriptures. But, I find it amazing that both followers and leaders of many faiths do not read what is considered to be their most sacred scriptures. My experience has been that many people, who think they know what their scriptures contain, have not read everything in entirety. As a result, Holy Scriptures becomes a counter cultural issue for most fundamentalist religions that preach their texts rather than teach their texts. Cultural morays, rather than systems thinking, become the fuel to interpret any issue. Anyone who seeks the truth is condemned to be against God. When asked, "Don't you believe the Bible is the word of God?" I always answer with a question to get more clarification of the question. I respond, "Are you asking me if all the words in the Bible are only spoken by God?" Most often my question is met with a statement, "It is a real simple question, can't you answer it?!!!" Then I have to respond "No." As the person questioning me stands in utter amazement that I am not a believer, I then show them in the Bible and read to them these verses.

> If thou be the Son of God, cast thyself down: for it is written, He shall give his angels charge concerning thee: and in their hands they shall bear thee up, lest at any time thou dash thy foot against a stone.
> Matthew 4:16 KJV

Also,

> Doth Job fear God for nought?
> Job 1:9 KJV

I then ask the question, "Are these God's words or Satan's words in God's word?" It becomes apparent that false profits, Satan, and many other evil doers have words in God's word. So I cannot say that God spoke all the words in the Bible, because God's word identifies the person speaking as Satan, a false profit, etc. When any enterprising system looks for solutions only by means of a particular cultural moray, we loose vital information and as a result we lack the ability to integrate all the ideas and meaningful content of our sources. It is not good enough to just look at cultural morays; rather we look into other sources of authority to remove bias in our integrative systems thinking. There exist normative theories that have worked in the past and will always work for the enterprise in the future. Before we accept a particular belief, we must always examine the sources of our doctrine before instituting dogmatic declarations that others must adhere to. Many religious enterprises have begun to become political activist as a result of miss-interpretation of verses taken out of contexts. Who should we follow, God or country?

Politics, Religion, and Money

With respect to whom we should serve God or Country, Jesus Christ answered this question when asked by the Pharisees.

> Matthew|22:15 Then went the Pharisees, and took counsel how they might entangle him in his talk.
> Matthew|22:16 And they sent out unto him their disciples with the Herodians, saying, Master, we know that thou art true, and teachest the way of God in truth, neither carest thou for any man: for thou regardest not the person of men.
> Matthew|22:17 Tell us therefore, What thinkest thou? Is it lawful to give tribute unto Caesar, or not?
> Matthew|22:18 But Jesus perceived their wickedness, and said, Why tempt ye me, ye hypocrites?
> Matthew|22:19 Show me the tribute money. And they brought unto him a penny.
> Matthew|22:20 And he saith unto them, Whose is this image and superscription?
> Matthew|22:21 They say unto him, Caesar's. Then saith he unto them, Render therefore unto Caesar the things which are Caesar's; and unto God the things that are God's.

Does the First Amendment of the United States Constitution allow religious organizations to support or oppose political candidates? Is it freedom of speech or do we just have the privilege to make a fair comment without fear of government reaction? We could debate the first amendment rights concerning this issue for a long time, it is not very clear. Under the First Amendment, every legally registered person in the United States has the privilege to practice being a citizen of the United States. Whether you are a famous musician, famous scientist, a famous writer, or religious leader; as a United States citizen, we have freedom to speak and make a fair comment about the issues. Just because famous people may not be qualified to make a fair comment about an issue or endorsement, our government more often supports the entitlement of everyone to speak freely. But we are more prone to listen to famous and well-known popular people. In order to answer the question, there are no provisions or explicit actions the Federal government may exercise to enforce unbiased endorsements of a political candidate by Churches under the first amendment. But, under section 501(c)(3) of the Internal Revenue Code, tax-exempt organizations are absolutely prohibited from supporting or opposing candidates for elected public office. Tax laws change from time to time, but in the year 2000 this code was challenged in court. A federal appellate court rejected a church's claim that the First Amendment's free exercise of religion clause allowed the church to urge the public to vote against a candidate. *Branch Ministries and Dan Little, Pastor v. Rossotti*, 211 F.3d 137 (D.C. Cir. 2000). Another case was *Bob Jones University v. United States*, 461 U.S. 574, 603 (1983). The Supreme Court held that "not all burdens on religion are unconstitutional;" however, State Courts may justify a limitation on religious liberty by showing that it is essential to accomplish an overriding governmental interest. The fact that a church may be motivated by its religious principles will therefore not prevent a church from losing its tax-exempt status and facing other penalties if it supports or opposes any candidate.

Now we need to answer another question. What does supporting or opposing a political candidate mean? May taxed-exempted organizations send money to a particular party (Republican or Democrat) as long as nothing has been said in favor of one party's candidate over another? What are the guidelines for the courts and the IRS to consider all of the relevant facts and circumstances in determining whether a church has supported or opposed a candidate? The Internal Revenue Service regularly publishes and updates its *Tax Guide for Churches and Religious Organizations.* While making donations to candidates, raising funds for candidates and endorsing candidates are prohibited, so are more subtle efforts to support or oppose candidates. In a more recent update the IRS provides the following examples of prohibited activities by churches:

> *Sermon.* Minister D is the minister of Church M. During regular services of Church M shortly before the election, Minister D preached on a number of issues, including the importance of voting in the upcoming election, and concludes by stating, "It is important that you all do your duty in the election and vote for Candidate W." Since Minister D's remarks indicating support for Candidate W were made during an official church service, they constitute political campaign intervention attributable to Church M.

> *Church Newsletter.* Minister B is the minister of Church K. Church K publishes a monthly church newsletter that is distributed to all church members. In each issue, Minister B has a column titled "My Views." The month before the election, Minister B states in the "My Views" column, "It is my personal opinion that Candidate U should be reelected." For that one issue, Minister B pays from his personal funds the portion of the cost of the newsletter attributable to the "My Views" column. Even though he paid part of the cost of the newsletter, the newsletter is an official publication of the church. Since the endorsement appeared in an official

publication of Church K, it constitutes campaign intervention attributed to Church K.

> *Candidate Invitation.* Minister F is the minister of Church O. The Sunday before the November election, Minister F invited Senate Candidate X to preach to her congregation during worship services. During his remarks, Candidate X stated, "I am asking not only for your votes, but for your enthusiasm and dedication, for your willingness to go the extra mile to get a very large turnout on Tuesday." Minister F invited no other candidate to address her congregation during the Senatorial campaign. Because these activities took place during official church services, they are attributed to Church O. By selectively providing church facilities to allow Candidate X to speak in support of his campaign, Church O's actions constitute political campaign intervention.

> *Voter Guides.* Church S distributes a voter guide during an election campaign. The voter guide is prepared using the responses of candidates to a questionnaire sent to candidates for major public offices. Although the questionnaire covers a wide range of topics, the wording of the questions evidences a bias on certain issues. By using a questionnaire structured in this way, Church S is participating or intervening in a political campaign.

Court decisions, IRS rulings and IRS publications provide the following additional examples of prohibited activity:

> *Statements*. Publishing or distributing written or printed statements or making oral statements on behalf of or in opposition to a candidate. Treasury Regulation § 1.501(c)(3)-1(c)(3)(iii); *Christian Echoes National Ministry, Inc. v. United States*, 470 F.2d 849 (10th Cir. 1972), *cert. denied*, 414 U.S. 864 (1973).

> *Evaluating Candidates*. Considering the qualifications of all candidates, selecting those determined to be best qualified or evaluating the candidates based on objective and nonpartisan criteria, and publicizing the results of that selection or evaluation. *Association of the Bar of the City of New York v. Commissioner*, 858 F.2d 876 (2d Cir. 1988), *cert. denied*, 490 U.S. 1030 (1989); Revenue Ruling 67-71.

> *Distributing Others' Evaluations of Candidates*. Distributing the evaluations of candidates by others, such as the views of the audience for a candidate forum. Technical Advice Memorandum 9635003 (Apr. 19, 1996).

> *Legislative Voter Records*. Publishing a compilation of the voting records of incumbents on a narrow range of issues, such as land conservation, and distributing the compilation widely among the electorate, even if the guide

does not include express statements in support of or in opposition to any candidate. Revenue Ruling 78-248, *Situation 4*.

➢ *Campaign Material*. Distributing voter education material prepared by a candidate, political party or PAC. Kindell & Reilly, "Election Year Issues," *IRS Exempt Organizations Continuing Professional Education Technical Instruction Program for FY2002*, at 372.

➢ *Allowing Use of Space, Services or Mailing List*. Selling or renting space, services or mailing lists to a candidate unless available to all candidates on an equal basis, also available to the public on the same basis, and provided on a regular basis (not provided for the first time to a candidate). Kindell & Reilly, "Election Year Issues," *IRS Exempt Organizations Continuing Professional Education Technical Instruction Program for FY2002*, at 383-84.

➢ *Loan Funds*. Making a loan to, or guaranteeing a loan to, a candidate, political party or PAC. Technical Advice Memorandum 9812001 (Aug. 21, 1996).

Many people who review these laws and cases may conclude that our government is too involved with religious organizations. Many argue that there are laws concerning separation of Church and State. Many fundamentalists argue that their rights are being violated. Freedoms have not been taken away from anyone. Churches are allowed to engage in strictly *non-partisan* election-related activities. Churches are to encourage their members to register to vote and to vote as long as they do not encourage them to support or oppose particular candidates or parties. I have visited many Churches, Synagogues, Temples, and other places of worship in my lifetime. One particular political issue that is talked about is abortion and the right to life issue. Overwhelmingly, the people I have talked to support the "right to life" political candidate and are encouraged by their religious leaders to do so. But looking at the abortion statistics published by religious organizations, the number of abortions do not necessarily go up or down when such candidates are elected and serve over a period of time.

There are two U.S. Supreme Court decisions during the 1973 year that challenged the present abortion laws in the United States. These cases are *Roe v. Wade* and *Doe v. Bolton*. Roe v. Wade is the case that more people talk about concerning this issue. But the combined efforts of the two rulings changed the legal climate radically to require abortion to be; (1) legal for any woman, regardless of her age, (2) legal for any reason during the first seven months of pregnancy, and (3) for virtually any reason thereafter. Also, since the 1973 ruling, the U.S. Supreme Court has upheld the constitutionality of state laws which regulate and limit abortion in the following ways; (1) requiring a parent to be notified or give consent before a minor daughter has an abortion, (2) subject to a judicial bypass option which allows a teenage girl to involve a judge rather than her parent(s), (3) requiring that women receive full medical disclosure of possible risks associated with and alternatives to abortion, (4) requiring that after receiving such information - adult women wait a period of 24 hours before having an abortion and that minors wait 48 hours, (5) prohibiting the use of state money to fund abortions for low-income women, except when the mother's life is threatened by continuing the pregnancy, or in cases of rape or incest when payment is authorized under the federal Hyde Amendment.

Many religious activists are in battle with our courts to have these rulings over turned or modified. Many claim that the United States has one of the highest abortion rates among developed countries. This could be true or not true. Many countries fail to report with accuracy what the numbers really are. But taking a look at the number of reported legal abortions for selected years between 1972 and 1997 we can look at the numbers for the United States. Here are the numbers according to the Abortion Surveillance Report provided by the Centers for Disease Control and Prevention's (CDC) January 7, 2000. I am adding an additional column to remind us who was serving as our presidents in the White House.

President	Year--Number
Richard Nixon	1972--586,760
	1973--615,831
Gerald Ford	1974—Not Available
	1975—Not Available
	1976--988,267
Jimmy Carter	1977—Not Available
	1978—Not Available
	1979—Not Available
	1980--1,297,606
Ronald Reagan	1981—Not Available
	1982—Not Available
	1983—Not Available
	1984—Not Available
	1985--1,328,570
	1987-- 1,353,671
	1988 – Not Available
George H.W. Bush	1989--1,396,658
	1990-- 1,429,577
	1991- -1,388,937
	1992--1,359,145
William Clinton	1993--1,330,414
	1994--1,267,415
	1995--1,210,883
	1996--1,221,585
	1997--1,184,758

Included in the report, roughly one-half of the women who had abortions in the U.S. had no other children. Forty four percent of the women who had abortions in the U.S. had at least one previous abortion and twenty percent of women who had abortions in the U.S. were married. Eighty percent were unmarried. The percentage of teenagers, nineteen years of age and younger having abortions began to drop in the 1980s, coinciding with the passage and enforcement of laws requiring a parent's involvement in their teenage daughter's abortion decision, but abortions continued to be at a higher level during the 1980s. The statistics concerning abortion adverse pregnancy diagnosis and patient care are not available. When I was admitted into one of our Nashville Hospitals to have a hernia operation (elective surgery-outpatient surgery), I was asked to take the time to evaluate the care and service I had received. Also, by the insistence of my doctor, he wanted to have two follow-up visits. Maybe my research to find this data concerning patient care and follow-up was not extensive enough, but I was unable to obtain data concerning patient perspective and their evaluation of treatment received.

The data seems to indicate that it does not matter which party or presidential candidate is supported and elected, abortion rates have not changed significantly over the years. What does the data and information indicate about improvement and progress of who is winning with respect to the issues? The data indicates very little. Anyone could conclude that the data only indicates that our leaders are creating the illusion of progress. How does this data provide information on where we need to improve our processes? Where is the data that can tell donators that their time and money toward a particular issue has fostered development? Nowhere in these reports does it indicate the long and short-term benefits of the process. No indicators are given to determine if this process is in the best interest of the United States citizens.

Both the evolutionists and creationist Christians disagree on the origins of our existence. However, evolutionist and creationist agree that when nature gives birth to a new generation, this is how nature improves itself. The process of natural selection is how nature improves. The issue is not whether you are for or against supporting abortion, the issue is "Are we doing anything that may be tampering with the process of natural selection?" Taking these statistics and comparing them to other species, what is the natural rate of miscarriages within certain populations?

In the 1984-year, were more female fetuses terminated than male? According to a 1990 Canadian study of 22,000 women who received prenatal diagnosis that they were carrying a child with Down syndrome, 88 percent of those women terminated the pregnancy. Much of this data reported cannot be relied on for fair evaluation and interpretation. My research in this area has determined that we have the worst statistical data concerning this census. We really do not have enough information to make the best decisions concerning this issue. All the information provided only spawns more questions.

Even though the "right to life" issue has gotten many religious people to vote for a particular candidate, organizations that are tax exempt are not to tamper with the voters decisions concerning political candidates. I have been dismayed to find leaders of many tax-exempted organizations urging their religious followers to specifically vote for a particular candidate, "the right to life" candidate. Like all organizations that are exempt from federal income tax under section 501(c)(3) of the Internal Revenue Code and eligible to receive tax deductible contributions under section 170(c)(2) of the Internal Revenue Code, churches are prohibited from supporting or opposing any candidate for elected public office. This prohibition applies to candidates for federal, state or local offices. The IRS enforces this prohibition through audits, fines, and loss of tax-exempt status. A church may also face financial penalties. The IRS may assess excise taxes on both the church and its leaders. If the church received investment or other non-contribution income during the year for which it is no longer tax-exempt, it may be required to file IRS Form 1120 (corporate income tax return) and pay tax on that income. State or local authorities may also demand taxes for that period as well, including property taxes. The Rev. Jerry Falwell, in the July 21, 2004 edition of his e-newsletter *Falwell Confidential*, cites Mr. Staver's views and states that Branch Ministries only lost its "IRS letter" for one day. This may or may not be correct. Other information sources say that the IRS revoked the tax-exempt status of Branch Ministries on January 19, 1995 retroactively to January 1, 1992 and the courts upheld that revocation.

Should religious organizations such as the Branch Ministries have to pay taxes to support issues and programs that they are in disagreement with? Could this be considered taxation without representation? When our first president, George Washington stopped the "whiskey rebellion" this was the cry of the people that were in opposition, "Taxation without representation." George Washington's comment was, "You have representation." This is true; we elect representatives who should serve the best interest of the people they represent. It was the people's responsibility to determine if their representatives were present and regularly voting on the issues. But all of this does not answer the question of how does an enterprise organization obtain tax-exempt status with our government. Many religious groups in the United States own a great deal of property. Other groups are making their moves to be recognized as a belief by faith organization. The shafarist group, SAFAR, standing for Secularism, Humanism, Atheism, Free thought, Agnosticism, and Rationalism claim that the government and the media are not acknowledging the world's fourth largest belief system and our government acts as if this group of people doesn't exist. In number of adherents it's behind Christianity, Islam and Buddhism but ahead of Hinduism. Globally it's 85% the size of Catholicism and in the United States of America, just a little smaller than Episcopalians, Presbyterians and Lutherans put together. Perhaps most astoundingly, given today's politics, in the U.S. it is roughly the size of the Southern Baptist Convention. This organization claims, "Its leaders are not invited to open Senate sessions, Politicians do not quote them and our news shows do not interview them. And while it is a sin, if not a crime, to be anti-Catholic or anti-Semitic, disparaging this faith is not only permitted, it is publicly encouraged." This organization has also stated, "So completely is this belief system excluded from our national consciousness that we do not even have a name for it. So let's give it one, shafarism - standing for secularism, humanism, atheism, free thought, agnosticism, and rationalism." Another issue they point to is, "Shafars are 850 million people around the globe and at least 20 million at home who are ignored, insulted, or commonly considered less worthy than those who adhere to faiths based on mythology and folklore rather than on logic, empiricism, verifiable history, and science." It appears that this group is bidding for power by the fallacy of ad populum. Ad populum is a fallacy that occurs when we appeal to people. There are several types of ad populum; glittering generalities, name-calling, soft-soap, snob appeal, plain folks, bandwagon, them verses us, and waving the bloody shirt. This was discussed earlier in the book. But often this appeal works to persuade a representative to change their vote if enough people are willing to reelect on the issue. The shafarist have included this appeal, "This might be considered just another of the world's many injustices were it not for the fact that the globe is currently exceptionally endangered by a madness driven by false prophets of major traditional mythologies such as bin Laden, Bush and Sharon. Seldom has organized religion been so ubiquitously harmful. Even in our own country the dismantling of our republic and its constitution is being led by an extremist Christian cabal that not only is a political travesty but a mockery of its own professed faith." Here is an example of yet another appeal, "But faith in religion is just one type of faith. Atheism can be called faith in evidence, agnosticism faith in doubt and science faith in logic. These are no less human faiths than those in an unseen God."

So often the question is present to our politicians, "Should a religious faith leader be allowed to intrude with impunity in such secular areas as politics or science and still claim the protection of reverence and law?" The Shafars answer is "no." The Shafarist say, "Once Southern Baptists, Catholics, Jews or Muslims enter the political arena, they are no more entitled to special protection or regulated rhetoric than a Democrat or a Republican." In other words Shafarist say, "If you want to pray and believe, fine. But to put a folkloric account of our beginnings on the same plain as massive scientific research is not a sign of faith but of ignorance or delusion. And if you want to play politics you've got to fight by its rules and not hide under a sacred shield." The Shafarist then ask the questions, "Is it worse to be anti-Catholic than anti-African? Is it worse to be anti-Semitic than to be anti-Arab? Is it worse to be anti-Anglican than anti-gay?" When answering such questions, we find ourselves answering with a preference toward one group over another. This type of questioning is sometimes refereed to as ***entrapment***. It is designed to catch the non-careful thinker off guard. There are a small group of leaders that encourage a hierarchy of empathy for certain type of groups over others. But our society has made efforts to eliminate prejudices.

So the Shafarist would like to consider that they are a faith based organization. It seems that faith is everywhere but many people sometime in their life have to have a world of evidence before they can come anywhere close to believing anything. Claims continue that people have seen visions of Jesus, that they have witnessed many miracles, seen the holy engravings, and have experienced many other theophanies. Much of the religious materials I have read are not in the form of a treatise or philosophical dissertation. Most is personal narrative with true claims to an archeological historical and sometimes the text is a pretentious historical. Only time will tell. In reference to the Old and New Testament texts, much has been written in support of the accuracy of the written word. This is known as an evidential method rather than a scientific method. The evidential method is used in the United States court system to prove or disprove witness's claims. Even though the evidential method contains scientific evidence, when in the absence of scientific evidence many will determine adjudication with written and spoken word. This is referred to as Christian Apologetics. One of the most well known people in the area of Apologetics is Josh McDowell. He wrote the book "Evidence that Demands a Verdict." As defined by Webster's New Collegiate Dictionary, Apologetics is "a branch of theology devoted to the defense of the divine origin and authority of Christianity." Josh McDowell has written some very interesting material; however, he does have some critics. Robert M. Price is one of them. Here is a quote from Price, "Apologetics as practiced by Josh McDowell is merely an exercise in after-the-fact rationalization of beliefs held on prior emotional grounds. . . . The more seriously one takes him as a representative of his faith, the more seriously one will be tempted to thrust Christianity aside as a tissue of grotesque absurdities capable of commending itself only to fools and bigots." The one thing I have learned about both sides of the issue is nothing ruins the truth like stretching it. When we tamper with evidence, stretch the truth, or force beliefs on other people; we are tampering with processes.

    Religious organizations over all do an outstanding job. The people who support them are usually wonderful, self-disciplined, and more often practice loving people rather than hating people. Religious organizations have provided wonderful day care centers, schools, hospitals, support medical research, can be counted on to provide relief to victims who have suffered tragedy, and most of all they are the most generous people with their time and money. Many members of religious organizations have benefited from attending a worship service. Famous singers such as Elvis Presley received voice training while singing in the church choir; the same could be said for so many other singers who started their careers in a similar fashion. Another interesting story concerning church and worship involves another scientist, Galileo. The development of the first clocks gave scientists the ability to perform experiments requiring the careful measurement of time. For example, it led to the first determination of the speed of light by Olaus Romer, within 35 years of Galileo's death.

> "The first clocks with the regularity and precision we expect from a timepiece were developed following a discovery by Galileo. He was sitting in church one day when a minor earthquake rocked the cathedral. The earthquake did no damage, but the long chandeliers suspended from the ceiling high above were set in motion. Galileo watched the long, slow swings and had an idea. It occurred to him that the time required for one swing did not depend on the size of the swing. As the swings became smaller they took just as long as the big swings had taken. He used his pulse rate to time each swing and became convinced that the time required for one swing was constant."

<u>Introduction to Physical Science</u>
McGraw-Hill (David M. Riban) page 84

Galileo does not record how he kept his heartbeat constant, nor does history record the reaction of the priest of Galileo's inattention to the sermon. But discovery, while sitting in church, of the constancy of the period of the pendulum became the basis for the first accurate clocks. I always wondered what may have happened if Galileo did not go to church that Sunday.

Even though people are benefiting from religious organizations, there is one particular issue that all religious organizations continue to be repeating offenders. The issue with religious organizations that becomes apparent is their inability to recognize special cause variations. As much as religious organizations and political organizations talk about changing things or not changing things, it becomes apparent that the human part of the enterprise changes the interpretation but the laws and the Holy Scriptures remains normative. I am remembering what Mark Twain once said "the Bible is like a Pharmacy, the practice changes but the content remains the same." Everyone has listened and heard the complaints against religious groups pushing beliefs on others that disagree with those opposing religious intervention. This is the real issue. Are religious organizations interfering or are they only attempting to intercede in the process of education, politics, and government. Much of the interfering is due to interpretation of certain passages of a religious text.

An example of interpretational differences of law and Scripture that affected both religion and politics was debated before and after America's Civil War. The southern culture said it is Biblical to have slavery and this was a conservative view of many of the members of southern churches. This issue was one of many that lead to a separation of the Baptist church. Religious texts have become a counter cultural issue for most fundamentalist religions. Cultural morays, rather than Scripture, became the fuel to interpret any issue. When any society begins to look for solutions only by means of our cultural morays, we loose vital information and as a result we lack the ability to integrate all the ideas. This is what I was referring to with fundamentalism and tampering with common causes. There exist normative theories that have worked in the past and will always work for the enterprise in the future. Before we accept the new theories, we must always examine the verified results of the old theories before instituting change.

With respect to tampering with processes, it is clear that intercession is the process that should be practiced and not interfering. There is a difference in interceding and interfering. When Jesus answered the question concerning who should we pay tribute, He did not criticize the government or people who followed a particular religion. This would have been an opportunity to declare a better form of government, but apparently Jesus did not foster unjust criticism. With respect to tampering with processes, it is clear that intercession is the process that should be practiced and not interfering. When people are at a low follower readiness and not willing to participate (model #2), we interfere with the plan (process) that is rarely considered. This is the plan that meets the benefit of others. The growth of the meaning in the word intercession (intercede) in the various languages can be highly suggestive. In earlier texts it meant "to strike upon" or "against." In a good sense it means "to assail anyone with petitions" or "to urge", and on behalf of another "to intercede." In the modern sense, it has become to mean "to assist others with a watchful eye in an un-interfering way that fosters development for all."

An illustration to better define intercession as opposed to interfering would be the responsibility to watch or baby sit a toddler. Let us say that we have been given the responsibility to watch a 14 month old baby that has learned to walk. While sitting outside watching the baby play, you notice that the child has started to approach (walk-toward) a busy street. It is obvious to many people that we should go and get the child before the child walks in front of a moving car. It is not necessary for the toddler to share in the painful experience and long recovery treatments involved when the child is hit by a moving car. When we remove the child from perusing their adventure into the street occupied by moving cars, we are not interfering with their experience to learn. I have never heard anyone say, "Let the child get hit, they will just have to learn the hard way!" A statement such as this is an absurd appeal to not interfere with the child's experience. It is not interfering with the learning experience of the child; it is the act of intercession on the behalf of the toddler.

This is an example that provides an obvious action to take, but when we debate religious issues, people often fail to decide to intercede. As a result, many religious followers only interfere to stop a natural work in progress due to a misinterpretation of scriptures or our laws. So this case is another example of tampering with processes. Political and Religious leaders continue to interrupt the processes and make changes before we have the opportunity to determine if a change is appropriate. The United States of America is the most charitable country in the world today. If one's religious enterprise fails to promote intercession over interfering, then this enterprise will loose the respect of others. What goes wrong with our religious enterprises? Many of the leaders of religion fail to understand the difference in intercession and interfering (tampering with people and processes). As for my belief, God loves everyone, but I prefer "fruits of the spirit" over "religious nuts."

Case #3: Federal Express - Zapmail

The story of Federal Express as told in the book <u>Absolutely Positively</u> is truly an amazing account of what is now an American icon. Federal Express is one of the best managed companies in the world and a great company to work for. Business people and corporations from all over the world tour the Federal Express hub in Memphis to learn and study the successful managerial practices of the best of the best. Federal Express had its origin while Fred Smith was attending Yale University in 1965. While at Yale, he wrote a term paper about the passenger route systems used by most airfreight shippers. This paper received a lower than average grade. But the paper was ahead of its time. The content of this paper was truly forward thinking on Fred Smith's part. Fred Smith also determined through research done for this paper "the need for shippers to have a system designed specifically for airfreight that could accommodate time-sensitive shipments such as medical supplies, critical pharmaceuticals, and computer parts for field service organizations as well as other service groups. This began the business of "just in time" supply practices. This company has received numerous awards for excellence in business. In 1990, Federal Express received the Baldrige award for outstanding service. Fortune magazine ranked Federal Express in their list of "World's Most Admired Companies" list, No. 8 (2005), ranked 2002-05"America's Most Admired Companies" list, No. 6 (2005); No. 1 on the Delivery Industry list (2005) "100 Best Companies to Work for in America" list (1998-2005); 2005 "Hall of Fame" for claiming a spot on this list every year since its inception. Also the company ranked in the "50 Best Companies for Minorities" list (2000-01, 2003). Just go to the Federal Express web sites, the list of awards are impressive to say the least.

Fred Smith served in our United States Military and served during the Vietnam War. After his tour of duty, August of 1971, he bought controlling interest in Arkansas Aviation Sales, located in Little Rock, Arkansas. This provided a model to determine the feasibility of getting packages and other airfreight delivered within one to two days. Many issues, inefficiencies, and dilemmas were documented to do a practical research study resolving the inefficient distribution system. These improvements that were identified in this study started a program of continuous improvement that would be the best practices that Federal Express uses today. Now an idea that had been born in a 1965 term paper was tested. Fred Smith had the model that revolutionized the shipping industry and now defines the speed and reliability we see today.

On April 17th 1973, Federal Express operations began and the company delivered 186 packages to 25 cities within the United States. The company's headquarters were moved to Memphis Tennessee. The Memphis airport granted an area for the Federal Express hub and the location was very good for weather conditions and geographical location. The company did not show a profit until July of

1975. In fiscal year 1983 Federal Express reported $1 billion in revenues, making American business history as the first company to reach that financial hallmark inside ten years of start-up without mergers or acquisitions. Fred Smith is a hero and so were the carefully selected people who served as executive officers of the organization. One of these officers was Jim Barksdale, COO of Federal Express, now president of Netscape. Jim Barksdale is another hero. He has an excellent understanding of the value of computer networks and why real-time access to information is critical for the successful operations of any modern business. One of the most important parts of the Federal Express infrastructure was their IBM computer network. When Jim Barksdale came to Federal Express, he brought with him a world of knowledge concerning the implementation of IBM computer products that aided in the success of Federal Express's business. I had always wondered where Jim Barksdale received his knowledge. It wasn't until I was serving as Vice President of Systems Development for The Potomac Group Incorporated that I discovered why Jim Barksdale had such an exceptional knowledge in IBM hardware and software and how to apply computer technology to drive the Federal Express business plan. When I took the job as Vice President of Systems Development with the Potomac Group, the Potomac Group used the JC Penney Shared services computer network (an IBM computer network) as their telecommunications carrier. One of the first things on my agenda was to meet with some of the people to discuss future plans for a medical healthcare product and the future needs of the company (Potomac Group). During the meeting I had the pleasure to meet Bernie Curran who was the Vice President of Marketing at JC Penney Shared Services. He shared with me a story about Jim Barksdale. While Bernie Curran was a manager at IBM in Memphis, he hired Jim Barksdale and several other Ol' Miss business college graduates. Mr. Curran only had great things to say about Jim Barksdale, heroes hiring heroes. One thing I have learned during my years of business practice, it is a big world but also a small world. People serving in an outstanding enterprise know all the heroes of other outstanding enterprises.

Zapmail

I was employed at Federal Express from October of 1983 to August of 1987. During my employment, I must say that this is one of the greatest companies a person could have the privilege to work for. This company has a great work ethic and to my surprise, not only did managers evaluate employees, but employees every quarter participated in evaluating their managers. What a brilliant concept that keeps everything in check. I was interviewed for a position as a field service engineer for a Federal Express project called Gemini, that later became known as Zapmail. Zapmail was a new technology business venture to provide same day electronic transmission of a document and provide same day delivery rather than over-night air delivery. With all this said about a company that never makes a mistake, what happened to Zapmail. Many business schools, business colleges, and business people, refer to this part of Federal Express history as a management failure. How could such a great company fail to make such an excellent idea work? This service would have moved Federal Express way beyond the forefront of document delivery services. A same day

2 hour guaranteed document delivery service was the next logical business step in a great business plan. It would certainly take the business world by surprise. This was the natural progression a company that was so successful and needed to do next. It would take over the facsimile machine business and would remove most of the overnight delivery from being sorted in the Memphis Hub. Workers at the Federal Express hub would then be able to concentrate on processing more large packages rather than processing over-night letters which was the larger portion of the revenue at Federal Express. Not only would Zapmail add to the revenue mix, taking overnight delivery service out of Federal Express would also take this market away from competitor businesses. Same day document transmission and delivery seemed to be the only way to take this business to the next level. So, how did the Zapmail project become the Achilles heel of an organization that had the Midas touch?

In order for Federal Express to provide a same day document service, it required a telecommunications network and high speed, high document quality facsimile computers to be located at strategic Federal Express locations, business centers, and customer offices. The telecommunications network Zapnet, (separate from the FedEx IBM network) consisted of Tandem Nonstop Guardian II mainframes strategically located as network hubs.

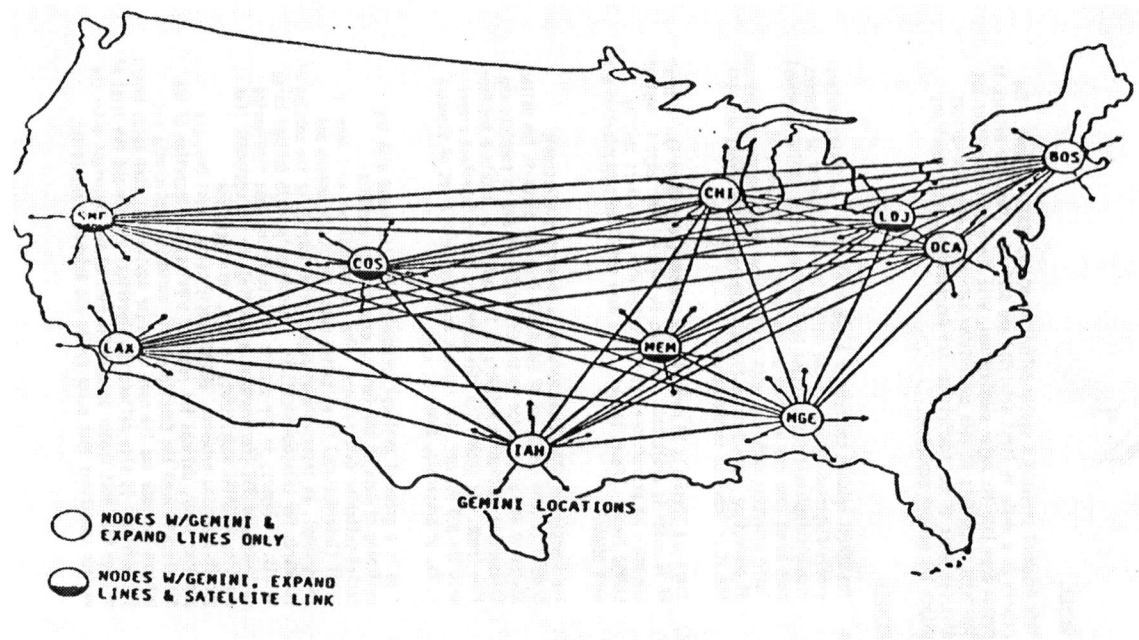

Figure 1. GEMINI System

The technology was much faster than existing facsimile machines and the document imaging as well as print quality was superior to other technologies. All was state of the art. This network continued to expand and grow. Other large cities had a mini-node network computer that would handle 300 to 500 customers on dedicated lines and dial-in capability. The network nodes were all connected to each other for fail-safe operations. If a network node became inoperable, then network traffic could route to other facilities. The Gemini equipment, later to be called Zapmail, was located at Federal Express facilities as well as Federal Express business centers. Bellow is a drawing from a technical manual that we had in training. As you will see, it consists of a document scanner, document printer, and a computer operating terminal (keyboard, CPU, and monitor).

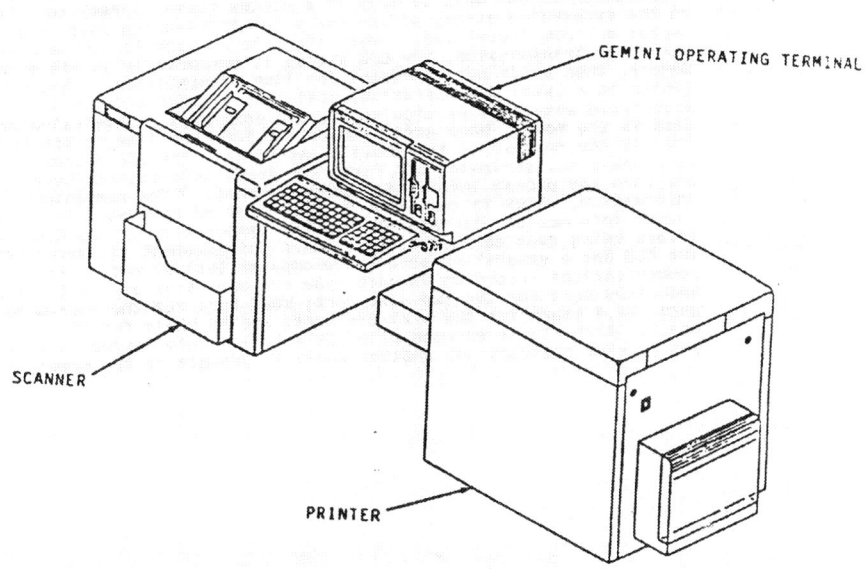

Four members from the first graduating class were asked to travel to Federal Express locations and survey the sites to determine if these sites were suitable to deliver the machines. Some sites where this machine would be installed was located in hotel rooms. If Federal Express did not have a business center or FedEx facility in an area of high document delivery, then the Zapmail machine would be located in a hotel room that allowed a FedEx courier to pick-up the document there and make a delivery without traveling to a location outside of the courier's route. The four people that were picked to do site surveys received a list of Zapmail locations from the FedEx Properties Management Department. We would then travel to the site, do a survey, and write down the pros and cons of the location. This information would then be used to accept or reject the site as suitable or unsuitable for a Zapmail machine. The four of us traveled all over the United States, all of us going in different directions to do our surveys.

There were some issues that occurred, but none of them would be show stoppers. During the time the network was being installed, the brake-up of AT&T occurred. Some speculated that this would slow-down the process of computer lines needed for the network. But everything continued as scheduled. Zapmail machines were made at the NEC plant in Japan. The Zapmail computers were then delivered to the Zapmail Electronic Products facility located in Memphis Tennessee. They were unpacked and went through a thorough "burn in" process. This was done to test the product and remove any final defects before the machines were sent to the field to be installed in approved site location. Japanese engineers from NEC were on-site at the Memphis facility to assist with troubleshooting problems during "burn-in." There were no interpreters to translate Japanese to English or English to Japanese. In order to let Japanese engineers know that a Zapmailer had a technical issue, we would hang a rubber chicken over the Zapmailer that had an issue. The NEC engineers responded to all issues quickly and produced an excellent product. There were no product problems discovered during the burn-in process.

Another issue that presented itself after Zapmail machines were delivered was activating the Zapmailers on the network. But this issue was quickly fixed and was an issue with the Paradyne-challenger 14,400 modem modulator/demodulator. A modem is a communications device that can be either internal or external to your computer. It allows one computer to connect another computer and transfer data over telephone lines. When connected to the network using this type of modem, the Zapmail machine encountered network errors and transmission of data did not occur. The result was documents scanned would not electronically leave the Zapmail machine. Some of the modems worked and some did not. Once a comparison of the modem boards was done, it was determined that a jumper that allowed LAPB (Link Access Protocol Balanced) to work was removed. This ended up being a simple fix. The jumper on the mother board was reconnected and all was well again. Problems came and were fixed quickly. However, there were four issues that would be the down-fall of this business adventure that would prove to be the most costly to Federal Express. As a result, these issues created a cash trap that would drain millions from the company's profits.

Four Issues Became Paramount and One of these Four Issues became very Expensive

There were four major issues that began to plague the Zapmail program that began to rob money from the revenue and created a cash trap for this organization. They were, (1) decoder errors in the network, (2) software downloads to the remote Zapmailer 2 machines, (3) limited number of pages at the Zapmail machines, and (4) print quality of documents for Zapmailer 1 machines. The Zapmailer 2 was located at customer sites that were not Federal Express facilities such as Law Offices, Real-estate offices, etc.

Issue 1 Decoder Errors

This issue did not plague the Zapmail project as much as print quality, but the Zapmailers 1&2 were blamed for what ended-up being a network issue. The error manifested itself when a document was printed at the Zapmailer 1 or Zapmailer 2. An example would be sending a 10 page document from Atlanta, Georgia to Nashville, Tennessee and one of the documents out of the ten sent would be partially blank and on the document it would say "Decoder Error – Call Technical Support." A customer support desk person would have the customer resend the document. This temporarily appeased this issue only to have the issue reoccur once again on another day. Customers did care for the fact that a document would be cut off at certain locations on the document. A certain percentage would be blank.

Engineers began to research the issue blaming the decoder error as an internal problem to the Zapmailers. I was asked by a station manager if I would look into the problem. This issue was causing a great deal of customer complaints. I began the investigation by tracing the wires marked "decode error" on the machine schematics that I had received in class. I found that the error originated on the CCU board. This was the Communication Control Board located on both the Zapmail 1 and 2 machines. According to the schematics, this was an issue that originates in the computer network and not at the local machines. I made several phone calls to the Memphis office to see if there were documents that recorded such issues during the "burn in" process. There was no documentation that decoder errors were an issue during the "burn in" process. However, several engineering experts blamed the Zapmailers for this issue and the network managers said dogmatically that it was not a network issue.

After doing additional research with network analyzers recording three months of data, it prompted me to write a memo (see exhibits). I simply posed a question for the network managers. I was asking what synchronization method we were using in the zapnet. I listed three synchronization methods, but there are other methods. These were the three most common. The reason I asked this question was because it became clear to me the decoder errors were "clock slips" occurring in the network due to lack of synchronization of all the network nodes in the zapnet. This memo circulated in the corporate office for about two working weeks. I received several answers. The one answer I found most amusing was the fact that the network manager responded with a software synchronization of the packets, I was asking about hardware synchronization. Apparently our network expert did not know the difference. However, mysteriously after this memo circulated, decoder errors became non-existent. I then received the reply that the network was synchronized with the Memphis network node being the master clock. What I find interesting about this issue is many network experts were unable to provide information and most of the information seemed to be just guessing. However, the memo worked. Decoder errors went away.

Issue 2 Software Downloads - Zapmailer 2 (Customer Locations)

Another customer issue that cost Federal Express much time and money was the Zapmailer 2 machines that were located at customer locations. Many of these machines were located in city businesses and other remote sites that were within a 100 mile radius of a city. Some machines were even further out than 100 miles. Customer Service Technical Representatives (CSTR) were located in the city area, but covered a hundred mile radius of that city and responded to customer calls by answering a pager and driving their Federal Express customer service vehicle to the customer site to do any necessary repairs.

Software engineers for Zapmail were constantly making improvements to the software (software is always changing – that is why it is the soft part of any computer product). Before the network managers pushed software upgrades via the network (downloads) the CSTRs would have to drive to all the Zapmail locations to upgrade the Zapmailers (a CSTR could have 60 to 100 machines in an area). The company could cut down the cost if we started downloading software upgrades using the network. Then CSTRs would not have to travel, costing time and money. It would save the operating expenses in gas alone by hundreds of thousands of dollars across the country.

So the network engineers began a process of downloading software upgrades via the network. Great idea, but it created an even bigger issue. When the software was downloaded at night, it would cause the Zapmailers to reboot, and they would be stuck in the middle of this reboot of the new software. When customers came in to their offices in the morning, they were unable to login (entering user name & password) to the zapmailer and send or receive documents. Of course, the customers would flood the customer support lines at the call centers and the customer support people would tell them to turn the machine off and then turn it back on again. When the customers performed this task, it wiped out all the software and documents. They could not logon to the Zapmailer to do any tasks. Then CSTRs in the field would get a page to manually download the software at the customer locations. We were right back where we started, driving all over the country fixing Zapmail machines by doing local software loads.

One day I received a call from Fred Mitchell. He was our lead engineer for our region. This guy is a hero. He researched this problem with several other people in Memphis and discovered that we should never have a customer turn the machine off and back on again. Fred Mitchell had located a button (inside the Zapmailer) that when pressed, it would reset the Zapmailer and the system would boot and the download was a success. The only problem is the customer could not press the button because the button was located on the inside of the Zapmailer which meant that someone would have to remove the covers from the Zapmailer to press this reset button.

Fred Mitchell developed a retrofit to have this reset button moved to the outside of the Zapmailer so the customer could press the button. His idea was great and ingenious. However, nobody listened to his idea, nor was he able to implement his idea. It was an idea that he tested with people in the field and it worked. Many of us decided to do the retrofit without the permission of corporate engineers. I put Fred Mitchell's idea to work in my area, and it solved the problem. My expense accounts for travel were the lowest in the nation. No more driving to the customer's location to fix the problem. This should have been a mandated retrofit in all regions, but it was ignored. Something so simple could have saved the organization millions of dollars. The cost of technicians driving to locations and the number of customer complaints continued to eat into the Zapmail profits.

(See Tom Oliver's Memo concerning this issue with the Houston Texas area.)

Issue 3 Limited Number of Pages Scanned

Zapmail officially started on July 2, 1984. One issue that was discovered was the limitation of the number of pages scanned for transmission. I witnessed this at the Federal Express business center in downtown Nashville. A law firm brought a 67-page document to be transmitted to another Federal Express business office in New York City. When the 67-page document was placed in the scanning hopper, the first 23 pages were scanned and then the Zapmail computer locked. Technical support in Memphis had already received several phone calls concerning this issue. Technical support told FedEx employees that documents that exceeded 20 pages should be divided into two or more transmissions. This also became the rule for customers that had the Zapmailer II. FedEx Zapmail trainers told customers to only transmit 20 pages at a time.

This issue, even though perceived by many customers and FedEx employees to be a big problem, later was easily solved at several service locations by the Field Service Technicians. The field service technicians had weekly regional conference calls. Several of the field service technicians discovered that a defragmentation software program fixes this issue. Fragmentation is caused by creating and deleting files and installing new software. Computers do not necessarily save an entire file in a single space on a disk; they're saved in the first available space. The zapmail computer was storing scanned documents to image files on the hard-drive. After a large portion of a disk has been used, most of the subsequent image files were saved in pieces across the drives volume. When files are deleted, the empty spaces left behind are filled in randomly as new files were created. This is how fragmentation occurs. The more fragmented the volume became on the hard-drive; the zapmailer would lock and not accept additional documents. There are two main types of disk fragmentation: file fragmentation and free space fragmentation. The zapmail system had issues with both types of fragmentation.

An image file with all its parts stored in one location on a disk is described as "contiguous." If a file is not contiguous, it's fragmented; broken into pieces that are scattered throughout the disk. This had an effect on disk performance because the disk head requires more time to move around to different points on the disk to read scattered file parts. This is a primary reason for the gradual degradation of system performance and caused limited number of pages to be scanned. It also caused customers to have to reboot the system on a frequent basis. A partially full disk contains unused space, known as free space. Ideally, this space would be available in a few contiguous portions of the disk. And while it's good to have free space, it's not good if it's fragmented. Free space fragmentation refers to file space that's broken into small pieces, rather than joined together. This type of fragmentation results in slowed performance because of the time it takes for the disk head to move to different points on the disk to find free space and then write the file. Fragmented free space also increases the possibility of file fragmentation; when a file is larger than the space it's being written to, the file fragments. So defragmentation is the process of rewriting non-contiguous parts of a file to contiguous sectors on a disk for the purpose of increasing data access and retrieval speeds.

Some of the field service technicians decided to take it upon themselves to purchase the software and scheduled the defragmentation to run at mid-night. This software fixed the issue. However, the Federal Express engineers at corporate were slow to listen to the field technicians and by the time (20 months later) engineers in corporate decided to take this software seriously, Zapmail closed prior to implementing this software. This was a big disappointment to several field service technicians because this issue lingered in the minds of many people to be non-fixable. If only the engineers at corporate had listened. This would have saved the company a great deal of money and customer complaining.

Issue 4 Print Quality - Zapmailer I (FedEx Facilities)

Print quality for the Zapmail 1 machines became a very big issue that ate into the organizations profits. The company spent over 20 million dollars trying to improve the document quality of the Zapmail 1 printers, which in actuality the print quality degradation was due to changes made to the technical procedures concerning preventative maintenance of the Zapmail 1 printers. The print quality issue brought about many false positives from the so called experts that were hired to monitor print quality. This was not the fault of management. Often I have read and heard stories in MBA programs that management was the reason for Zapmail failures. This is not true. The failure was due to changing a process without regard to first understanding and then being understood.

CASE STUDIES

I had done a great deal of research on my own concerning the print quality issue. I wanted my customers in the middle Tennessee area to have the best printed documents in the country. When engineers came out into the field to present a new procedure to improve print quality, I tracked issues that were a result of this new procedure. It appeared that this new procedure only added to another issue, statistical control. This procedure designed by the engineers in Memphis headquarters, caused the manufacturing settings to be out of statistical control. As a result, the new adjustments caused alarms on the printer to go off and sensors reported paper jams that were not there. This procedure of new adjustments to the printer spawned all kinds of research into the area of print quality. Kodak was hired to be consultants, new engineering groups formed that needed expensive testers to test the printer laser power, toner properties, testing the selenium drum in the printer, and additional changes to printer quality procedures.

I rejected these new procedures and decided to follow the original settings provided to me in the first training class. These were the procedures that NEC had provided. They seem to work well and put all of my printers back into statistical control. But I discovered another issue during my research. This printer that was designed for Federal Express Zapmail was apparently not so new technology. The print engine was similar to the Royal 122 printer copier. One of these printers was located in one of the Nashville Federal Express facilities. I made a comparison of the two print engines and they were identical accept for one thing. The Royal copier had a neutralizing corotron and the Zapmail 1 printer did not. I got the permission from my field service manager to order the parts to add the neutralizing corotron. I retrofitted five of five printers in the Nashville area. To my amazement, the installation was easy because the printer casing for this component was already engineered in the design. It was as if some one just had it taken out. Everything was already retrofitted to put it back in the printer. This was puzzling, but I found out what the issue was later.

I began to track the success of the print quality. All the issues with print quality had gone away. All I did was use the adjustment procedures provided by NEC (rejected by the new Zapmail Engineers) and added the neutralizing corotron. Why were we doing so much research and spending money on print quality if this was all we needed to do? I sent my findings to the engineers in Memphis. It was rejected over other schools of thought. Nobody cared about the results. So I decided not to push the issue. It was working for me, why bother.

Then something caused a turn in events. Bruce Erlandson (hero) was the training instructor in Memphis. They trained the field technicians. I was in the first class and Bruce requested my presents in Memphis to evaluate improvements to the training. On January 14, 1985 Bruce Erlandson drafted a memorandum requesting that I attend the 16th class to come to Memphis for training. This was to add input and discuss with Bruce how training could be better improved and what could be added to the class that field engineers would find most helpful. It was while I was attending class that I brought to the attention to others that the procedures for print quality were wrong. During class I observed many students struggling with the new procedures and this was causing printers to fail. One of the other instructors blamed students for failing to follow instructions, but the students were following the instructions. The instruction only created poorer print quality. The class went to lunch feeling discouraged that the printers were not working correctly. Many of the printers were sounding alarms, so the instructor just shut the printers off. I stayed in the class room while everyone else went to lunch. I began to do the procedures provided by NEC before FedEx engineers changed these procedures.

Bruce Erlandson came down stairs because he heard I did not go to lunch with the class. He asked me what I was doing. I told him that I was making the correct adjustments to the Zapmail 1 printer to fix all the problems. He then asked me, "You mean you use a different procedure than what we are teaching by the Engineers?" I said yes I do. The old NEC procedure is better than the procedures we have now. I began to explain to Bruce that many changes had been made to print quality procedures. As a result we have purchased equipment that was not needed. Bruce asked me if I had proof of this. I told him I needed to go to my car, get all the research documentation I had done, and I would meet him in his office.

I began showing all of my research documentation and testing I did concerning all the issues with print quality. I also shared with Bruce all of the many contradictory schools of thought that were circulating all across the country. Many of these were false positives and false cause and effect ideas that had destroyed a printer that was at one time in statistical control. I showed him that there was no proof of printer drum fatigue, laser power issues, and continued to destroy the espoused theories that had been circulating for years. I also informed Bruce of the neutralizing corotron and how successful it improved print quality in the Nashville area. Bruce was not only impressed, but he was convinced that we should do testing here at the Zapmail facility in Memphis. Bruce then introduced to me Wayne Chase. Wayne was one of the technical writers for Zapmail. Bruce wanted Wayne to review my work and prepare a document that could be presented to the Zapmail technical-engineering group. Wayne then invited me to eat lunch with him.

Wayne began to share many interesting stories that shed some light on the many things I had uncovered. He had been writing all the technical documentation for these engineers at corporate. He commented that they were ruining the Zapmail system rather than making improvements with all the changes they were making to the system. He also commented, "You know that neutralizing corotron you where talking to Bruce about? I am going to show you the NEC prototype and you will note that it was included in the original designs." He then informed me that in the early days of Zapmail (Gemini) an engineer had it removed from the production of the current Zapmail printers. This was to reduce cost in production. The Federal Express engineer that recommended the removal got a lucrative reward and recognition for saving on the production cost. Wayne was against the recommendation. Now you have the proof that this Federal Express engineer made a bad decision for the company. Maybe it is not too late to put it back the way it should have been from the beginning. I totally agreed with Wayne. I told him that the mistake was to make changes without having a through understanding of the system. Now these changes that seemed to be harmless and thought to be helpful has turned this project into a monster.

When we got back to the Zapmail warehouse, Wayne had the supply room people bring us the Zapmail prototype. Wayne was correct. The original design included a neutralizing corotron. The removal of this part to the print engine was causing all the print quality issues with the Zapmailer 1s. I began to setup the testing. Wayne was looking at my notes. He asked me what all these math equations were and these computer programs I had written. I informed him that I was testing data compression techniques. I have found a way to keep the high resolution of documents at the Zapmail machines, but the reduction in data would reduce the bandwidth of the document transmissions on the network. He asked me if he could take the information to some people that were working on network issues. I said okay.

I continued to do testing and two days later Wayne came back to check on my progress. He also shared with me that engineers who he could trust, tested my data compression techniques and they worked. He said if we could fix these printer issues and use these data compression techniques, we could save millions of dollars that were being misdirected toward issues that were totally unfounded. He seemed very excited. I shared his excitement.

After testing, the results were outstanding. Without the help of Wayne Chase, it would have taken longer to record the results with such accuracy. He also guided me in the testing. The print drums were being replaced as a result of early image denigration and drum fatigue (not true). We compared the prototype and proved that a vital component to the print engine was removed. The engineer that made this disastrous decision was now a manager. He was promoted and given a big bonus for removal of this component. Due to the fact that nobody bothered to try and understand what this print engine component does, it was removed as a cost saving in manufacturing of $15.00 per printer engine. We proved that this component is an important part of the print engine mechanics. The part that I put back into the printer engine was called a cleaning corotron. After testing, it was easily proven that this is why we were loosing millions of dollars a year replacing printer electronic boards and printer drums.

My research was correct technologically, but it did not sit well with those that had committed to the incorrect removal of the original placement of the cleaning corotron. So it was not politically correct to correct the problem because it would mean abandoning the false philosophy that motivated their self interest enterprise, thus losing integrity of their eliteness in the company's political arena. I had several meetings with different management groups, and it was decided to not implement the idea. The time spent in these meetings was listening to engineer's (supposedly experts) perversion of the truth and planning how they could keep these ideas from the attention of executive management. Implementing the idea would have put several careers in jeopardy. I then used my "open door policy" to speak with Tom Oliver, the new Vice President of Zapmail. Chuck Winston (VP) and Jim Vaughn (VP) had been fired previous to my meeting with the new vice president. After my meeting, I was told that I may have some good ideas, but they were going to take a different plan. I was informed that the engineers were experts and we would continue to make the present procedures work.

On a Sunday, approximately two years later, Fred Smith announced that the Zapmail program would be shutdown because it was costing the company too much money to support and maintain. Interoffice politics and the failure to stop the tampering of processes was the downfall. A political environment is one in which "who" is more important than "what." When the boss proposes a new idea, the idea gets taken seriously. If an employee proposes a new idea, it is ignored. The politics with the management group reeked with the odor of dishonesty and perversion of the truth. Self-interest of a few managers was paramount to cover their mistakes and the cover-up is what prevailed.

In terms of my personal mastery, I focused on the means as well as the results of my findings. The process of interacting was very important. I watched these middle managers privately slip into "being in the barrel." I know to this day, that if the executive management had been presented with the facts and not the generalizations of middle management, Federal Express would have a profitable Zapmail service today. The middle management group lacked a spirit of openness. Openness is a characteristic of relationships, not individuals. If openness is a quality relationship, then building relationships characterized by openness may be one of the most high-leveraging actions to build organizations characterized by openness. Middle management at Federal Express killed the goose that laid the golden eggs, openness.

Conclusions

Reading this case people find it absolutely amazing that such a small change to a small component could grow exponentially out of statistical control. People refuse to understanding that tampering with processes leads to such an expensive disaster. The removal of a vital component caused many people to research in the wrong direction. It created false positives that people escalated as universal truths. Peter Senge, in his book The Fifth Discipline," presents a question that I have always asked myself, "How can the internal politics and game playing that dominates traditional organizations be transcended?" This question has been an everyday question I ask while employed at many fortune 500 companies. The concept that stands out the most is that of openness. Wayne Chase was open to hear my results and was open to resolve issues. So many others were not open, they became closed to new ideas and chose to hide what they thought would protect them rather than the organization. There were many problems that existed as this start-up project got off the ground. Key engineers and decision makers were unqualified to do the jobs they were hired to do and this resulted in tampering with processes. The best Zapmail employees were the people hired from within the company. They were the heroes struggling to get out of the chaos. The people hired from outside the company claiming to be experts, tried to change the way Federal Express does business the best, which is by serving others rather than supporting personal special interest.

For years after the "so called" failure of Zapmail, many experts have attempted to speculate and explain the failure. Contrary to what one will read on the Internet and what professors teach in our business schools and colleges, the information they have provided concerning the failure of Zapmail is totally inaccurate. Marketing experts dismiss this business venture as "poor pre-market planning." Others say that everyone already had a FAX machine, what made Federal Express think people would buy their FAX machine? I have researched sites on the web for years and read books on the subject, but these are examples of people who think they are acting intelligent, but are only conceptualizing with misinformed *schools of thought*. These experts have committed the availability error. Zapmail was more than just a FAX machine. I personally installed hundreds of Zapmailers in law firms, real-estate office, and places like Georgia Pacific and Healthcare Corporations of America. Even though they already had a FAX machine, they removed the old technology in favor of the new technology and service. The customers told me that the print quality was better on Zapmail (no wax paper curling), it was faster, you could store documents and retrieve to print later, and when the machine was broken; you got the machine repaired same day and a Federal Express courier came immediately to pick the documents up and send it from another Zapmail site. What a service.

Review the documentation in the exhibits. Review the letter from the Law offices of Farris, Warfield & Kanaday. This is a law office that already had several FAX machines. Why did they replace all of their FAX machines with a Zapmailer if all Federal Express had was a FAX machine? This was a very well thought out product. The service and technology revolutionized the industry. It put pressure on other companies to provide a better product. Prior to Zapmail FAX machines could not store document images (there was no Adobe Reader back then). You did not have to re-scan documents or worry about "Did my document get there?" You could broadcast a single document to thousands of different locations. A customer did not have to have a Zapmailer to receive a document. The Zapmail technology was compatible with other FAX machines. The zapnet (the computer network) was a precursor to the Internet and World Wide Web (email messaging and electronic bulletin boards). New data compression techniques were developed and the Zapmailers had password security. Users of the Zapmailer could create group policies for other users of the Zapmailer. Documents had encrypted keys to promote confidentiality; and all this technology decades before Microsoft had a windows product or Active Directory software. This concept and technology was ahead of its time. Many of the people that were at Federal Express during this time took these ideas that they were exposed to and have done very well to advance their careers in the computer industry. I am truly grateful that I had an opportunity to work at a great company such as Federal Express and had the opportunity to be exposed to such great technology. Read the documents in the exhibits. This was a project that was very well thought out, but a small group of people pretending to be experts, destroyed this great idea with their false positives and inter-office politics.

***Note:** After Reading this case and the selected documents, the reader will realize that there has been a great deal of miss-information concerning the failure of Zapmail. It was actually a very well thought out product and service. It was a technical marvel that was ahead of its time and working well for the customer.*

I have additional documentation concerning this case. It has been left out due to the massive volume of the content. I have included documents that may be of interest to the reader. I have saved all of my original technical manuals for the Zapmail machines, hundreds of pages of technical research concerning print quality, and still have my notes taken in class during technical training. These materials are available upon request.

CA – Sunday November 20, 1983

Federal Express asks FCC approval of electronic document relay setup

WASHINGTON (UPI) — Federal Express plans to build a vast, $1.3 billion space age delivery system that will "beam down" letters and documents now carried by its fleet of planes and land couriers.

In an application filed with the Federal Communications Commission, the small-package delivery company revealed details of an electronic document relay service it is already building and plans to start up in July 1984.

The recent filing also reveals that between January 1985 and 1995, the Memphis-based company intends to completely bypass many fuel-gobbling delivery trucks and jets. It wants to launch two of its own satellites linked to a nationwide network of 50,000 Earth stations to distribute the information "packages."

The Federal Express Satellite Network, which the company says "bears a close analogy to Federal Express aircraft operations," would at first transmit just documents and data, but would likely be enlarged to include telephone and video services.

"We're very excited about the satellites and would like to start building as soon as possible," said Allen McArtor, vice president of Federal Express satellite systems.

The company, which now delivers 240,000 packages each day, expects the electronic document service to generate $1.3 billion a year in revenues by 1988.

If the predictions hold true, the system would be a serious challenge to American Telephone & Telegraph Co.'s post-divestiture data and teleconferencing services, and electronic mail services such as the one launched this year by MCI.

An MCI spokesman, however, denied the two systems would compete for customers. "We're an information highway and they'll still be a document service. There isn't anything you can do with a satellite that you can't do cheaper with fiber optics and microwave," he said.

In the FCC filing, Federal Express proposed to build three and launch two medium-powered Ku-band satellites, which would transmit and receive information from four regional teleports in Memphis, Colorado Springs, Colo., and unspecified locations in California and the Northeast.

Article announcing Zapmail from the business section of the Commercial Appeal – Memphis Press (November 20, 1983)

July 2, 1984 Congratulations Letter
Signatures of Fred Smith and Jim Barksdale

The official start of Zapmail

CASE STUDIES

Federal Express Corporation
Box 727
Memphis, Tennessee 38194

901 369-3600

DATE: July 27, 1984   TO: Thurman White

FROM: C.D. Winston

SUBJECT: **BRAVO ZULU**

Congratulations! ZapMail is successfully launched on July 2nd thanks to your outstanding efforts. As you know, Bravo Zulu is a Navy slogan for a job well done – as this was done.

We installed over 1,000 ZapMail systems; activated 950 systems; connected over 1,300 data subscriber lines, and 83 data trunk lines to ten operating switching nodes; activated over 1,200 2WPSTN circuits; completed over 700 retrofits; and repaired over several hundred individual maintenance items. This record is truly outstanding and has rarely been accomplished in the annals of U.S. business history. Our achievement is one to be proud of for many years to come.

During the five weeks preceeding 2 July, we attacked and overcame every obstacle---scratched photoreceptor drums; polygon motor failures; unstable operating software; downline load bugs; node database errors; zip to MPN errors; copy quality adjustments; lack of dedicated data lines; delay in 56 kbps line delivery; poor data line quality; modem problems; computer software bugs; and other individual situations. Our ability to overcome these obstacles and achieve our goal of a successful ZapMail introduction on schedule is a direct measure of your dedication and resourcefulness. In speaking with you on several occasions, I asked you for this full measure, and you responded. For this I am grateful and the Corporation in staying ahead of the competition.

I know of the long hours and personal sacrifices you endured and I wished it could have been otherwise, but now is the time to pause for a brief moment to look back and realize what we have accomplished. We have successfully implemented the most advanced and largest fully integrated information network ever made operational at one time. You have certainly proven that the newest Division in the company has as much "purple blood" as anywhere in the Corporation.

Again, my personal thanks goes to you for your individual efforts in keeping Federal Express the leader!

Sincerely yours,

Charles D. Winston
Sr. Vice President
Electronic Products Division

A letter from the Senior Vice President of Electronic Products.
This letter states many of the issues that we had to overcome during start-up of Zapmail.

LAW OFFICES
FARRIS, WARFIELD & KANADAY

FRANK M. FARRIS, JR., P.C.
CHARLES H. WARFIELD, P.C.
THOMAS P. KANADAY, JR.
JAMES G. MARTIN III
STEPHEN W. RAMP
ROBERT N. BUCHANAN, III
STEPHEN K. RUSH
ROBERT D. TUKE
WARREN H. WILD, JR.
G. MICHAEL YOPP
JULIAN L. BIBB
A. STUART CAMPBELL
DANIEL W. SMALL

WILLIAM B. DRESCHER
VICTOR S. JOHNSON, III
PAUL E. BIDEZ
RACHEL L. STEELE
BENJAMIN R. SEARS
CORNELIA A. CLARK
H. NAILL FALLS, JR.
B. RINEY GREEN
CHARLES A. GRICE
JANE L. DAVIS
BRADLEY A. MacLEAN
ROBERT C. GOODRICH, JR.
DAVID J. WHITE

SEVENTEENTH FLOOR
THIRD NATIONAL BANK BUILDING
NASHVILLE, TENNESSEE 37219

TELEPHONE (615) 244-5200

August 14, 1984

Mr. Trip Boone
Account Executive
Federal Express
566 Mainstream Drive
Metrocenter Office Park
Nashville, TN 37228

Dear Trip:

    I want to thank you and your associate for putting on such an impressive demonstration of your company's electronic system for transferring documents. I certainly believe this approach will be very helpful to this law firm. I hope to give your system a test run in the very near future. I would appreciate your keeping me informed of the developments in this system including when and under what terms a unit might be available for installation on a trial basis. I am confident that this service will be a very useful tool to the legal profession. Again, I thank you for your courtesy.

                              Sincerely yours,

                              FARRIS, WARFIELD & KANADAY

                              Stephen K. Rush

SKR:cs

Letter from the Law Offices of Farris, Warfield & Kanaday
This is a law firm that had FAX machines, but recognized that there was definitely a need for better services and technology. I was the associate referred to in this letter. The Zapmail II machine replaced this law firm's facsimile machines.

CASE STUDIES

Federal Express Corporation
Box 727
Memphis, Tennessee 38194

901 369-3600

January 25, 1985

It's been a number of months since that first ZapMail document was zapped through our Federal Express network.

We've come a long way, have learned a lot and, with the launch of the ZapMailer 2, feel we are definitely on the way to an even more prosperous road for our company.

Oftentimes, the doers of hard work may feel that their toil is unnoticed. That is not the case at Federal Express, nor will it ever be.

In fact, you are among a select number of individuals whose diligent efforts to assist in the successful startup of ZapMail last summer have been recognized.

And it is through this recognition that we are awarding you a certificate of achievement for your work with the startup of ZapMail.

Congratulations, and keep up the good work as we strive to meet our goals with ZapMailer 2.

Frederick W. Smith
Chief Executive Officer

Jim Barksdale
Chief Operating Officer

January 25, 1985 Letter from Fred Smith and Jim Barksdale
This letter also announces that we will move forward with the Zapmail II image computer that will be installed at customer locations.

Federal Express renews commitment to ZapMail

Despite its losses, system believed wave of future

By David Flaum
Staff Reporter

Federal Express Corp. will lift its moratorium on the sale of ZapMailer machines Oct. 1, revamp ZapMail, its two-hour document delivery service and begin selling facsimile machines that will work with the ZapMail system, officials said yesterday.

The Memphis-based express package delivery firm halted sales of the machines in March with officials saying they wanted to re-evaluate the business. Federal Express has reported ZapMail losses of more than $130 million in each of its last two fiscal years.

The recommitment to ZapMail shows "our complete dedication to the fact that we feel electronic transmission of documents is the wave of the future," said Armand Schneider, a Federal Express spokesman.

The company's stock had risen earlier yesterday on rumors that it was about to resume ZapMailer sales. The stock closed at $63.125, up $2.50 for the day.

After the stock market closed, Federal Express officials said the company will convert the 7,000 ZapMailers in service so that they may send to and receive from Group 3 facsimile machines. Group 3 machines produce the highest quality document reproductions among facsimile machines, said

The conversions will take six to eight months and give ZapMailer users the ability to send to 400,000 to 500,000 other facsimile machines, Schneider said.

The company will also sell two types of facsimile machines of its own, he said.

ZapMailer machines still have an advantage over both the Federal Express facsimile machines and others, said Schneider. Owners and renters of the ZapMailers may send documents to persons who have no facsimile machines or ZapMailers through Federal Express offices and the company delivery system, he said. Facsimile machine owners will not be able to do that but may transmit to other facsimile machines and ZapMailers.

The company will use its Zap-Mail transmission system, too. Instead of using its own phone line system, the company will have facsimile machine users and ZapMailer owners and renters send the transmissions between machines on their own telephone lines.

That will increase the company's same-day document delivery service capacity, said Frederick W. Smith, chairman and chief executive officer.

Another article from the business section of the Memphis Commercial Appeal – Federal Express Renews Commitment to Zapmail despite loses.

FEDERAL EXPRESS

AUG 16 REC'D

Federal Express Corporation
Box 727
Memphis, Tennessee 38194
901 369-3600

Bob, I'm not the right person on this. I can help with some things but not...

cc Ray Grantham

INTER-OFFICE MEMORANDUM

DATE: August 2, 1985

TO: Don Wallace
Jim McKinney
Ed Moelder

FROM: Thurman White
Bob Christie

cc: Ray Grantham
Fred Mitchell

SUBJECT: DECODE ERRORS-NETWORK SYNCHRONIZATION

I would like to emphasize the importance of preventing loss of synchronization, or clock slips in our Network. A lot of time and money has been directed in solving the Decode Errors with respect to the Imager I and II machines.

This is not where the problem exists. The problem is harbored in our Network. The effect of synchronization (clock slips) errors on digitized voice is not serious until the clock misalignments reach values in the order of 1 part in 100,000. However, digitized signals from voice band modems and voice or data signals which have been coded to maintain security or eucrypted or modified, etc., are highly susceptible to clock slips. High speed modem data are generally phase modulated like our modems and a single 8-bit slip in the digital data is producing a phase shift of approximately 81 degrees. Not only is the data coded, it's also scrambled further because the modem loses synchronization. Such clock slips give audible blips in the voice signal and cause problems in the Decoding equipment. There are several possible methods for synchronizing a network of independent switching Nodes. I feel we need to look into several possible methods and study to be sure what method our Network is employing.

Listed below are a few of our own suggested methods:

1) PLESIOCHRONOUS SYNCHRONIZATION-Supply each Node with a clock so accurate that the difference between it and other clocks is so minute that the slips don't occur. This technique is called plesiochronous synchronization. It is expensive to implement since the clocks are expensive and must be redundant at each switch. Nevertheless, this method is the one chosen by the CCITT for international digital transmission in Europe and the gateways to the East. The clocks must be stable to within 1 part to 100,000,000,000.

AUGUST 2, 1985
DECODE ERRORS-NETWORK SYNCHRONIZATION
PAGE TWO

2) PULSE STUFFING-To do pulse stuffing network-wide, as is done in higher-level multiplex systems. This would require every channel at every digital switch to be stuffed separately on transmit. Such an approach is effective, yet very expensive and may not be economically feasible, but could be looked into.

3) MASTER/SLAVE-The method adopted for the North American network and the one we may need to use is that of master/slave synchronization. The master timing frequency reference is maintained in Hillsboro, Missouri, which is their geographical center of the Network. From there, the master timing reference is sent to selected switching centers, which become slave timing centers over dedicated transmission facilities. From these slave centers, the timing reference is forwarded to lower level centers over existing digital facilities. (We might want to try this in Memphis.)

[handwritten: 6:20 D-Am Memphis Node]

Could you please let us know what kind of Network Synchronization we presently use or if we have a system?

We feel we must be aware of the many methods employed in Network Synchronization. We must exhaust all possibilities and gather accurate information on precisely what the Network does or doesn't do. If not, our customers will experience a growth in Decode Errors as a result of a growing Network.

Regards,

Bob Christie
Sr. Manager-MidSouth District
EPO Field Service Division
COMAT:3041
PHONE: 901-762-7608
BC/lf

Thurman White
Sr. STR
EPO Field Service Division

CASE STUDIES

Federal Express Corporation
Box 727
Memphis, Tennessee 38194

901 369-3600

INTEROFFICE MEMORANDUM

DATE: August 22, 1985   TO: Thurman White

FROM: Don Wallace   cc: Ray Grantham   Fred Mitchell
                            Jim Colson   Chuck Colter
SUBJECT: RESPONSE TO "DECODE ERROR –   Paul James   Harry Shiers
         NETWORK SYNCHRONIZATION" MEMO   Bob May

In response to your memo, see attached, I do not share your opinion that clock synchronization is the major contributor to our decoder error problems. I have analyzed actual document images before and after a decoder error has occurred and have discovered that a pathological pattern exists whereby the last 3 bytes of a 1024 bytes X.25 packet is overwritten. This pattern has been the predominate culprit for most decoder error documents that I have examined in the past few months. This would appear to be problem with either the IPS or Tandem software rather than a "clock synchronization" issue. There may be merit to your claim, but I have not seen any evidence to support it. Also, I find it difficult to believe that clock slippages could escape the CRC checks of the bit-oriented X.25 protocol. There is a 10^{-10} probability that an error is missed by the CRC check.

Don Wallace
Manager, Network Analysis
Telecommunications
COMAT: 3522   PHONE: (901)-797-5674
INTERNAL PHONE: 222-5674

DW/jw
0956W

I would think a Network Manager would know the difference in Hardware Synchronization and Software Synchronization

Thurman White — CST

Network Issues

Copy of the DECODE ERRORS memo I sent and the Response.

ZEROS AND HEROES OF BUSINESS

Federal Express Corporation
Box 727
Memphis, Tennessee 38194

901 369-3600

INTER-OFFICE MEMORANDUM

DATE: January 14, 1985   TO: Bob Christie
FROM: Bruce K. Erlandson   cc: Chuck Colter
SUBJECT: <u>FIELD SERVICE INPUT TO IPS-1 TRAINING</u>

In return for our good work in producing the EPD Field Service Manual for you under short notice, I am asking a favor in return. I respectfully request the services of Thurman White from January 15th to February 6th within the Training Department at 3394 Winchester. We are currently administering New Hire Class #16, and on January 15th we will begin the IPS-1 Technical portion. We are making a concerted effort to complete the documentation of this course, however, I feel that without an experienced Field Service input that we may miss the mark somewhat. I propose that Thurman White audit our IPS-1 Technical portions and advise us of areas of omission, obsolete information, and areas where greater or lesser emphasis need be addressed. Thurman sat through Course #1, has played a major role in IPS-1 installations, activations, servicing, and has taken the initiative to educate himself to broaden his understanding of his work world. Therefore, I believe Thurman can provide us meaningful insights into how we may need to adjust our IPS-1 Training program.

Thank you for considering what is an important request to us, and please advise as soon as possible on your response.

Thank you very much,

Bruce K. Erlandson
Bruce K. Erlandson
Manager, Technical Training
Electronic Products Division
PHONE: 922-4498
COMAT: 38194/4411

BKE/gal

To: Bruce — Thurman will be in Class Jan. 21 thru Feb. 6. It's the best I can do! Bob

cc: Chuck Colter

0677G

Inter-Office Memorandum from Bruce Erlandson
Requesting my Services
(Bruce Erlandson was the Manager over Technical Training)

CASE STUDIES

Federal Express Corporation
Box 727
Memphis, Tennessee 38194

901 369-3600

INTER-OFFICE MEMORANDUM

DATE: February 14, 1985   TO: Mike Williams
                                       Ray Grantham
FROM: Bob Christie   Jim Colson

SUBJECT: IPS PRINT QUALITY PROBLEM PROPOSAL   cc: Harry Shiers
                                                   Chuck Colter
                                                   FSM's
                                                   Wayne Chase
                                                   Thurman White

Since an inordinate amount of time and resources have been spent on the print quality problem, the MidSouth District is proposing a plan to correct the considerable deficiencies of the problem. I realize that there are seven million ways to fix the print quality problem, since they are all inter-related with each other. You can change one variable and it will change everything.

I am also aware that Dr. Williams has spent a great amount of time and emphasis on coming up with a new toner and developer along with some other modifications from Kodak. I commend his efforts. However, I do believe that this proposal would not only enhance Dr. Williams' proposed plan, but also benefit the field service organization. Therefore I am recommending that we proceed with this plan in an expeditious manner.

I know it is more impressive to spend large amounts of money and solve problems than it is to correct an adjustment. If money is no factor, then let's redesign the system, create an empire for Engineering and Print Quality, and impress everyone with our increased status. But if money and time are critical, let's fix the adjustment. If I can be of any assistance in any way to explain these procedures to anyone, please feel free to call me. I have numerous pages of documentation and supporting evidence.

Regards,

Robert C. Christie
Sr. Manager - MidSouth District
EPD Field Service Division
COMAT: 3041
Phone: 901-762-7608

BCC/cep
attachment

Inter-Office Memorandum concerning Zapmail Print Quality

```
                ELECTRONIC PRODUCTS
FEDERAL         SERVICE BULLETIN              [XX] ROUTINE
EXPRESS                                       [  ] URGENT

DATE  12-19-85    SUPERSEDES   N/A                              NO. 1P-010
AUTHORIZED BY    CHUCK COLTER, SENIOR MANAGER, SERVICE SUPPORT
DOCUMENTS EFFECTED   N/A

DISTRIBUTION   ALL FIELD SERVICE MANAGERS, CSTRs, and NODE TECHs

    SUBJECT:  RETURN OF FAILED ZAPMAILER -1 AOMs
                       ACTION IS REQUIRED

    The Acousto Optical Modulator (AOM) for the Zapmailer-1 is in drastically
    short supply.  This is due to useage that has greatly-exceeded the forecasted
    failure rate.  Currently, the AOM is considered a consumable part and costs
    $388.11 each.  The manufacturer's part number is: FNG-500120-0A00.  FEC part
    number is: 012103 0020.

    The AOM is being studied for possible repair by Depot Maintenance.  Therefore,
    until further notice, please return any FAILED AOM's to EPD Material Support,
    following the procedures used for repairable parts.
```

An Electronic Service Bulletin

This document is very interesting. It provides an example of the over run costs of Zapmail due to false positives. The Acoustic Optical Modulator was being replaced as a failed part. There was no problem with the AOM itself. These computer boards were being removed because technical support told field service technicians that these boards were bad and causing poor print quality. In fact, I never removed one from any of my Zapmail machines. The problem was not with failed components, it was an adjustment of a variable resistor that caused the problem. When engineers in Memphis changed the printer quality procedures, the procedures instructed technicians to re-adjust a resistor on the AOM board. As a result of making changes to original procedures, the new process created more problems that led to other problems. Tampering with the product brought about inaccurate information that created a chaotic situation.

CASE STUDIES

Federal Express Corporation
Box 727
Memphis, Tennessee 38194

901 369-3600

INTEROFFICE MEMORANDUM

DATE: July 25, 1986

FROM: Thurman White

TO: Harry Shiers

SUBJECT: Cleaning Corotron Part Numbers

First I would like to thank you for getting a COA started concerning the cleaning corotron and the Imager 1 printer. The pages following this letter are from the IPB manuels of the Royal 122 and 130R. These printers, like ours, is made by Konishiroku and I was told by the people at Royal that the part numbers are Konishiroku part numbers. However, I could not get a part number for the corotron rail assembly.

Royal does not order this part separately, because it is sent to thier field techs as one unit preadjusted at the manufacturer. Hopefully the information I am sending will be of help to you. If you have any questions please call 615-256-8038 or reach me using Field Service Dispatch.

Thank you,

Thurman White
Sr. CSTR
37228/MQY/TN

ZEROS AND HEROES OF BUSINESS

Documentation concerning the Neutralizing Corotron

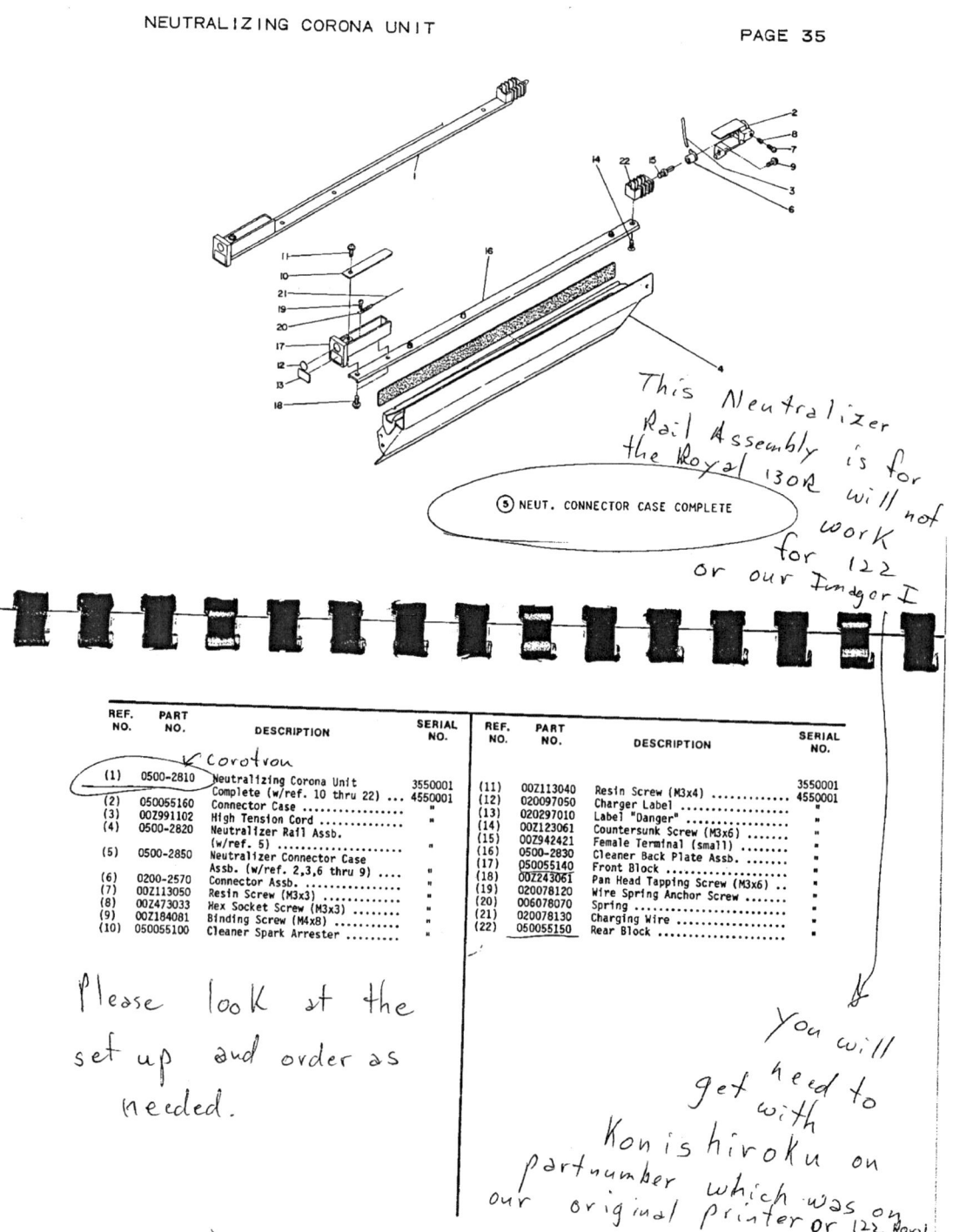

Federal Express Corporation
Box 727
Memphis, Tennessee 38194

901 369-3600

INTEROFFICE MEMORANDUM

DATE: January 20, 1986   TO: Mike Williams

FROM: Bill Conkel   cc: Chuck Colter
                                     Ace McInturff
                                     Harry Shiers
                                     Bill Baggett

SUBJECT: ZAPMAILER-1 FOURTH COROTRON

I am writing in reference to your memo on Electrometer Adjustments of January 13, 1986, to Ace McInturff.

If I might make a suggestion regarding testing of the fourth corotron, I have a theory. I feel that a considerable part of the toner mess being caused in the ZM-1 is due to the conveyance unit vacuum motor exhaust port. As you may be aware, this port blows from the rear at the exact location of the fourth corotron's future placement. This causes loose toner to be blown toward the front, landing on the door and other parts in the front. My theory is that the fourth corotron may only be acting as a "wind break", preventing the exhaust air from stirring up toner as much.

In talking with Bill Baggett about this, I suggested that after he has completed the required testing that he run the same sort of test with the fourth corotron voltage lead unplugged. This might give us a clearer picture of exactly what benefit this device is providing. Of course, I realize that this is your "shot" to call.

I thought you should know.

Best regards,

Bill Conkel

Bill Conkel
Sr. Technical Analyst - Service Support
Electronic Products Division
PHONE: (901) 922-6233
COMAT: 38194/MEM/TN-3523

BC/dh/0077f

OPEN DOOR COMMUNICATION FORM

05073

If more space is needed, attach additional sheets with this form

FOR EMPLOYEE RELATIONS USE

DATE RECEIVED	JULIAN DATE	JOB CODE
11-22-85		

Completed 12-4-85

It is the policy of Federal Express to have an Open Door process in which employees can communicate their ideas and concerns directly to management. This process should facilitate interaction between management and employees for informal resolution to concerns.

Please fill this form out completely and forward the first three copies to EMPLOYEE RELATIONS, COMAT 1811, who will then forward your issue to the appropriate managerial employee to address it. You will be receiving a response from this person within 14 calendar days from his or her receipt of the issue.

ANONYMOUS ISSUES WILL NOT BE ADDRESSED
PLEASE PRINT OR TYPE CLEARLY

EMPLOYEE NAME	EMPLOYEE NO.	JOB TITLE
Thurman Richard White	29901	Sr CSTR

DIVISION/REGION	DEPARTMENT/COMAT NO.	PHONE
Delta Region	EPD field service	615 256 8...

OPEN DOOR ISSUE *(Please explain below, in detail)*

Date: 21 Nov 85

Mr. Tom Oliver Vice President EPD

I respectfully request a meeting to express in detail the need for having a <u>field service engineer</u> to research and accumulate accurate updated information for the Zapmail Techs. in the field.

Please see the attached letter and information. I could save the company alot of money and time.

Thurman White CSTR
Nashville, Tenn. MQY 37228

RESPONSE

Please respond to the above issue on this form and return WHITE COPY to EMPLOYEE RELATIONS, COMAT 1811, within calendar days of your receipt.

RESPONDENT'S NAME	TITLE	EMPLOYEE NO.	ORGANIZATION CODE	PHONE
T. R. Oliver	Sr Vice President	10524		225-3130

11/29/85

Thurman,

I've asked Ron Crawthern to have you visit with us

CASE STUDIES

Delta Region   EPD field service   615 256 805

OPEN DOOR ISSUE *(Please explain below, in detail)*

Date: 21 Nov 85

Mr. Tom Oliver Vice President EPD

I respectfully request a meeting to express in detail the need for having a <u>field service engineer</u> to research and accumulate accurate updated information for the Zapmail Techs. in the field.

Please see the attached letter and information. It could save the company alot of money and time.

           Thurman White   CSTR
           Nashville, Tenn. MQY 37228

RESPONSE

Please respond to the above issue on this form and return WHITE COPY to EMPLOYEE RELATIONS, COMAT 1811, within 14 calendar days of your receipt.

RESPONDENT'S NAME	TITLE	EMPLOYEE NO.	ORGANIZATION CODE	PHONE
T. R. Oliver	Sr Vice President	10524		225-3130

11/29/85

Thurman,

I've asked Ray Grantham to have you visit with us in Memphis as soon as I get back from my trip over Thanksgiving.

Signature: Tom O.

DISTRIBUTION: White — Employee Relations Copy (To Respondent)
Yellow — Respondent Copy
Pink — Employee Relations Copy
Goldenrod — Employee Copy

Inter-Office Memorandum

Date: 21 Nov.1985
To: Mr. Tom Oliver
From: Thurman White
Subject: Zapmail Program Improvements

    I would first like to thank you for giving me the opportunity for using the Open Door Policy.I would also like to express my enthusiasm that I share with you in wanting Zapmail to be nothing less than excellent service for our customers.I have been with the Zapmail/Gemini program for over two years.During that time I travelled extensively setting up Zapmail in twenty states.I was in the first class of Gemini technicians and during that time had the privilege of meeting you and Dave Anderson at a play at Germantown High School.After the play we talked enthusiasticly about Gemini and its successful future.During the two years I have witnessed some of the inefficiencies that have developed in the Zapmail/Gemini program.This is why I am writing to you.

    I first want to refer to my memorandum dated August 2,1985 concerning Decode Errors. Decode errors were a real problem in our Network.I decided to research this problem.As a result of my research I sent in the attached memorandum.In late August I received a response that I was wrong yet at the same time I received the response,the Network stopped having decode errors.I believe someone took credit for my hard work.

    Also concerning my memorandum dated February 14,1985 on IPS1 Print Quality Problem. Please Mr. Oliver take the time to read it and understand it.Our original Imager 1 printer had cleaning corotron.Our engineers asked N.E.C. to remove this very important part of the printer.With proof in the memorandum of the need to have the cleaning corotron placed back into the printer, why has it not been taken care of.

    I believe in this company and share with you the concern to improve the Zapmail program.But accurate intimate knowledge is a prerequisite to the future success of this program.Accurate information has been made available but not being used.My manager,Bob Christie has beenthe perfect example of the best manager a man could have.Bob Christie has backed me in everything I do.Bob Christie has helped me solve work problems as well as personal problems.He has gone beyond the call of duty for me and others many times. But, we are only a cry in the dark.I have picked two examples of the many other ideas I share with alot of the other CSTRs.The problem is not field managers, but it is with inaccurate information that we use as Gospel.

    There is so much more that needs to be addressed, but would take to much time in this letter.I am proud to be an employee of Federal Express EPD and have found an exciting career with Zapmail technology.I feel real good about our future with Zapmail now that we have a Vice-President who listens.

Thank you

Thurman White CSTR

BNA 37228

FEC-O/S-104
2042730233

CASE STUDIES

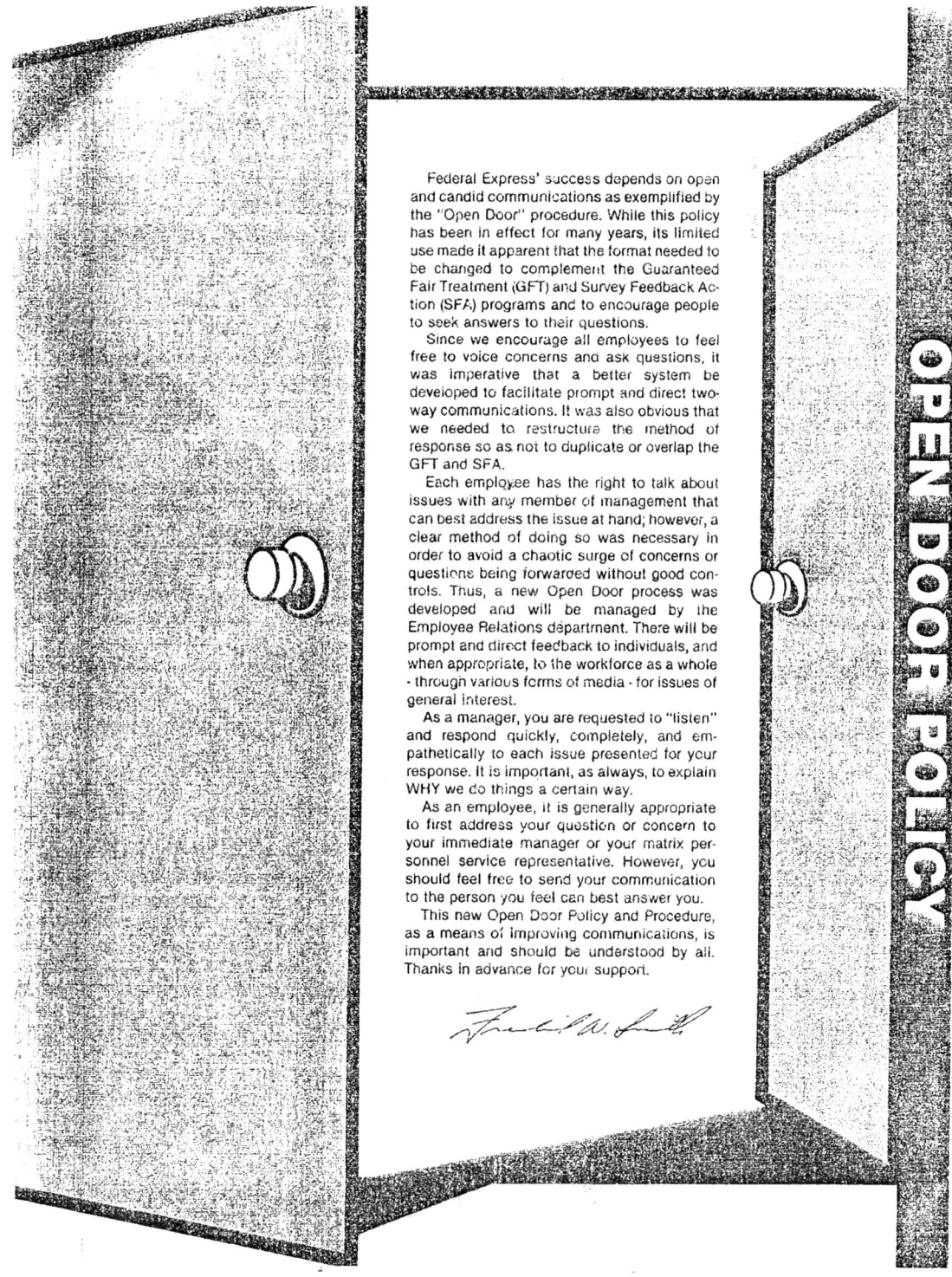

Federal Express' success depends on open and candid communications as exemplified by the "Open Door" procedure. While this policy has been in effect for many years, its limited use made it apparent that the format needed to be changed to complement the Guaranteed Fair Treatment (GFT) and Survey Feedback Action (SFA) programs and to encourage people to seek answers to their questions.

Since we encourage all employees to feel free to voice concerns and ask questions, it was imperative that a better system be developed to facilitate prompt and direct two-way communications. It was also obvious that we needed to restructure the method of response so as not to duplicate or overlap the GFT and SFA.

Each employee has the right to talk about issues with any member of management that can best address the issue at hand; however, a clear method of doing so was necessary in order to avoid a chaotic surge of concerns or questions being forwarded without good controls. Thus, a new Open Door process was developed and will be managed by the Employee Relations department. There will be prompt and direct feedback to individuals, and when appropriate, to the workforce as a whole - through various forms of media - for issues of general interest.

As a manager, you are requested to "listen" and respond quickly, completely, and empathetically to each issue presented for your response. It is important, as always, to explain WHY we do things a certain way.

As an employee, it is generally appropriate to first address your question or concern to your immediate manager or your matrix personnel service representative. However, you should feel free to send your communication to the person you feel can best answer you.

This new Open Door Policy and Procedure, as a means of improving communications, is important and should be understood by all. Thanks in advance for your support.

Box 727
Memphis, TN 38194
901 369-3600 Date: January 15, 1988

To: Fred Mitchell
Manager of Field Service
Telecommunications
Memphis, Tenn. 38194

From: Thurman Richard White
Subject: Resignation and two weeks notice.

Please accept this letter as an offical letter of resignation from the company and a two week notice for employee separation beginning January the 31st, 1988. I will be starting employment with another company starting February 1st, 1988.

This reignation is because I am seeking care opportunity with a group I have consulted for off and on for about two years. I have had a good job with Federal Express and have no bitterness toward management nor company policy. Please accept this resignation as a personnal carreer move on my part, and not as a hostile letter of departure. Federal Express has been real good to me and gave me the opportunity to grow in the field of data communications. Thank you for the opportunity to be an employee with a great company and an excellant work group. I will be looking forward to your reply and for instructions on what are the proceedures that I need to take in order to pursue care opportunity with another group.

Thank you
Thurman Richard White
Sr. FSTR
Telecommunications
Nashville, Tenn. 37228
(615) 256-8038 office
(615) 331-8514 home

CASE STUDIES

Case #4: MediClaim Incorporated

The Arkansas Medicaid Bid

MediClaim, Incorporated was a software, hardware, computer (end-user stations and networks) development company, based in Nashville, Tennessee. The company is dedicated to developing computer products specifically designed for State Medicaid programs. MediClaim, Incorporated was established for the purpose of saving any State's Medicaid program money, assisting health care providers in solving their technical problems associated with eligibility verification and claims submission, and most of all to bring the provider in closer to the way Medicaid does business so State Medicaid can watchdog provider Medicaid activities.

The heroes in this case study are Martin Poe, Carl Olsen, and Marty Poe. Carl Olsen, President of CMS Inc. a shared partner of MediClaim Incorporated was involved with developing telecommunications technology. Marty Poe was President of MediClaim Incorporated and I was the Chief Information Officer and product development engineer for the company. Martin Poe financed our ideas and was the business advisor and overseer for the company's operations. Carl Olson did the telecommunications development for access to State Medicaid data bases.

Prior to MediClaim, I was Vice President of Systems Development for The Potomac Group located in Nashville, Tennessee. One well known person who was both a shareholder and a member of the board for the Potomac Group was Bill Frist M.D. (now Senator Bill Frist). He was at this time a heart and lung transplant surgeon for Vanderbilt University Medical Center. While serving as vice president with the Potomac Group, I developed some of the first and only Medicaid eligibility products in the industry that, at that time, was being used in eight States. I also served as a Medicaid Specialist with a healthcare billing agency for several years. During that time I learned a great deal about Medicaid billing and started provider programs to get indigent patients, at the hospital on a Medicaid program. As an independent consultant in this Medicaid industry, I had worked for over six years, solving provider problems with Medicaid billing and had developed computer products that identify the providers self-pay write-off as a Medicaid billable.

MediClaim Incorporated first began services in the State of Florida. The plan was to go to the hospital's business offices; get a list of patients treated and released that had not paid their bill, and run these "self-pay write off" accounts through our system. Even though it was beginning to be a very lucrative business, healthcare providers were becoming angry that they had to split money we recovered (50/50). Providers that we were servicing felt it was their money, not MediClaim's money. We were taking 50% of money that the business offices declared non-payable. We were able to recover more money because we combined eligibility verification with the billing of the heath care claim. The research and theories of why healthcare had issues was coming to light and we began to cash in on our discovery.

HCFA (The Health Care Financial Administration) began to discourage organizations such as MediClaim from practicing our science on the health care issue of billing errors created as a result of not having access to the eligibility files. HCFA began to discourage organizations from being both an eligibility agent and a billing agent. In order to stay in business, we were asked to charter the company as an eligibility agent or a billing agent for the health care providers that were our customers. This was not a hard fast ruling, but it had me worried because this could drastically affect our business plans for the future. This was a downside for MediClaim, but the upside was the fact that HCFA was looking for organizations willing to provide technology in the areas of eligibility and claims capture. State Medicaid Directors and HCFA had targeted 3 main problems with the Medicaid system that needed systems technology. They are an EVS Eligibility Verification System, ECC Electronics Claim Capture, and ECM Electronic Claims Management. So the providers wanted access to the State's eligibility files and they wanted to submit health care claims and track the results of payments of pending payment.

Identification Of Problems With State Medicaid

Three (3) main problems that Medicaid Directors have targeted.

1) Eligibility Verification System - Requirements

> A) Must have on-line / daily update access to eligibility file at the Fiscal Agent. Presently, if a Medicaid Recipient goes off eligibility in the middle of the month, Medicaid has to pay for coverage on the remaining days even though the recipient is not covered.
> B) There is an increase of FTEs (Full Time Employees) at the eligibility unit. This increase is a result of the large number of providers needing eligibility information. Medicaid workers having to spend a great deal of time with answering phone calls and answering questions that providers have concerning eligibility.
> C) Third Party Unit Collections and Third Party Liability Cost Avoidance. Because of the lack of access to the TPL file, providers will bill Medicaid as a primary payer when in this particular case Medicaid is a secondary payer. Most TPL Units work the TPL payment for the health care provider and attempt to collect the primary payment.

2) Electronic Claims Capture

> A) Adjudication fee of $ 0.25 per claim is charged to the State Medicaid for processing the input. If the claim is rejected, and the provider

resubmits, an additional $ 0.25 is charged. Medicaid feels that the cost could be reduced if the claim went in right the first time.

B) With 185% of poverty (benefits), TPL participants will play a very strong role in Medicaid. Claims will need to be routed for electronic submission to the correct fiscal agent or organization that reviews and sends payment on the health care claim.

3) Electronic Claims Management

A) The number one provider complaint of the doctors and hospitals is "where is my claim and why is it pending, etc." Tracking the claim at the provider location would reduce State cost.

B) Tracking Take-Backs. Another responsibility of the TPL Unit is to track take-backs. A take-back is when a provider received money from Medicaid as a primary (should be secondary) and the provider must bill up to the amount of the take-back before Medicaid will make a payment.

When I read this information, I was ecstatic with joy. The product that we had already developed and were using in the State of Florida was being requested for bids by HCFA. This was amazing to me. I wanted to turn all of our attention to participating in the bid process. I was convinced that our product would win in every state across the nation. Knowing that MediClaim may not be able to continue doing eligibility and claims processing as a business, we could now turn our attention to selling the product to State Medicaid programs. My fellow business partners were reluctant, but very supportive. Even though we were making money, I told everyone we could make more money if we start participating in the bid process to sell MediClaim's product to the States. We could make millions of dollars and there would be very little development costs involved because we meet all of the HCFA requirements. The first state to put this out for bid and a request for technology in this area was the State of Arkansas. I contacted the Arkansas Department of Human Services and asked them to send me the RFB (Request for Bid). Once I had received the RFB, it first appeared to be very overwhelming. There was a great deal of writing to be done and the bid required documentation and had hundreds of questions that required a response. I asked Marty Poe if he would assist me. He was so supportive that he closed his lucrative sporting goods business to help me do the bid. However, you will see that I was wrong and my friends were correct. I should have continued to do our Florida operation and not devote time to bidding our product. The bid process can be very political, costly, and most of all corrupt. Even though my friends were reluctant, I wanted to turn our attention to the Arkansas bid. I can never thank them enough for all the work and dedication to me my friends gave, but this bid would be my Waterloo.

The Political Environment in the State of Arkansas
The Evolutionary Process to Bid the Technology and Historical Background

Bill Clinton (42nd President of the United States) was the governor for the State of Arkansas at the time of this bid offering. EDS was the fiscal agent (Medicaid Claims Processor) operating in the State of Arkansas. EDS has always had the reputation of being one of the greatest organizations in the area of computer technology and services. This was the company that Ross Perot had founded. EDS had always built on its strong services heritage of meeting, and exceeding clients' needs every day, and driving their business performance all along the way. EDS has always proved they never give up until the job is done for their clients. But things had changed within the ranks of EDS by the time of this bid offering. If you remember, Perot sold EDS in 1984 to General Motors for $2.5 billion. He retained ownership in the company, which made him GM's largest individual stockholder and a member of the board of directors. From the start, Perot and GM head Roger Smith quarreled, and Perot criticized the quality of GM automobiles (Perot was right). In 1986, GM bought out Perot's stock for $700 million with the agreement that he could not compete with EDS for three years. Perot ignored the agreement. Two years later, he started a new computer service company, Perot Systems, which operates in the United States and Europe. So Ross Perot was no longer president of EDS. At the time of this bid offering Les Alberthal was president of EDS. On April 28, Les Alberthal, who joined EDS in 1968, was named president and chief executive officer, and Mort Meyerson became vice chairman. On Dec. 1, Ross Perot, Mort Meyerson, senior vice president Bill Gayden and chief financial officer Tom Walter left EDS. The buyout cost GM $742 million.

In May 1989, while Vice President of the Potomac Group, I had a meeting with the Department of Human Services (Arkansas Medicaid) and demonstrated POSD technology (Point of Sale Device-*see picture*-these are credit card terminals). Present at the meeting was Tom Jewart (of EDS) and Ray Hanley (Assistant Medicaid Director for Arkansas. This was nearly two years prior the Arkansas RFB (August 1, 1991). The reason I mention this meeting, that was nearly two years prior to the bid offering, is because the outlined technology that was later to appear in the Arkansas RFB resembled the technology that Tom Jewart (EDS) and Ray Hanley witnessed during my presentation. Ray Hanley often drew pictures during meetings and he drew this one during my demonstration. After I completed the demonstration (1989 meeting), Ray Hanley turned to Tom Jewart of EDS and asked, "Why was this technology not part of the proposal from EDS.

CASE STUDIES

I left The Potomac Group and stopped serving as Vice President of Systems shortly after this meeting, due to many disagreements with some of the other officers of the company. However, the technology that I had engineered was not going to go away. I decided to take the technology to a higher level and started MediClaim Incorporated with several business partners. We began operations in the State of Florida to do Medicaid eligibility and health care claims submission. It was the summer of 1990 that we did a demonstration of our technology for the State of Alabama. They liked what they saw, but suggested that we do the demonstration for the State of Arkansas, because they were the leaders in selecting such innovations. So the people of MediClaim scheduled a meeting with the State of Arkansas Medicaid Department, on October 4, 1990. Present at the meeting was Ray Hanley. I had saved his picture of the "better mouse trap." After showing Ray Hanley the improved system, Ray Hanley asked us to meet with EDS (Fiscal Agent contracted to do Medicaid MMIS) in Ray Hanley's office. The demonstration we did for Ray Hanley, was a live demonstration of our Florida Medicaid System. The meeting with Tom Jewart and EDS concluded with Tom Jewart saying they (EDS) could do the technology and wanted MediClaim, Incorporated to do the training and installation of their product. My comment was, "Oh, I did not know you guys had a system. If EDS would have us do the training, then I need to see the product." Tom Jewart replied, "Well...our system is still under development." Tom Jewart also informed us that the State of Arkansas had already asked EDS to develop this type of technology (the MediClaim Florida Product) for the State of Arkansas.

On July 22, 1991 I made a phone call to Tom Jewart at EDS in Arkansas. EDS had had an additional year to come up with the Medicaid technology requested by the State of Arkansas. I called EDS to see when MediClaim, Incorporated could start training the health care providers of the State of Arkansas to use the EDS product. Tom Jewart of EDS informed me that the State of Arkansas was putting the project out for bid. EDS still had not produced a health care product for the State of Arkansas. Our product was up and running in Florida and had been during this time period. I then called Ray Hanley and asked him how MediClaim, Incorporated could get on the bid list for the AEVCS project. Ray Hanley was very cooperative and Federal Expressed a copy of the IFB to MediClaim, Incorporated.

The AVECS Bid
(Automated Eligibility Verification & Claims Sub-mission)

On August 1, 1991 the Department of Human Services Division of Medical Services (Medicaid) put out an IFB (Invitation for Bid). This IFB was a request for computer technical development companies to develop software/hardware for the Arkansas AEVCS (Automated Eligibility Verification & Claims Sub-mission) project. This bid outlined and requested software services and development which MediClaim Incorporated had developed and is presently being used in the Medicaid industry. EDS at the time of the RFB, was the fiscal agent contracted by the State of Arkansas Department of Human Services Division of Economic and Medical Services to be the Fiscal Agent for the State of Arkansas. EDS is contracted to store Medicaid Eligibility records and process medical claims for the State of Arkansas.

When Marty Poe and I reviewed the RFB in August of 1991, it was uncanny how much this bid was requesting, was already demonstrated in the May 1989 meeting that I attended and did a demonstration of the technical capabilities for the Medicaid Departments. At this time, we had elevated the technology to a higher level. I had a feeling that we were going to get the contract and easily win. We had some modifications to make to our system, but these would be minor changes to MediClaim's product.

There were over 60 companies on the list that expressed an interest in this bid offering. After Arkansas sent copies to companies expressing an interest to bid, many companies on the list requested a meeting for "Questions and Answers" Of all the companies on the list, nine attended this meeting. MediClaim attended this meeting to try and get some more exposure. Martin Poe took four people with him to the meeting. MediClaim attended, asked questions, and then met with other companies. The people, who attended the meeting in Arkansas, saw this as an opportunity to prove their ability to advance technologically in the field of health care. The AVECS bid was considered to be the way of the future. But other companies during the Offers Conference (Questions & Answers), August 14, 1991, one of the questions that came up was the conflict of interest between the Fiscal Agent EDS holding the files and the State allowing them to bid on AEVCS. MediClaim, Incorporated did not submit this question. But as you can see many of the potential bidders backed out because they felt that the IFB was home cooked from the Fiscal Agents (EDS) prospective. In actuality, it tried to resemble the product we had demonstrated twice to this department in Arkansas.

After returning from the meeting, Marty and I continued to labor, working many times all night long, answering every section of the bid. But I must say, because of Martin Poe and Marty Poe, this was the best response to an RFB I had every seen. Marty Poe had included in MediClaim's proposal a plan to implement Medicaid software, point of sale devices (POSD), and network technology to interface with the MMIS (Medicaid Management Information Systems) data base. Marty made an offer that was too good to be true. He proposed a transaction processor that would allow eligibility checks and claims submission at no extra cost. Because the State of Arkansas had not included any computer network plans in the RFB, the next logical step was to make a telecommunications solution for the end-user computers. Arkansas had not considered new telecommunications technology. We were using a transaction processor that would save the State time and money. Marty Poe put an offering in our proposal that we knew the State could not refuse. This was our ace of spades and would guarantee our win. So on August 14, 1991 MediClaim, Incorporated sent our letter of intent to bid on the AEVCS project.

September 9, 1991 9:00A.M. was the Public Opening to bring your response to Arkansas. We brought our proposals. To everyone's surprise only two companies actually prepared proposals for the AEVCS project. This was an IFB for the state of the art technology, a model of a national health care product, and technology that will be the wave of the future according to Ray Hanley. Why do you suppose that the State of Arkansas did not receive a large number of proposals from a large number of companies? MediClaim believes it is because of the overwhelming unfair advantage for EDS to be permitted to bid on this IFB. For nearly three years EDS had cost the State of Arkansas a tremendous amount of money delaying implementing technology that they cannot develop. As a result of the EDS presence in this bid, many companies declined to put in a competitive bid.

DURING THIS MEETING MEDICLAIM MAKES A VERBAL PROTEST TO HAVE THE EDS BID THROWN OUT - BECAUSE THEY DID NOT FOLLOW BID PROCEDURES

Martin Poe was brilliant during this meeting. This is a man that is bigger than life. Martin Poe has several outstanding businesses to his credit. He protected our hard work and took control of the meeting. The people that represented EDS at this meeting were rude and arrogant. These people were not at all like the old EDS of Ross Perot. Rebecca O'Neal began the meeting; she made a suggestion to read to the group the bid pricing. I agreed to let her read our bid to the group. Martin Poe politely asked if she would read the EDS bid prices first. The people representing EDS said, "Our bid pricing is confidential. Know one is to read our bid to anyone." Martin Poe replied, "Then our bid is confidential also." Everyone looked puzzled that anyone would challenge EDS. Martin Poe made several interesting points at this time. Martin Poe verbally protested the price on the EDS bid. Martin said that the EDS price was bogus. Why would anyone purchase a product that did not exist? He emphasized that MediClaim knew what the cost would be because we have a real product operating in Florida. EDS is not doing this anywhere in the country. How do we know that EDS can produce the product? EDS then agreed to read their bid pricing. EDS "lowballed" the price. Their pricing was lower than ours. Martin Poe continued the verbal protest and stated that it is not over yet. There is a requirement to have a live demonstration of the technical requirements outlined in this RFB. Martin Poe also pointed out that to award a bid based on pricing alone would be ludicrous. Why would anyone spend tax-payers money on a product that doesn't exist? During this time we received little cooperation from the State officials. If it were not for Martin Poe calling Senator Bradford (of Arkansas) and convincing the senator to demand a demonstration, MediClaim Incorporated would not have been given a chance to do a live demonstration and EDS would have won the bid because of a lower price. But what was the State buying? Senator Bradford was the only official in the State of Arkansas that demanded a demonstration. Martin Poe asked the senator, "Why is it that the Department of Medicaid says this IFB is so important, yet they do little to get involved with the AEVCS process? The bid says **must demonstrate**."

On October 11, 1991 the State of Arkansas scheduled the Oral and Live Demonstration. MediClaim, Incorporated did a live demonstration of the Medicaid project with a different Fiscal Agent operating for the State of Florida (Consultec). The evaluation committee was there and I must say that they were the first professional people we had met in this process. They understood the States needs, Medicaid problems that needed to be solved, asked intelligent questions, were well dressed, could articulate and demonstrated their knowledge in the areas of Medicaid billing, eligibility, third party liability, and over all project objective. The evaluating committee said, "They had never seen such an outstanding demonstration." (Note: Evaluation in the Exhibit). Marty Poe also took time to explain that MediClaim, added into our bid a free computer network system for the State of Arkansas Medicaid Department. The EDS front-end communications only accommodates a limited number of Medicaid transactions. MediClaim has a network computer system that we want to give to the State free. This network is flexible and accommodating. It is designed to tie in all Human Services programs at no extra development cost to the State.

After the demonstration, it was apparent to all five of the Arkansas evaluators, that MediClaim, Incorporated was truly established for the purpose of assisting health care providers in solving technical problems associated with eligibility verification and Claims processing for Medicaid, Medicare, and independent third party payers. They could see for themselves that MediClaim is dedicated solely to the health care industry and specifically to health care providers. The evaluators were in agreement with MediClaim. We shared value in the idea that health care providers must be provided the ability to verify payment sources and shorten accounts receivable aging to enable them to operate more closely to the way third party payers operate. Following our demonstration, EDS had nothing to offer. I have provided the evaluators comments of MediClaim's product and the EDS product. The evaluators saw no demonstration of hardware or software. The State was going to buy vapor-ware from EDS. EDS had ignored the mandate in the RFB that stated in numerous places "must demonstrate."

CASE STUDIES

On September 11, 1991 MediClaim mailed an official bid protest letter in accordance with the bid protest procedure to Mr. Ray Hanley, Assistant Medicaid Director. On September 20, 1991 MediClaim received written response from Ray Hanley to MediClaim's bid protest letter. His response was evasive, noncommittal, and did not address the issues under protest. After receipt of Mr. Hanley's response several phone calls were placed to Mr. Hanley to have his response be clarified. After no communication or cooperation from Ray Hanley concerning the public bid and receiving information from Rebecca O'Neal and Edward J. Erxleben, that Ray Hanley's department's credibility and honesty left a lot to be desired.

On October 17, 1991 via telephone Rebecca O'Neal had informed MediClaim, Incorporated that EDS had been awarded the bid. However, MediClaim, Incorporated continued to protest EDS's conformity to the bid i.e. did EDS meet all mandatory software requirements and demonstrate completely as mandated in the IFB on October 10, 1991. This is just one of many issues we questioned. Having the superior product and implementation approach as scaled by the evaluators, MediClaim, Incorporated failed to receive the bid due largely to the fact that MediClaim, Incorporated followed the bid in pricing all categories of service in Pricing Schedules A-H of the Arkansas IFB. These prices where mandatory and breakdowns were requested (Gantt Chart). EDS failed to make proper entries into the pricing schedules. Many of their pricing answers were "N/A" (Not applicable) for mandatory requested prices on software and services. EDS, for the most part, only priced hardware related to this BID. Because MediClaim understood the bid and responded to all of the pricing questions (AS REQUIRED), MediClaim was penalized and EDS was awarded automatic 100 points for low bid. EDS had a lower BID because they failed to respond to all of the pricing questions. In addition to the omitted prices of EDS, they were lower in pricing computer hardware equipment (mandated in the bid) because they conspired with Verifone to get lower prices from the POSD vendor. Verifone quoted a lower price for computer hardware for EDS. Verifone did not lower their pricing for MediClaim. More importantly EDS could not fulfill the mandatory software requirements during the live demonstration.

On the day that EDS was awarded the bid, Martin Poe contacted Arkansas attorney Bob Brooks. MediClaim Incorporated begins proceeding to prepare a lawsuit against the State of Arkansas Department of Human Services. MediClaim listed the State Purchasing Statutes and Bidding Statutes that had been violated and not adhered to.

* The bid was subject to the Arkansas Purchasing Law and Regulations, 19-11-201 et seq.

* Accordingly, pursuant to section 19-11-244 of the Arkansas Purchasing Law and Regulations, MediClaim, Incorporated, makes protest of its failure to receive the award of the bid.

*   First, the AEVCS Project Bid (APB) was to be a bid for state of the art technology in implementing a statewide point of sale claim transmission and eligibility verification system.

*   In accordance with the Invitation For Bid (IFB) on the APB, MediClaim, Incorporated, fully complied to all sections of the IFB and was extremely capable in performing all functions of the IFB to specifications requested to be implemented by November 1, 1991.

Section IV of Appendix "C", and Analysis Document flow chart on page 47, of Appendix "C". Therefore, failure to so comply should cause EDS's bid to be rejected according to Section 1.11, of the IFB. Thus leaving MediClaim, Incorporated the only successfully bidder.

*   MediClaim, Incorporated in addition to submitting a bid price, further included a cost efficient alternative ("option") bid price in their IFB for the Arkansas Purchasing Department to consider. It is apparent from the evaluation scores, that the sole determinative factor in awarding the APB to EDS was price. If MediClaim, Incorporated's option price was considered by the Arkansas Purchasing Department, MediClaim, Incorporated's bid prices would have been extremely competitive to that of EDS and thus allowed MediClaim, Incorporated to win the APB award. However, the Arkansas Purchasing Department did not consider the option bid price of MediClaim, Incorporated, and further informed the evaluation committee not to consider the option. The failure to so consider the option in MediClaim, Incorporated's IFB was in conflict and violation of Arkansas Purchasing Law Regulation Section 19-11-229(f) and R7: 19-11-229.

*   MediClaim, Incorporated's option conformed to all requirements of the IFB; therefore, it should have been considered in the evaluation and awarding of the APB. If this would have been done, MediClaim, Incorporated would have received the APB award.

*   EDS should not have been allowed to bid on the IFB due to a severe conflict of interest. Allowing EDS to bid was violation of competitive bidding as outlined in Arkansas Purchasing Law and Regulation Section 19-11-201 ET seq. Further, 45 CFR Part 74 Appendix G of Attachment O-Procurement Standards of OMB Circular A-102 of the Uniform Administration Requirements for Grants in Aid to State and Local Government States, in pertinent part states

> "All procurement transactions...
> shall be conducted in a manner that
> provides maximum open and free competition."

CASE STUDIES

In light of this Federal Regulation it was an obvious conflict to allow EDS a Fiscal Agent and writer of IFB specifications to bid on the IFB. The conflict is therefore, first; EDS is a Fiscal Agent of the State, second; EDS wrote the technical specification that were utilized in the IFB, third; EDS was evaluated, scored, and otherwise given points toward their IFB and implementation ability of various specifications EDS wrote for the IFB. These factors create a very high degree of unfairness and deter open and free competition. Further, cost association with the APB will be supplement with Federal Funds via the Health Care Finance Administration (HCFA), the Federal Regulation can not be overridden by Arkansas State Law regardless of what HCFA states. Further, in review of Arkansas State Law, there is found no law-giving rise to EDS's ability to so participate in the APB due to their obvious conflict.

* The Federal Regulation and Rules pertaining to the APB should have been adhered to and thus EDS would have been unable to participate by submitting their bid due to the obvious conflict. MediClaim, Incorporated accordingly would have received the APB award.

* Finally, MediClaim, Incorporated, protest the award of the APB to EDS on basis of MediClaim, Incorporated's original bid protest filed on September 11, 1991. The Arkansas Purchasing Department allowed EDS to continue through the bid process without giving a complete answer to MediClaim, Incorporated protest based Arkansas Purchasing Law and Regulation Section 19-11-144. The answers MediClaim, Incorporated received was extremely evasive and non-conforming to the actual facts giving rise to the protest. This provided an unfair advantage to EDS because EDS failed to adhere to all requirements of the public bid.

* Therefore, such failure to respond to MediClaim Incorporated's protest and to disqualify EDS allowed EDS to continue through the bid process and ultimately receive the APB award, this action taken was in total conflict with Arkansas State Purchasing Law and Regulation 19-11-201 et seq.

* In addition, according to Arkansas Purchasing Law and Regulation R1: 19-11-217(A), the authority is vested in the State Purchasing Director, Mr. Erxleben, to assure the quality Assurance of commodities to be purchased. More particular the Regulation states:

> R1:19-11-217(A) State Quality Assurance, Inspection and Testing.
>
> The State Purchasing Director or Agency Purchasing Official shall assure that commodities and services conform to necessary specifications, terms and conditions in the following situations:

(2) Before delivery when bidder has responded
to an Invitation for Bids and/or received a
contract award.

The word "shall" is determined by the Arkansas Purchasing Law and Regulations as meaning the imperative. To this date, Mr. Erxleben, State Purchasing Director, has failed to adhere to this State Purchasing Law. Mr. Erxleben did not exhaust all the resources that were available to him (at tax payers expense) to assure that commodities and services conform to necessary specifications, terms and conditions as outlined in the Arkansas bid. Mr. Erxleben had the resource of a State selected five (5) member evaluation team and did not even consider the written comments of these evaluators. The evaluators commented that EDS had no product nor did they have a network. The evaluators wrote that MediClaim had the product which was asked for and that MediClaim had good ideas on how to save the State money and accommodate future growth.

In order to prove our allegations, we needed to enter a discovery. Our attorney, Bob Brooks, asked the Department of Human Services to have all documentation ready that pertained to this bid. The most important information we could obtain would be to get documents pertaining to any collaboration between EDS and the Department of Human Services. I had suspected that there must be correspondence between the two entities. For the last three years I had been talking to The Department of Human Services and they shared with me information concerning EDS involvement with doing the development. Our attorney needed proof of this. So it is obvious that forcing the Department of Human Services to have all documents ready for our review, then we could find proof of our suspicions of unfair bid practices.

I left for Little Rock Arkansas with a Nashville attorney that was working with Bob Brooks (MediClaim's Arkansas Attorney). We traveled all day Monday to work the rest of the week searching for the appropriate documents. I thought it would only take six to eight hours to find everything we needed. When we came to the office where the documents were, the office was full of boxes with papers (supposedly) pertaining to the bid. There must have been at least one hundred boxes. So we started to search for the documents we needed. As we started to search, it was forever an overwhelming task. I was so discouraged, that I called Martin Poe in the Nashville office. I told him what these guys did to us. I was so upset I could hardly think. Martin told me to calm down. I told him we will be here for a whole year looking for the right papers. He told me again to calm down and he would make a phone call and have everything taken care of. He then told me to go to lunch and enjoy myself and not to worry. I then told the people in the room (workers for the State of Arkansas) that I would be going to lunch and would be back at 1:00 p.m. to start working again. They could see my discouragement and were gloating. They locked the door behind us and then everyone went to lunch. All I did during lunch was to complain about the unfairness of it all.

I then came back from lunch. The Arkansas State employees unlocked the door. When I entered the room I walked in the back at the table that had thousands of documents I had been reading and reviewing. When I looked down, the documents we needed were sitting on top in plain view. To this day, I do not know how Martin Poe did it. It was taken care of. I had the evidence that was crucial proving collaboration and unfair bid practice. Now that we were in possession of these documents we could prepare a case that will prove the following:

> Because, the State, HCFA, and EDS collaborated to create a solo bid for EDS, there is proof of a CONFLICT OF INTEREST. MediClaim, Incorporated will sue the State of Arkansas on the issues of a conflict of interest.

> In addition, failure on EDS' part to complete the bid on the day of bid opening should have been enough to throw the bid out. MediClaim, Incorporated was ignored when we protested this issue in particular.

Martin Poe's inside contact strategically placed other documents that contained information that EDS was asking for more time to develop the technology. These documents are also located in the Exhibits section of this case. Earlier in this case, I mentioned that Marty Poe offered the state a network at no additional cost to the State. EDS had promised that they would do the computer networking and already had an agreement with the State to develop an On-Line Transaction Processor. One of the documents that were made available was concerning this issue. The state had awarded the contract, which did not go out for competitive bid, to EDS concerning computer networking for the AVECS end-user computer that would be located at Hospitals, Doctor offices, Dentists offices, and other health care provider groups. We now had documents that showed EDS's inability to have the OLTP (On-Line Transaction Processor) computer available as scheduled and that EDS has already dictated to the State for more time to implement their technology. Remember, MediClaim did live demonstrations with our products through our network that we offered to the State for free. It was apparent that Martin Poe's contact or contacts were very angry with the way tax payer money was being wasted. Apparently, this insider or insiders wanted the unethical practices to stop.

After discovery, we filed a complaint. MediClaim, Incorporated wanted a fair and impartial review of EDS's and MediClaim's proposal and product and how they conform to the requested bid. We wanted an impartial ruling. As time continued to pass, EDS asked for an extension to deliver the product. In one of the documents you will note that EDS was requesting a July 7, 1992 implementation date.

Legal Preparation for MediClaim Incorporated

After the discovery, attorney Bob Brooks (Arkansas) began to prepare a case. He researched several cases and one case styled was Blue Cross and Blue Shield of Maryland verses United States Department of Health and Human Services 718 F. Supp. 80 (D.D.C. 1989). Where in HCFA was sued for declaratory and injunctive relief for the improper award of a contract regarding maintenance and enhancement of a Medicare Common working file. The members of MediClaim Incorporated wanted to pursue this case.

June 17, 1992 MediClaim, Incorporated files its complaint against the Arkansas Department of Human Services. DHS by law has ten days plus three day mail time to answer the complaint.

July 8, 1992 the Department of Human Services filed its motion to dismiss along with its memorandum brief in support of its motion. MediClaim Incorporated has ten days to respond plus three days for mailing.

July 23, 1992 MediClaim Incorporated files its amended complaint along with its response to motion to dismiss accompanied with memorandum in support of response to motion to dismiss. The Department of Human Services by law has ten days plus three day mail time to respond to MediClaim's amended complaint as well as reply to MediClaim's response to motion to dismiss.

August 4, 1992 The Department of Human Services files motion for enlargement of time to respond to MediClaim's amended complaint and to reply to MediClaim's response to motion to dismiss. The Department of Human Services is granted ten days by the court.

August 4, 1992 MediClaim, Incorporated files motion for preliminary injunction along with its memorandum brief in support of the motion. The Department of Human Services has ten days plus three days mail time to respond.

August 18, 1992 The Department of Human Services responds to motion for preliminary injunction along with memorandum brief supporting their response. The Department of Human Services files motion to dismiss amended complaint along with their memorandum in support. MediClaim has ten days plus three days mail time to respond to The Department of Human Services response to motion for preliminary injunction and motion to dismiss amended complaint.

August 20, 1992 received The Department of Human Services supplement to Department of Human Services response to motion for preliminary injunction.

August 24, 1992 MediClaim, Incorporated files motion for enlargement of time to answer response to preliminary injunction and motion to dismiss. Time extended to September 8, 1992.

We passed summary judgment, and now it was time to take depositions. The State of Arkansas would take the depositions of MediClaim Incorporated first. After Martin Poe and I gave our depositions, it was time to take the depositions of the people of the State of Arkansas. But many things had changed during these legal proceedings. Medicaid director Terry Yamauchi was dismissed as director over the Department, the law firm had removed Bob Brooks as our attorney and put Dean Worley in charge of our case, and Bill Clinton (Governor of Arkansas) was running for President of the United States.

Marty Poe and I prepared deposition questions for our Arkansas attorney (now Dean Worley) to ask key people working for the State of Arkansas. We called our new attorney to confirm a date and time to come to Arkansas to take depositions. All of a sudden, the attorney began to act hostile with our suggestions and terminated the call. We then tried to contact him and we were ignored. On this same day, we received a fax from the firm that was a termination letter. The firm had terminated their involvement with the case and would not have anything to do with the people of MediClaim Incorporated. We were worried but not discouraged. We began to call other law firms all over the State of Arkansas, and nobody would have anything to do with us. We then turned our attention to the news media. Nobody wanted to report the story. The last person we talked to concerning the AVECS bid was on April 15, 1992 - Trint Gillies of CBS.

CBS
555 West 57th Street
9th Floor
New York, New York 10019

We were dropped like a hot potato and nobody would have anything to do with us including our last contact, CBS news. In conclusion, the letters and other documents in the exhibits, are a demonstration of the many Directors, Commissioners, and leaders of America's healthcare system. They dictate the rules, recommendations, and enforce policies. A few managers that were the decision makers in this bid process, made a conscience decision to spend tax payer money for non-existent computer equipment and computer software, did not participate in the live demonstration, refused to address questions asked by their own employees, and did not consider alternatives. How can anyone make a decision without taking the time to gather all the information? Why would any leader ignore other alternatives? How can managers make a conscience decision to purchase a product that they themselves did not test or use? They did not even come to the live demonstration of a product that was in existence and being used in another State. What an incredibly ignorant decision to make. Would anyone in their right mind buy something that they could not see first and test with their own hands? This is the sign of a zero. I do not know of anyone that pays for something if they haven't seen it and tested it first.

More importantly, why would anyone award a bid based on a price (alone) of a product that was not available for a demonstration?

These documents are a demonstration of leaders in a large organization that supported self-interest rather than act in the best interest of the people of the United States. Wesley Harris (Hero) and the other four evaluators (Heroes) were the only people working in the best interest for the people of Arkansas. His letter is well written and makes many very interesting points that managers at all levels of this bid need to explain to the taxpayers of Arkansas as well as to the United States. Read the documents and make your own conclusions.

Arkansas Department of Human Services
Division of Economic and Medical Services

P.O. Box 1437
Little Rock, Arkansas 72203-1437

Bill Clinton
Governor

Terry Yamauchi, M.D.
Department Director

Kenny Whitlock
Division Director

MEMORANDUM

TO: Bill Carpenter, Administrator
System & Support

FROM: Wes Harris, MPAI
MMIS

DATE: October 24, 1991

SUBJ: AVECS Evaluation Committee

September 12, through September 13, 1991
The Evaluation Committee, Wes Harris, Glenda Higgs, Cathy Lyon, Sandra Smith and Linda Whitaker, convened to begin the task of reviewing the bids received in response to the AVECS IFB. Ed Merck advised the bids had not been released by State Purchasing due to unexplained technicalities and related proprietary issues.

The Committee members familiarized themselves with the IFB requirements on these dates. Noting the specifications for the AVECS were developed by OMS/EDS and having been advised EDS was a respondent, the committee felt EDS had a distinct advantage over any other potential respondents. The committee was additionally concerned regarding the rumored $6,000,000 differential in the price of the bids received by State Purchasing and the likelihood of the Committee's efforts being an exercise in futility. These issues/concerns were discussed at length with Mr. Merck.

September 16, through September 17, 1991
The Evaluation Committee convened and were informed the bids had not been released by State Purchasing.

September 18, through September 20, 1991
The Evaluation Committee convened and reviewed the bid response received from Electronic Data Systems.

The Committee felt it was apparent EDS's foreknowledge of the AVECS requirements governed their response. We found several areas, i.e., staffing and programming costs, we felt were left open-ended to potentially allow for amendments after contract award.

"The Arkansas Department of Human Services is in compliance with Titles VI and VII of the Civil Rights Act and is operated, managed and delivers services without regard to age, religion, handicap, sex, race, color or national origin."

Based on the nature of questions to be utilized in scoring the bid responses, the Committee requested a presentation/demonstration by the respondents.

September 23, through September 24, 1991
The Evaluation Committee convened and were advised the second bid response had not been released by State Purchasing.

September 25, through September 26, 1991
The Evaluation Committee convened and reviewed the bid response received from Mediclaim. The Mediclaim response verified the Committee's belief of the controversial nature of the AVECS IFB. The Mediclaim response required an oral presentation/system demonstration due to the proprietary nature of the information requested.

September 26, 1991
The Evaluation Committee submitted a written request for a presentation by both respondents. The Committee felt a presentation/demonstration would allow both respondents the opportunity to demonstrate their understanding of the AVECS requirements, State objectives and their respective system's capabilities. It was felt the presentation would allow a comparison of the bid responses to the respondent's actual knowledge and capabilities.

September 27, 1991
The Evaluation Committee prepared questions for the respondents pursuant to the areas the Committee specifically wanted addressed at the time of the presentations.

September 30, through October 1, 1991
Three members of the Evaluation Committee convened to contact references supplied by Electronic Data Systems and Mediclaim.

October 10, 1991
The Evaluation Committee attended a presentation/system demonstration given by Electronic Data Systems.

The EDS presentation consisted of an elaborate oral presentation which on several occasions contradicted information supplied in their written response. An equipment demonstration consisting of an overhead slide presentation and opportunity to observe card swipe capabilities was also provided. The Committee felt EDS's responses to questions raised regarding staffing and programming costs confirmed the potential for future add-on costs to the AVECS contract. The Committee had requested a hands on demonstration of the equipment the respondent proposed to use in this project. EDS was not prepared for this. The EDS staff member in attendance responsible for programming the equipment reported he had not been advised of the demonstration until four days prior to the presentation. When questioned as where the breakdown in communication occurred, the programmer reported it was within EDS. This information was not provided in the presence of any other EDS personnel. Subsequently, the Committee was not able to observe or use the equipment proposed.

October 11, 1991
The Evaluation Committee attended a presentation/system demonstration presented by Mediclaim.

Mediclaim did not give a polished oral presentation and their professionalism was seriously lacking. There was a great deal of emotionalism exhibited based upon Mr. White's previous dealings with OMS/EDS personnel. Their system demonstration was excellent. They displayed their equipment at arms length of the Committee and encouraged hands on participation in the demonstration. The Committee observed and participated in an actual eligibility transaction and claim submission interfaced with live claim files of the Florida Medicaid Program (Consultec). Prepared questions submitted by the Committee were answered to satisfaction. When pressed by the Committee regarding cost, Mediclaim responded with several alternatives in procuring an AVECS. Each of these alternatives could have resulted in considerable cost savings to the State; however, due to the specifications of the IFB, the Committee was prohibited from taking any of this information into consideration.

October 14, 1991
The Evaluation Committee convened to complete the scoring of the Electronic Data Systems and Mediclaim bid responses. It was felt by all members of the AVECS Evaluation Committee that due to the pricing formula it was unlikely the respondent with the best software and system expertise would be awarded the AVECS contract. The completed score sheets and all information pertaining to the review were turned over to Ed Merck at this time.

Mr. Harris has made some excellent points concerning pricing and the true award of this bid. I have excluded the original scores and evaluator's comments, but these are on file and can be provided. The evaluation committee scored MediClaim higher in all categories except pricing.

These documents were obtained during the discovery phase of the law suit. Filed are hundreds more that are just as implicating of unethical bid practices. The interesting thing about these documents and memorandums is the fact that the original EDS price in the APD (Advanced Planning Document) was very close to MediClaim's bid price for AEVCS. Marty Poe had priced the cost perfectly. One reason why the MediClaim price was higher is due to the fact that the Arkansas AEVCS bid specifically requested Verifone computer equipment. Verifone Incorporated gave EDS a lower price than they gave MediClaim Incorporated. Also provided, were documents showing the EDS failed to provide a product and continues to ask for more money to do the AEVCS project. The State of Arkansas did not hold EDS to the bid price.

Shortly after my meeting with Ray Hanley (Arkansas-Medicaid) in the summer of 1989, the Division of Economic and Medical Services began to plan for technology that would give the States Federal matching funds.

DIVISION OF ECONOMIC AND MEDICAL SERVICES

MEMORANDUM

TO: Ray Hanley, Assistant Deputy Director

FROM: Bill Carpenter, Administrator, Systems & Support

DATE: September 22, 1989

SUBJ: EDS Electronic Benefit Transfer Proposal--Cost Benefit Analysis

---

My purpose in writing this memo is to brief you on a meeting held two weeks ago with regard to the above subject. It will also provide you with a preliminary cost benefit study which shows the cost effectiveness of the proposal, and, informs you of actions that we believe will result in even more favorable cost benefit justifications.

Summary of Meeting

The meeting was held on September 8, 1989, in Kenny Whitlock's office. Those in attendance were Kenny Whitlock, Tom Jewart, Frank Loftus, Bill Freeburn, Jerry Evans and myself.

To briefly summarize the proposal, EDS plans to establish an integrated system that will both improve recipient access to Medicaid and significantly increase our service to providers while simultaneously saving substantial administrative and program dollars. The proposal is fully described in the booklet prepared by EDS which was given to you by Bill Freeburn.

Preliminary Cost Benefit Study

The figures cited below were put together quickly and consolidate easily verifiable costs and savings. It is a simplistic, although accurate first glance at project cost effectiveness.

Obviously, more detailed work needs to be pursued before writing and submission of an Advance Planning Document, which HCFA will require before providing federal match. Incidentally, Larry Lawson confirmed that 50% FFP would be available, at the least, if we can demonstrate favorable cost benefit ratios. The FFP could be as high as 75% to 90%. He also stated

CASE STUDIES

Memo to Ray Hanley
September 22, 1989
Page 2

his opinion that a competitive procurement would be required because of the size of the project and federal regulations described in Section 11 of the State Medicaid Manual and within federal procurement regulations. This process could take 6 months or more.

The costs and estimated benefits are described in the table below:

COSTS

5,700 provider units X $700 each= $3,990,000

BENEFITS

EDS Reduced Claim Processing Rates= *Occurs because 90% ECS rate will require less data entry*	$ 700,000
Pre-editing Cost Savings #1= *Ineligible/Benefit Limit*	$ 800,000
Pre-editing Cost Savings #2= *Prescription Drugs*	$ 480,000
Pre-editing Cost Savings #3= *TPL Pay and Chase*	$ 400,000
Date Specific Eligibility=	$2,800,000
Postage Savings Recipient Denial=	$1,000,000
Other Postage/Production Savings= *Recipient ID Cards*	$ 540,000
Total Estimated Benefits/Savings	$6,720,000

EXCESS OF BENEFITS/SAVINGS TO COST

Benefits/Savings Minus Cost= $2,730,000

As you can see from the above table, it is conservatively estimated that some $2.7 million can be saved through various cost diversions during the four year period between January, 1990 and December, 1993, as a result of implementing the Electronic Benefit Proposal submitted by EDS.

Memo to Ray Hanley
September 22, 1989
Page 3

Kenny Whitlock was interested in the cost effectiveness of this project during the current biennium, July, 1989 through June, 1991. Because of the huge outlay required to purchase the provider microcomputer/point of sale devices, I would think that it would be difficult to achieve more benefits than project costs during this period. I would guess that the only way this could be achieved is through gradual purchase and implementation of the provider units (e.g., start with 1,500 units during the first year) and for the date specific eligibility savings to be greater than expected.

Actions Which May Result in More Favorable Cost Benefits

As I have mentioned to you and Kenny, I believe the savings due to date specific eligibility could be greater than $675,000 per year.

Sara Mingledorf in the Alabama Medicaid program studied this during the past several years. This study looked at the entire universe of claims paid past the case closure date. She estimates that $3.0 to $4.0 million would result with their program. They have nearly 400,000 eligibles compared to our 265,000 (both unduplicated counts). Their expenditures are $550 million compared to our $485 million. If their ratio of date specific eligibility savings to total expenditures were applied to Arkansas expenditures, we could expect around $2.6 million in savings.

This, combined with the prevelent belief of experts that savings for date specific eligiblity are generally higher than you expect, point to further study. We are now in the process of looking at this. The methodology involves getting from ACES/OIS a complete identification of the recipients for FFY 1989 who had eligibility segments during the year that were closed. We will get recipient name, recipient ID, add date and close date. Then, EDS will apply the results to FFY 1989 paid claims to identify the medicaid payments made on behalf of these recipients after case closure. Tom Jewart estimates that 35 hours would be required for EDS to accomplish this. This information should be available during the next couple of weeks.

In the meantime, we will begin putting together the advance planning document. I think we also need to discuss the details of the project with Larry Lawson of HCFA. These actions will be taken if you approve.

BC:mac

cc: Connie Alexander files / bcc: Bill Freeburn

CASE STUDIES

DIVISION OF ECONOMIC & MEDICAL SERVICES
MEMORANDUM

TO: Ray Hanley, Assistant Deputy Director, OMS

FROM: Bill Carpenter, Administrator, OMS Systems & Support

DATE: March 19, 1990

SUBJ: Attached Report Entitled, "Automated Eligibility Claims Submission", Dated March 2, 1990

The purpose of this memo is to transmit the above captioned report. It requests that you, Kenny Whitlock and any other appropriate agency personnel, review the document and provide us with feedback.

Also attached, is a copy of the AEVS/EBT Preliminary Work Plan, dated February, 1990. Note that one of the tasks is "Detailed Plan Selected and Finalized", which was due February 28, 1990. The attached report is the "deliverable" that satisfies that task. We hope your comprehensive review and comment can result in the identification of specific adds, changes or deletions to the document. These changes will then be incorporated into the next deliverable, the Advance Planning Document, which will be submitted to the Health Care Financing Administration (HCFA).

One item that is not included within the report is the Cost Analysis. This includes the detailed analysis of project cost and benefits that would justify whether the project is worthwhile from a monetary standpoint. This section of the report cannot be completed until the DHS-357, dated March 8, 1990, is processed by DHS Office of Information Services (OIS). On March 9, 1990, Kenny Whitlock requested a high priority via a memo he sent to OIS. A copy of the memo is attached. We anticipate that this project will be complete by March 30.

Our agency comment should be complete by the first week in April. Realistically, this is the date in which changes to the attached document should be completed, and, the finalization of an Advance Planning Document, suitable for submission to HCFA.

Note the Statement of Confidentiality on page 2 of the report. This statement emphasizes EDS' desire to keep details of this document strictly confidential since proprietary information is involved.

Please contact me if you have any questions. Also, let me know if you would like us to perform any additional work on this project.

BC;mac

cc: Tom Jewart
    Ed Merck
    Connie Alexander

Attachments

*Connie,
Please review carefully. My project file is available. Risk to Agency is considerable, so be critical. Due 30 Mar.
Thanks,
Bill*

This document mentions an Advanced Planning Document. It is obvious that EDS had several years to have a product demonstration ready. Also, HCFA was apparently reviewing the Advanced Planning Document with Arkansas Department of Human Services.

Division of Economic and Medical Services
MEMORANDUM

TO: Ray Hanley, Asst. Deputy Director, OMS

FROM: Bill Carpenter, Administrator, Systems and Support

DATE: June 22, 1990

SUBJ: AEVCS Advance Planning Documents dated June 11, 1990

Attached to this memo are three copies of the AEVCS Advance Planning Document.

As we discussed by phone, I will keep one copy and forward an additional copy to Sarah Mingleddrff in Alabama.

As I mentioned, this document has changed from previous versions in that the cost of the equipment fell by $100,000 to $2,049,810. This was the result of a last minute price reduction offered by VeriFone. These figures are in the possession of Larry Lawson at HCFA.

As a reminder, we obviously have not received "sole sourcing" authority from HCFA. Therefore, there remains some possibility that HCFA would cause us to conduct a competitive procurement. In view of this, we would not want the equipment pricing information released outside this agency. I am virtually certain that this would be a violation of state procurement regulations.

Let me know if you have any questions.

BC/mm
cc: Connie Alexander
    Ed Mercki
    Files

Sarah Mingledorff is mentioned in this document. I mentioned our meeting with Alabama in the case study. Sarah Mingledorff was the person MediClaim had the meeting with.

CASE STUDIES

Arkansas Department of Human Services
Division of Economic and Medical Services

P.O. Box 1437
Little Rock, Arkansas 72203-1437
FAX (501) 682-6571

Bill Clinton
Governor

Terry Yamauchi, M.D.
Director

Kenny Whitlock
Deputy Director

June 28, 1990

Ms. Sarah Mingledorff
Director, Data Management
Alabama Medicaid Agency
2500 Fairlane Drive
Montgomery, Alabama 36130

Dear Sarah:

At your request, I have attached a copy of Arkansas' Advance Planning Document entitled, "Automated Eligibility Verification and Claims Submission". This APD was submitted to the Health Care Financing Administration, Region VI, on June 11, 1990.

We believe the attached Advance Planning Document is comprehensive and self-explanatory. It should require little elaboration. One point should be added. The detailed pricing information related to EBT POS devices has been omitted. This information is viewed as proprietary by our fiscal agent, Electronic Data Systems Federal. The State of Arkansas obviously has not received "sole sourcing" authority from HCFA. Therefore, there remains some possibility that HCFA would cause us to conduct a competitive procurement. In view of this, we would not want the equipment pricing information released outside this agency. Only after sole sourcing authority is granted by HCFA, will we release pricing information for this project.

We trust this information will be useful to you. Please contact us if you have questions.

Sincerely,

Bill Carpenter

Bill Carpenter, Administrator
OMS Systems and Support

cc: Ray Hanley
    Tom Jewart
    Files

"The Arkansas Department of Human Services is in compliance with Titles VI and VII of the Civil Rights Act and is operated, managed and delivers services without regard to age, religion, handicap, sex, race, color or national origin."

ZEROS AND HEROES OF BUSINESS

DIVISION OF ECONOMIC AND MEDICAL SERVICES
MEMORANDUM

TO: Ray Hanley, Assistant Deputy Director, OMS

FROM: Bill Carpenter, Administrator, Systems & Support

DATE: October 10, 1990

SUBJ: Automated Eligibility Verification & Claim Submission APD--HCFA Verbal Response to our September 28, 1990 Letter

---

The purpose of this memo is to document a summary of a phone call I had late this afternoon with Phil Koether, HCFA Region VI, regarding the above captioned topic.

On September 28, 1990, we submitted a letter to Mr. J. C. Street of HCFA that responded to problems/issues related to the AEVCS project. Phil reported that a preliminary phone conference would be held tomorrow between Region VI and Baltimore Central Office. The purpose is to address our responses and to formulate HCFA's position regarding the future of the project. Phil assured me that we will have an opportunity to provide our input with regard to the questions discussed before a final decision is made.

Phil asked me several questions related to our September 28 responses. First, from dot point #5 (9/28/90 HCFA letter), related to the "current transaction charge estimates and costs to be used for calculating them", he wanted a detailed look at the development and operational costs charged by EDS. I anticipated EDS would insist on this, but did not include it in the 9/28 response at EDS' request.

At the transaction costs and volumes cited in EDS' memo of May 31, 1990, EDS stands to gross $5.4 million from this project during the next 3 years. This excludes the $2.0 million we can expect from reduced claims processing rates. We need to know how much of this gross revenue would be for development and operational expense and how much would be for profit and overhead. The way to get this information is to ask EDS for Developmental costs by line item and for Operational costs by line item for each year of the project (similar to the method used in obtaining costs for the fiscal agent contract). By copy of this memo to EDS, I am requesting they provide this information.

Second, Phil questioned whether the provider eligibility queries would go back for greater than 1 year. I thought we had the capability to go back for 24 months and told him that. HCFA sent us an "all-states" letter that limited queries to one year, along with several other restrictions. I assured him our project personnel had the letter, were reviewing it's requirements and would fully comply with it's contents. This item was discussed at last week's AEVCS project meeting.

Third, he asked if the additional cost EDS mentioned in their May 31, 1990, letter to us had been completely identified. I told him that EDS had estimated the total costs at around $500,000 for ". . cards, card production, publishing of support material..", and, ". . field training. .". This information has been communicated verbally to me by EDS. By copy of this memo to EDS, I am requesting they provide this information.

Fourth, regarding the competitive/sole source procurement issue, dot point #1, Phil offered several comments or posed added questions. He asked why the State and EDS had elected to use only two companies as sources for the equipment. I emphasized (1) the economies that would result by sole source procurement, and, (2) our belief that the two companies represented the best products available. Also alluded to the other items in our letter.

No wonder EDS had the price advantage, HCFA and Arkansas Department of Human Services had been working on pricing two years prior to the competitive bid.

Letter to Ray Hanley
October 10, 1990
Page 2

Phil asked, if the project would continue if competitive procurement were required. He further queried whether EDS would/could continue the project if another source of equipment were selected. I responded that the project would continue. According to what I have been told, EDS is flexible with regard to working with another equipment vendor, however, they believe the equipment identified represents the best. EDS has indicated that compatibility problems might result from selection of another vendor, but, they could in all likelihood be worked out.

Phil added regarding the competitive/sole source issue that HCFA Baltimore Central Office officials are divided on whether to authorize federal funds for buying ADP equipment for providers. For that reason, they may take the position this equipment is not ADP for MMIS purposes, and, may elect to authorize limited or no FFP for the project. In the event the project is not funded by HCFA, he suggested alternative project planning should be developed (a number of possibilities exist).

The other points in the letter were acceptable from Phil's perspective. I closed by emphasizing the features, advantages and benefits of the project. Added emphasis was given to the automatic generation of TPL claims on the provider's behalf and future on-line Prescription Drug and Prospective DUR claim processing.

Phil told me he personally believes the project should be approved and will take whatever action possible to achieve that outcome. He believes we have better than a 50/50 chance of receiving some level of FFP for the project. He will give us a progress report on the meeting sometime tomorrow afternoon.

Let me know if you have questions.

BC;mac

cc: Tom Jewart
        Ed Merck
        AEVCS Project File
        files

DIVISION OF ECONOMIC & MEDICAL SERVICES

MEMORANDUM

TO: Ray Hanley, Assistant Deputy Director, OMS

FROM: Bill Carpenter, Administrator, OMS Systems & Support

DATE: October 12, 1990

SUBJ: AEVCS Phone Contact with Phil Koether, HCFA, Region VI

This is to follow-up our memo of October 10 in which I noted to you that Region VI would conduct a conference call with their Central Office regarding the disposition of the AEVCS project.

After the conference call (conducted yesterday), Phil Koether reported to me this morning that he was "... 95% confident ..." that Arkansas would be approved for 75% FFP on our AEVCS project. This, of course, is unofficial since it has not been placed into writing and only reflects Phil's opinion. However, it is very encouraging.

Phil also noted that HCFA would insist on us conducting a competitive procurement. This has always been HCFA's stance on procurements this large. They believe, in spite of the convincing information we have put together, that the competitive market place will produce the best possible outcome. We will contact DF & A State Purchasing next week to begin involving them. Additionally, we will begin other work next week associated with producing an RFP. It is estimated that this development will add an additional three months to the project. We expect to implement sometime during the July to October 91 time frame.

Other questions resulting from Phils call were related to: monitoring transaction charges to the provider; provider survey's on equipment; mandating 100% provider participation; EBT component of project and legal assurances on claim or back of check. More information on these items will be provided at a later date.

Phil concluded by saying Arkansas would be looked at closely because of their "pioneer" role with the AEVCS project. It was because of our APD that HCFA is about to add new material to the State Medicaid Manual that will lay the groundwork for HCFA participation in POS projects for all states. Because of the "pilot project" nature of the AEVCS, we can expect to receive a lot of detailed review from HCFA. They will be especially interested in the provider's reaction to the AEVCS and in cost benefit information.

Of course, this is very good news for DHS DEMS, however, it will continue to place more concentrated work demands on Systems & Support as well as other parts of DHS, DEMS and OMS. I would expect that part of our strategy in meeting these demands is to construct a formalized project work team composed of representatives throughout OMS. It would not hurt either to get a replacement Programmer Analyst.

BC;mac

cc: Tom Jewart
OMS Admin.
Ed Merck
Files

I find this document interesting because Arkansas is trying to receive Federal matching of funds for their "pioneer role" with the AEVCS project. MediClaim Incorporated had already implemented the technology in the State of Florida. How is this pioneering? Also, HCFA makes a decision to put this out for a competitive bid (give me a brake–how fake).

CASE STUDIES

DIVISION OF ECONOMIC AND MEDICAL SERVICES
MEMORANDUM

TO: Ray Hanley, Assistant Director, OMS

FROM: Bill Carpenter, Administrator, OMS Systems and Support

DATE: June 13, 1991

SUBJ: AEVCS Project Update

As requested in this weeks OMS Staff Meeting, the following text explains work recently completed on the AEVCS project. It also identifies several tasks/issues/problems that must be overcome before the project can continue.

REQUIREMENTS ANALYSIS VOLUME PROBLEMS

The attached draft memo dated May, 1991, was given to Tom Jewart on May 14, 1991. It lists 10 issues that block State approval of the EDS AEVCS Requirements Analysis document.

Tom Jewart responded to these questions in his letter to me dated May 24, 1991 (copy attached). His response did not address all issues clearly. On June 3, 1991, we sent Tom a letter (copy attached) that addressed these problems. On Thursday, June 6, 1991, a meeting was held between Systems and Support and EDS to discuss these problems. The meeting was some three and one half hours in duration and required EDS to produce a significant amount of responses/information for the project to proceed. Tom understands the issues and will respond quickly. I am asking Tom by copy of this memo to respond in writing with regard to a date in which this information can be obtained. Systems and Support is working with both EDS and OMS personnel to coordinate and solve other problems.

INVITATION FOR BID PROBLEMS

The AEVCS IFB was submitted to both the Health Care Financing Administration and the Arkansas Department of Computer Services. HCFA's Phil Koether offered forty two comments via a phone call on May 9, 1991. Sanford Cothren of DCS offered twenty three comments on May 17, 1991. These questions are included as an attachment dated 5/23/91.

These IFB problems are generally minor obstacles and can be corrected quickly. The most significant obstacles are associated with attaining answers from EDS and state staff which will allow us to accept the Requirements Analysis volume, and, in attaining added EDS supplied information that will allow us to complete both the revised Advance Planning Document and AEVCS Invitation for Bid.

Another significant problem is in developing a seperate IFB to competitively secure the plastic ID cards. This was discussed in our meeting with EDS on June 6, 1991. We are now working with both New York and Massachusettes state representatives to secure information necessary in producing an IFB.

I will work with Tom Jewart to determine when all of this information can be obtained.

BC:mac

cc: Tom Jewart
    Ed Merck
    Patty O'Malley
    Files   Attachments

EDS gets all this special treatment. Phone calls, participation in Advanced Planning Documents, updates…..Why has MediClaim not been treated with the same equal opportunity?

DIVISION OF ECONOMIC AND MEDICAL SERVICES

MEMORANDUM

TO: Ray Hanley, Assistant Director, OMS

FROM: Bill Carpenter, Administrator, OMS Systems and Support

DATE: July 19, 1991

SUBJ: AEVCS Project --Revised APD Cost Benefit Analysis

I have attached revised pages from the AEVCS project APD to be submitted to HCFA today. These pages include the revisions presented to you and Tom Jewart in my office yesterday. These new calculations have been collected during the past several weeks. Unfortunately, they represent significant changes from those in the first version of the APD submitted to HCFA in 1990.

The first two attachments are entitled "Cost Benefit Analysis". The first shows Benefits/Savings Minus Cost of $6,020,625.60. The second shows Benefits/Savings Minus Cost of $2,050,448. This represents a reduction of benefits in the amount of $3,970,178. This is primarily because of the changes in federal regulations that allow telecommunications cost to be passed through to HCFA and paid with 75 percent federal funding. Previously, these costs were to be paid by providers. Other costs have been added that were previously to be absorbed by EDS. These new costs are either to be shifted to the winning contractor of the IFB upon which we are now working, or, paid to EDS to cover added costs they have recently identified.

The second two attachments are entitled "Estimated Transaction Prices". The first shows old transaction prices (Eligibility--$0.21; Pharmacy--$0.24; Other Claim--$0.29) that would be charged to providers which include telecommunication charges. The second shows new transaction prices (Eligibility--$0.10; Pharmacy--$0.15; Other Claim--$0.15) that would be charged to providers which exclude telecommunication charges and assumes HCFA will pay them. Total yearly cost of transaction fees under both scenarios is document under the notes section.

Note also that several changes have been made to the benefits expected to accrue as a result of this project. These changes were made in recognition of the substantial increase in claims volume and numbers of medicaid recipients due to program expansion during the past year or so.

Let me know if you have any comments/instructions in response to this information.

BC:mac

cc: Tom Jewart
Ed Merck
Patty O'Malley
Files

Attachments

Two months prior to the bid opening and this memo is negotiating transaction pricing with EDS. EDS as not been awarded the bid yet, what is going on with this memo?

CASE STUDIES

COST BENEFIT ANALYSIS

The following table shows the associated hardware costs and the benefits derived from automated eligibility verification and claims submission.

COSTS

	Administrative	Programmatic
Total Cost to Purchase Equipment	$2,286,750.00	
POS Device Maintenance	200,000.00	
POS Help Desk/Programming of POS	175,000.00	
Recipient ID Card Production	500,000.00	
LTC MMIS Changes to Accomodate AEVCS	67,252.00	
Billing Manual Changes	280,550.00	
Added SE's To Modify MMIS Due to AEVCS	200,000.00	
Telecommunications Transaction Charges	4,320,000.00	
Total Project Costs	$8,029,552.00	

Handwritten annotation: AEVCS — $3,161,750.00

ESTIMATED SAVINGS OVER FOUR YEARS

	Administrative	Programmatic
Potential EDS Reduced Claim Processing Rates	$3,000,000.00	
Date Specific Eligibility		$4,500,000.00
Postage Savings from mailing fewer Recipient Denial letters	840,000.00	
Other Postage Savings from not mailing paper Recipient ID Cards	1,740,000.00	
Savings by category	$5,580,000.00	$4,500,000.00
Total Savings		$10,080,000.00

EXCESS OF BENEFITS/SAVINGS TO COST

Benefits/Savings Minus Cost	$2,050,448

ZEROS AND HEROES OF BUSINESS

Arkansas Department of Human Services
Division of Economic and Medical Services

P.O. Box 1437
Little Rock, Arkansas 72203-1437

Bill Clinton
Governor

Terry Yamauchi, M.D.
Department Director

Kenny Whitlock
Division Director

January 30, 1992

Mr. Phil Koether, Systems Analyst
Health Care Financing Administration, Region VI
Financial Management Branch
1200 Main Tower Building
Dallas, Texas 75202

Dear Phil:

This correspondence follows up a letter sent to you on January 14, 1992. That letter asked for HCFA approval of the AEVCS contract. We are supplying other HCFA requested information which applies to that contract.

You requested in our phone conversation several days ago for a modification of the APD to reflect the bid amount of EDS. Additionally, you requested changes made to the AEVCS professional services contract between EDS and the State.

I have attached a copy of the revised Cost Benefit Analysis section (page 10) from the APD document submitted to HCFA last July. It includes increased requests for funding of $490,548 due to higher than anticipated project costs received in EDS' business/technical proposals for the AEVCS project.

Also attached are several changed pages from the professional services contract. These changes are all minor in nature and have no substantial impact on the contract. The reasons for the changes are described in the attached letter from myself to Mr. Bob Batson of EDS.

Finally, you noted in a conversation with me this morning that HCFA would not approve the enhancements/rates described in Pricing Schedules A, B & C of the EDS bid. You stated that each enhancement would be viewed as a separate procurement requiring prior HCFA approval. We acknowledge and will comply with this requirement.

Let me know if I can provide any further information or assistance.

Sincerely,

Bill Carpenter, Administrator
DHS DEMS Office of Medical Services

cc: Ray Hanley

"The Arkansas Department of Human Services is in compliance with Titles VI and VII of the Civil Rights Act and is operated, managed and delivers services without regard to age, religion, handicap, sex, race, color or national origin."

Still referring to the Advanced Planning Document (two years ago) not holding EDS to their bid price submitted September of 1991.

CASE STUDIES

ARKANSAS MEDICAID
Advance Planning Document — Cost Analysis

COST BENEFIT ANALYSIS

The following table shows the associated hardware costs and the benefits derived from automated eligibility verification and claims submission.

COSTS

	Administrative	Programmatic
Total Cost to Purchase Equipment	$1,874,284.00	
POS Device Maintenance	418,108.00	
POS Help Desk/Programming of POS	1,124,276.00	
Recipient ID Card Production	235,630.00	
LTC MMIS Changes to Accomodate AEVCS	67,252.00	
Billing Manual Changes	280,550.00	
Added SE's To Modify MMIS Due to AEVCS	200,000.00	
Telecommunications Transaction Charges	4,320,000.00	
Total Project Costs	$8,520,100.00	

1,542,384

3,652,298.00

ESTIMATED SAVINGS OVER FOUR YEARS

	Administrative	Programmatic
Potential FA Reduced Claim Processing Rates	$3,000,000.00	
Date Specific Eligibility		$4,500,000.00
Postage Savings from mailing fewer Recipient Denial letters	840,000.00	
Other Postage Savings from not mailing paper Recipient ID Cards	1,740,000.00	
Savings by category	$5,580,000.00	$4,500,000.00
Total Savings		$10,080,000.00

EXCESS OF BENEFITS/SAVINGS TO COST

Benefits/Savings Minus Cost		$1,559,900.00

OMS

Third Revision January, 1992

ZEROS AND HEROES OF BUSINESS

M E M O R A N D U M

TO: Bill Carpenter, Administrator, Systems & Support

FROM: Ed Merck, Manager, Contract Monitoring

DATE: April 8, 1992

SUBJ: AEVCS Cost Benefit Analysis Estimate

A rough estimate of a revised Cost Benefit Analysis after recent changes to the AEVCS concept, as I understand it, is:

```
COSTS

    Cost to Purchase Equipment                  1,605,256
    POS Maintenance/Help Desk/Programming         647,904
    Recipient ID Card Production                  226,150
    LTC MMIS Changes for AEVCS                     67,252
    Billing Manual Changes                        280,550
    Added SE's to Modify MMIS for AEVCS           200,000
    Telecommunications Transaction Charges      4,258,000
    Total Project Costs                         7,285,112

ESTIMATED SAVINGS OVER FOUR YEARS

    Potential FA Reduced Rates                  2,500,000
    Date Specific Eligibility                              3,750,000
    Postage Savings--fewer
        Recipient Denial letters                  700,000
    Other Postage Savings--not
        mailing Recipient ID Cards              1,450,000
    Savings by category                         4,650,000  3,750,000
    Total Savings                                          8,400,000

EXCESS OF BENEFITS/SAVINGS TO COST

    Benefits/Savings Minus Cost                            1,114,888
```

There are costs associated with our current inability to perform normal maintenance/modification work to the MMIS. The dedication of experienced MMIS SE's to AEVCS work has resulted in a decline in support of work requested by the OMS staff, beyond my ability to evaluate in terms of costs.

Cost figures were reduced to reflect provider survey results which seem to indicate no purchase of the microcomputer interface. The reduction of costs for both purchase and maintenance

CASE STUDIES

of the PNC330 is approximately $1,400,000. It should be noted that if that is added back in to these figures, the costs exceed the benefits. The data for ID Card Production and Telecommunications Charges are reduced to reflect the shortened time period remaining from the startup date and the end of the four year period.

There has been recent communication concerning the obligation of the State to purchase equipment for the Voice Response System. Costs for that have not been included.

Savings figures are reduced by converting previously estimated savings over a forty-eight month period to a 40 month period. No adjustments were made for any changed claim volume, since previous estimates included projected increases.

Consideration should be given to the plastic ID card costs. If it is to be the case that 68% of the providers will not have equipment to read the cards, it may not be cost beneficial to change the card production system. Date specific eligibility can be implemented without the plastic cards.

cc: Patty O'Malley

Arkansas, Patty O'Malley, mentions something very interesting in this document. Verifone Incorporated gave EDS a lower price on the PNC330 computer terminal. This was the terminal that the bid requested. Even though we did a demonstration of personal computer software that could be sold at one-tenth the cost of these terminals, MediClaim had to include Verifone technology in our bid pricing.

Arkansas Department of Human Services
Division of Economic and Medical Services

P.O. Box 1437
Little Rock, Arkansas 72203-1437

Bill Clinton
Governor

Terry Yamauchi, M.D.
Department Director

Kenny Whitlock
Division Director

MEMORANDUM

TO: Tom Jewart, Executive Program Director, EDS

FROM: Bill Carpenter, Administrator, OMS Systems & Support

DATE: April 16, 1992

SUBJ: HCFA Request for Detailed Status Report on AEVCS Project

I have attached a FAX copy of a letter sent by HCFA Region VI. The letter is dated yesterday and requests by the end of next week a detailed status report. In order that the State may prepare a timely response to HCFA, please address the questions/issues in the HCFA letter thru written analysis by close of business Wednesday, April 22, 1992.

As you can see, HCFA has mentioned the possibility of either suspending or disallowing funding for this project. To prevent this, a detailed status report on the AEVCS should be accomplished which shows reasons for project delays, a revised cost benefit analysis based on current information with new project milestones and justifications and summary of current provider reaction.

Many of these issues have either been previously documented or will be as a result of the AEVCS project meeting held yesterday. However, it would be beneficial for us to meet for the purpose of systematically coordinating and planning an appropriate response. I propose Monday at 3:30 P.M. for this purpose. Let me know if this time is acceptable.

Please contact me if you have questions.

BC;mac

cc: Ray Hanley, OMS Deputy Director
Chuck Wilson
Patty O'Malley
Ed Merck
files

Attachment

"The Arkansas Department of Human Services is in compliance with Titles VI and VII of the Civil Rights Act and is operated, managed and delivers services without regard to age, religion, handicap, sex, race, color or national origin."

Seven months later, EDS has not produced the technology to do the AEVCS project. HCFA is thinking about pulling the Federal matched funding because no progress has been made to deliver a product.

CASE STUDIES

DIVISION OF ECONOMIC & MEDICAL SERVICES

MEMORANDUM

TO: Ray Hanley, Assistant Director, OMS

FROM: Bill Carpenter, Administrator, OMS Systems & Support

DATE: May 4, 1992

SUBJ: Summary/Analysis of May 1, 1992 Meeting with Dudley Meadows, DF&A Purchasing & Property Management

The purpose of this memo is to summarize a meeting held on Friday, May 1, 1992, with Dudley Meadows regarding the change in scope and direction of the AEVCS project.

Attending were Ed Merck, Patty O'Malley and myself from DHS and Dudley and Becky O"Neal from DF&A. The meeting was prompted by my memo to Dudley dated April 28, 1992. A copy of that memo is attached.

The issues discussed were (1) the EDS change in direction and scope regarding offering the option of Emerald software on providers Medicaid billing systems and addition of eligibility card readers, and, (2) the April 20 EDS letter (copy attached, along with February 7 state memo that may have prompted it) regarding status of the AEVCS contract.

Dudley believes from reviewing the issue that the best course of action is to stop the AEVCS contract between DHS DEMS and EDS. He will seek confirmation from Ed Erxlaben on this recommendation before it is formalized. Additionally, he is unsure whether by state law if DHS/DEMS will be bound by any final recommendation/decision. The basis for his recommendation is that the scope and nature of the contract at procurement compared to now has drastically changed. He believes that MediClaim and perhaps other potential bidders could claim they were not party to the final requirements of this contract at procurement time. If they were party to existing, proposed changes, Dudley contends, they could build a case that their organizations could have offered a cheaper price and better service. Refer to our memo of April 28 to Dudley for more background.

The April 20 EDS letter was also briefly discussed in which EDS contends there is no contract because the state changed it after signing. Actually, the contract was not changed after signing. The change was not agreed upon by DHS DEMS so the proposed wording was removed. Dudley advised us to bring the letter to the attention of our Office of Chief Counsel.

Memo to Ray Hanley
5/4/92
Page 2

I would suggest we wait with respect to taking any action regarding the AEVCS contract. The written response from DF&A Purchasing and Property Management should first be evaluated. We should then thoroughly examine all of our alternatives before deciding on a course of action. Some of the available alternatives include the following:

- Stop the contract and re-bid immediately
- Stop the contract and roll AEVCS into the next fiscal agent contract
- Continue the contract in the present direction and risk law suits from MediClaim and perhaps other potential AEVCS bidders
- Negotiate changes to the project direction that would not be so onerous

A number of considerations exist that affect our course of action. One important consideration is that EDS may claim, if we stop the contract, that we owe them for the development completed to date. This would include changes to the MMIS (including OLTP development) and work currently completed by the EDS Payment Services Division. Perhaps this should be weighed against any liability that may exist from MediClaim or other affected bidders. Another important consideration is that coming up with a suitable solution for providers and simultaneously assuring procurement integrity may be difficult. Be aware that I am also under obligation to report the outcome of this meeting to Phil Koether of HCFA.

Contact me if you have questions.

BC; mac

cc: Bill Freeburn
Bruce Hurlbut
files

Attachments

Another interesting document, MediClaim Incorporated demonstrated all of this technology as well as made these suggestions to Arkansas Medicaid Department. Not once has anyone called MediClaim Incorporated to resolve the very issues we warned the evaluation committee during the September 1991 demonstration.

CASE STUDIES

Thursday, May 14, 1992

EDS

Mr. Bill Carpenter, Administrator
Systems & Support Section
Department of Human Services
101 E. Capitol, Suite 470
Little Rock, Arkansas 72201

Dear Mr. Carpenter:

I have prepared this letter in response to Mr. Dudley Meadows' letter of May 7 in which he stated his belief that the scope of the Arkansas AEVCS project "has significantly been altered from the original Invitation For Bid." We have not been provided the information given to Mr. Meadows that led him to this conclusion. It is our position that the scope of the Arkansas AEVCS project has not been altered in any way whatsoever.

In our response to the Invitation for Bid, EDS/PSD agreed to provide point-of-sale (POS) devices, terminal application software, magnetically-encoded recipient identification cards, and training and Help Desk services. The Arkansas IFB denoted four categories of POS equipment: full-function, microcomputer interface, limited function, and printers. The equipment EDS/PSD has proposed for each category fully meets or exceeds each requirement of the original IFB. The IFB also provided the estimated quantity of POS devices needed in each category. As the State was careful to identify that the POS equipment requirements were "estimated", it also required the bidders to provide unit costs that could be applied to any device quantity to compute a total cost.

The concerns that led to Mr. Meadow's letter have their origin in the results of the provider survey which we conducted on behalf of the State. This survey which was conducted in March was not part of the IFB proposal, and was performed at no charge to the State. However, it was conducted because the State wanted to confirm its original estimates for specific POS devices. The survey of three rural counties indicated a strong demand for the full-function terminal, a moderate demand for the limited-function terminal, and weak demand for the microcomputer interface terminal. The requirements for the full-function and limited-function terminals appear to be in alignment with the State's IFB forecast. The demand for the microcomputer interface (the VeriFone PNC 330) is well below the original expectations.

I gave my views in previous correspondence to the State that the lack of demand in this very narrow survey did not necessarily indicate a lack of overall demand for the PNC 330. However, I do believe it is evident that the original forecast for the placement of 2,900 of these units will not be achieved. This does not change the scope of the bid, it only changes the quantity ordered.

As a result of the three-county survey, you asked me to consider additional ways that we could support the provider community. At a meeting on April 14, both you and Bill Freeburn asked me to investigate ways in which EDS could meet the needs of providers who had invested in a PC-based system, but who did not have a need for a PNC 330.

Bill, you shared with me your concerns regarding the providers' lack of a card swipe mechanism on their PC. As you recall, there is no requirement to swipe a card, as the provider can keystroke the same information in order to access the AEVCS system. However, for reasons of convenience and transaction speed, I suggested that providers could procure and attach a card reader to their PC if they wished. You asked me to research the cost for such a device in case the State chose to offer that enhancement to providers who might choose the PC software solution.

Payment Services Division
TR-04-151
18111 Preston Road

Mr. Bill Carpenter
May 14, 1992
Page 2

I provided you with that information in my April 21 memorandum as you directed. EDS/PSD has responded to the State's request for information: it is not proposing to change the IFB to incorporate a card reader device.

In response to your request to suggest "creative ways in which we can work with the PC-based providers", I suggested a stand-alone PC software interface to AEVCS in a memorandum to you dated April 21. This was a constructive suggestion to strengthen the State's program and to better support the State's provider community. This suggestion carries no commitment by EDS or by the State. It certainly does not alter the scope of the project in any way, as there is no additional cost associated with this option.

It is important to note that the PC software is not a replacement for the PNC 330, and has not been positioned as such. The PNC 330 gives the provider the capability to communicate with the data network. His system would have to be changed to communicate with the PNC 330. However, many providers do not wish to change their systems and desire to use their own telecommunications capabilities already in place. For those providers whose PC-based systems have no modems, the PNC 330 may present an attractive solution.

Given that we proceed with the PC full-function software solution, it will probably reduce the amount of Emerald devices that would otherwise have been deployed. If a provider's system does not interface to AEVCS, then he would need to rekey the claim onto an Emerald device. If we provided software to emulate the Emerald's functions on his own system, it would eliminate the need for another Emerald device, saving the State money.

Currently, the fiscal agent gives to providers a free stand-alone software package to enter ECS claims. Tom Jewart, the Executive Program Director, has planned for some time now to provide the same stand-alone PC package interface with AEVCS that providers now enjoy with ECS. The need for a PC-based software package to support practice management systems is not related to the lack of demand for the PNC 330. Instead, it reflects the tremendous ECS growth experienced in the State's Medicaid claims (now over 60%); and it underscores the State's posture in supporting its provider community.

I am sure that Mr. Meadows has the best interests of the State in mind. However, I do not believe that the information provided to Mr. Dudley is a complete reflection of what has actually occurred. The changes and suggested program revisions associated with the AEVCS initiative have all been originated by the State of Arkansas, have been limited in number, and have been consistent with the scope of the Arkansas AEVCS IFB.

Sincerely,

Chuck Wilson

J. CHARLES WILSON
EDS Project Director for Arkansas AEVCS

cc: Bill Carpenter   Bill Freeburn   Ray Hanley
    Martha Hulse   Tom Jewart   Phil Koether
    Frank Loftus   Dudley Meadows   Ed Merck
    Patty O'Malley   Kenny Whitlock

CASE STUDIES

Thursday, September 3, 1992

Mr. Ray Hanley, Director
Office of Medical Services
Arkansas Division of Economic and Medical Services
Seventh and Main Street
P.O. Box 1437
Little Rock, Arkansas 72203

Re: Interim Extension of Two SEs for Sixty Days

Dear Ray,

This letter requests your approval to extend the time period for two SEs supporting MMIS for 60 days. One of the two SE's time frame expires today, therefore, this proposal will extend that SE from September 4, 1992 to November 4, 1992. The second SE contract will expire on October 9, 1992, therefore, this proposal will extend that SE through December 9, 1992.

We propose that the State approve the interim extension for the use of these two on-site SEs. These SEs will continue to be used to work on the State's MMIS projects. The cost per month for each SE will be $5,706.67. The CPU resources for the two additional SEs would be billed to the State at the contract rates up to a maximum of $2,000 per month per SE.

Please indicate your approval by returning this letter with your signature. Please let me know if you have any questions.

Sincerely,

Mark Noble

cc: Bill Carpenter
Tom Jewart
Susan Robertson

Approval for Extension of Two SEs
Approval: _____ Ray Hanley _____ Date: 9/3/92

Approval for Extension of Two SEs
Approval: _____ Bill Carpenter _____ Date: 9/8/92

101 East Capitol Avenue, Suite 300
Little Rock, Arkansas 72201
(501) 374-6608
Fax: (800) 457-4454

EDS is asking for more money. Why is the State of Arkansas refusing to hold EDS to their original bid pricing?

Arkansas Department of Human Services
Division of Economic and Medical Services

Donaghey Plaza South
P.O. Box 1437
Little Rock, Arkansas 72203-1437
Telephone (501) 682-8375

MEMORANDUM

TO: Kenny Whitlock, Director, Services

FROM: Ray Hanley, Assistant Director

DATE: September 28, 1992

SUBJ: DHS-357 #3868 - Date S[...]

My intent in writing this memo is to [...] Systems (OIS) told you in August, 199[...] ready for implementation until June of 19[...]

As you are aware, the AEVCS project will be implemented beginning in late October. It will be operational state-wide by April of 1993. Our staff has been working with Economic Security and OIS since early 1990 to achieve implementation of date specific eligibility to no avail. In late May of this year, our staff prepared a memo for you to Gordon Page that clearly outlined the "imperative" of achieving date specific eligibility by October, 1992. A copy of that memo, which was sent to Mr. Page, is attached for your review.

It has been estimated that AEVCS date specific eligibility will save some one hundred thousand dollars per month. A date specific implementation delay until June of 1993 will reduce AEVCS savings by up to nine hundred thousand dollars. This is over half of the anticipated savings of one million seven hundred thousand dollars that AEVCS promises to bring.

In the AEVCS state-wide implementation meeting last Friday, Donna Johnson and Geoff Allen stated that date specific eligibility will be delayed by a pregnant programmer who will leave work in April, and, by OIS' inability to hire additional programmers. I am not sure that HCFA Region VI will be very sympathetic.

EDS states they are prepared to do whatever it takes to immediately implement date specific eligibility. Also, the Office of Information Services, in their August 5 correspondence to you, implys that EDS has not told them what needs to be on a test tape for date specific eligibility. The fact is that OIS will make this determination when they complete the project. EDS will then modify their system to accomodate the new OIS record.

What can be done to expedite completion of the date specific eligibility project?

RH;mac

cc: Bill Carpenter
    files

Caring People. . . Quality Services

"The Arkansas Department of Human Services is in compliance with Titles VI and VII of the Civil Rights Act and is operated, managed and delivers services without regard to age, religion, handicap, sex, race, color or national origin."

Why is AEVCS going to be implemented in April of 1993? The bid said that companies must begin an aggressive role-out of equipment immediately. This is nearly two years after the bid awarding.

CASE STUDIES

FRIDAY, JULY 10, 1992

COVER STORY
Recovery is sweet music to Nashville

TWITTY: Country music produces jobs, money.

By Kevin Maney
USA TODAY

NASHVILLE — If this city is what economic recovery looks like, the next few years are going to be real yawners.

Conway Twitty, for instance, has to struggle to say just how the boom in country music has affected that industry's home city.

Dressed at his office in a crisp orange T-shirt, white shorts, white baseball cap, white sneakers and white socks pulled to his knees, he notes that his concerts are selling better, Nashville recording studios are busier, record sales are jumping.

"It means jobs. It means money," says Twitty, who has had 54 No. 1 hits and has invested in several businesses. "I don't know how much it'll bring into this town this year, but it's got to be up there."

Middle Tennessee, anchored by Nashville, is surging into full-fledged economic upturn well ahead of nearly everywhere else in the nation. But ask people in the region's big industries — music, medicine, automobiles, real estate — and they have the same trouble defining the surge as Twitty. The recovery has definitely arrived, they say, but it's kind of mushy and very low-key.

Retail vacancies have inched down to 13.5% from

Please see COVER STORY next page ▶

CHRISTMAS IN JULY: National Tape founder Jerry Hutchinson, left, and salesman Jimmy Gray are handling holiday orders.

By Marcy E. Mullins, USA TODAY

ABOUT NASHVILLE
State capital
Size: 533 square miles, slightly larger than Los Angeles
Population: 510,784
Unemployment: 5.1% in April, vs. 7.2% for the USA
May median home price: $88,522, vs. $100,900 for the USA
Median rent: $359, vs. $374 for the USA
Major employers: State, county and federal governments; Vanderbilt University; city and county public schools; Opryland; Kroger; Nissan; Shoney's; South Central Bell; Bridgestone

An article about MediClaim Incorporated in the money section of USA Today.

COVER STORY

Nashville picks up economic beat

Continued from 1B

15% a year ago, while home sales are up 16% from last year. Jobs in the area grew 1% the first quarter. "We have overall slow and steady growth," says Anna Grimes of the Nashville Area Chamber of Commerce. "It's a mirror of what prognosticators are predicting for the rest of the country."

In fact, hardly anybody in Nashville seems excited about what's happening. "We went into the recession sooner, so we're coming out of it sooner," shrugs Ted Welch, a top real-estate developer. "We're back toward a normal path up now."

Beneath the ho-hum surface, though, lurk a lot of numbers and anecdotal evidence that show a regional economy gaining strength, slowly but surely.

Real estate has been one of Nashville's biggest sore spots. In the 1980s, office buildings sprouted like dandelions. "By '85, construction had spiked up three times higher than you'd expect in a bull real-estate market," Welch says. But that made for a glut. Vacancy rates hit a horrendous 25%. Cranes disappeared from the Nashville skyline. Contractors went under. "I don't believe there's been a speculative office building since I brought one on-stream in 1987," says Welch.

Now, though, a few cranes have appeared above the city. Office vacancies are down to 18.5% — still high but better. Office, retail and road construction are more active south of Nashville toward Franklin, the area's emerging suburban hub.

"We had a serious downturn in construction," says Robert Margo, professor of economics at Vanderbilt University in Nashville. "That seems to have played itself out."

The scene had been as bleak for homes, too. Home sales and prices dove the past few years. Now, home sales are up 16% from the same period last year and home prices seem to have stopped skidding. In May, the median price was $88,522, up slightly from $87,700 last year.

"We're seeing a major shift from what was a buyers market to a sellers market in some areas," says Shirley Zeitlin, whose Zeitlin & Co. is one of the area's bigger residential brokers. "For the first time in a long time, I'm seeing some instances of several offers on a house. I haven't seen that in years."

Real estate isn't rising only because supply dried up. More people are working — in April, Nashville's unemployment rate dipped to 5.1%, vs. 7.2% for the nation. A number of area industries are creating jobs and bringing in money.

Music is the most visible. Nashville has 170 recording studios, 1,500 music-publishing companies, offices for every major music label, CD- and cassette-duplicating plants and a community of singers, musicians and songwriters. The genre this year has snagged 12.5% of the $7.8 billion (annual revenue) recorded-music market, up from 9.5% in 1987.

True to form, it's hard to find ebullient displays of the industry's surge. But National Tape shows what's happening all over town. National makes cassettes for most of the music labels, and its two production lines are quietly humming 24 hours a day. "We're already running orders for Christmas," says salesman Jimmy Gray. "That's some of the earliest we've ever seen." National will open a new plant by year's end.

Car manufacturing is having a major impact on middle Tennessee and Nashville. Saturn, in Spring Hill, about 45 minutes southwest of Nashville, has shifted into high gear the past year. Its cars, noted for high quality, are selling faster than the company expected when the plant opened in 1990. Monthly sales zoomed from 10,204 in January to 21,038 last month. Two shifts of production employees are working 50-hour weeks to keep up.

Saturn hasn't added many new employees to the 5,000 that have been on staff, but it may eventually have to add a third shift. "We're slightly behind, but that's a good problem to have," says spokesman Bill Betts.

At the same time, the region's other auto plant is expanding. Nissan's facility in Smyrna, about 45 minutes southeast of Nashville, just finished a $490 million plant expansion and rolled its first Altima cars off the new assembly line. The plant added about 2,000 employees for the Altima line. Total Nissan employment in Smyrna: 6,000.

The region's other big economic engine is a highly entrepreneurial health-care industry centered in Nashville. "That's a big reason the economy here never went through too deep a downturn," says Margo. "Nothing slows down health care in our country anymore."

Nashville is home to Hospital Corp. of America, a privately owned medical monolith that runs 145 hospitals and will bring in about $5 billion in revenue this year. Around HCA and Nashville's several big, leading-edge hospitals, hundreds of companies such as MediClaim have sprung to life.

MediClaim is a highly speculative small venture that is building a system that would allow doctors and hospitals to electronically research and instantly file medical-insurance claims. In these times of cautious lending, such a firm would have a tough time borrowing from banks. But in Nashville's medical-oriented community, it has been able to find 12 private investors to get the company going. "I came to Nashville because I heard all the innovative health-care programs were coming out of here," says Richard White, the brains behind MediClaim's electronics and a Memphis native. He stayed when he found the people and money to back his work.

Nashville has many other strengths and weaknesses, of course. Its low cost of living, central location and fairly new infrastructure are helping attract business, such as a Lockheed mail-processing center that will add 1,380 jobs. Its sparkling new airport recently became an American Airlines hub.

On the downside, Nashville suffers from a low-performing school system and an often-ragged downtown. Many locals complain that the region is losing country-music tourist business to Branson, Mo., a center for live country acts.

Add it all up and Nashville has a mixture of economic good and bad that is making it react the way most of the country will when recovery comes to other areas, says Margo.

In other words, recovery may look a lot like Wyley Randall, a big, bearded man who sits with his guitar each day outside Houndogs hot-dog stand in the middle of the music district playing tunes for passers-by, making his living on tips. How's the economy treating him this year?

"Better'n last year, I guess," he says, then launches into a beer-soaked Hank Williams Jr. song: "Country-music singers/ are a real close family."

CASE STUDIES

I mentioned Carl Olsen as a hero in this case. Here is information concerning his role in the bid process. He worked with MediClaim to develop a computer network dedicated to the Health Care Industry.

Inactive Clients and Sample Projects (Partial List)

Alltel Corporation

Provided ATTEND-1 Test Set

ARCO

Procurement analysis of multiple PBX voice network

AT&T

Competitive analysis/market study of network switching systems

Children's Mercy Hospital, Kansas City

Design, procurement and implementation of new telecommunications system (voice and data) for the hospital.

Macy's of California

Design, develop and install a multi-site voice network surveillance system for real-time monitoring of 23 node PBX network interconnected via T-1 service.

Mitsubishi Electric

Design, procurement and implementation of voice and data communications networks. Included PBX implementation project, IBM and WANG data communications networks (contiguous US and international).

NYNEX Service Corporation

Database purification analysis for Enhanced 911 (E911) service system.

Pioneer Electronics USA

Design, procurement and implementation of voice and data communications networks. Included several PBX implementation projects, multiple host (IBM/HP) data communications networks (contiguous US) over several years.

St. Lukes Hospital, Kansas City

Design, procurement and implementation of new telecommunications network and infrastructure (UTP, Coax, Fiber) and new PBX system.

MediClaim's Telecommunication Group

The CMS Group, Inc.
Client Reference

Active Clients and Sample Projects (Partial List)

Pacific Bell

On-going database purification and analysis project to validate customer billing for all active customers (14,000,000 lines).

Central Office (CO) Switch Load transition management services, line database loading for Northern Telecom DMS100 and AT&T 5ESS Switching Systems. Currently have over 200,000 lines scheduled for conversion. (See enclosed brochure).

Provide Responder 200 for remote contact closure for one of Pacific Bell's large customers. (Product brochure enclosed).

Indiana Bell

Database purification and analysis for central office conversion projects from analog electronic (1AESS) to digital systems.

Ohio Bell

Database purification and analysis for central office conversion projects from analog electronic (1AESS) to digital systems.

C&P Telephone Company of Maryland

Provide ATTEND-1 Test Set. (Product brochure enclosed).

Siemens Stromberg-Carlson

Execute switch database loading for Siemen's client companies (Ameritech, Bell Atlantic, etc.) for switch conversions from existing electronic switches to Siemens EWSD digital CO.

CASE STUDIES

CENTRAL OFFICE

COMPARING DATA ON CO CUTOVERS

Conducting automated data base comparisons prior to a conversion can eliminate a lot of headaches and most customer complaints.

BY CARL OLSON

CENTRAL office conversions are synonymous with increased labor costs and customer complaints. Even a small flaw in a synchronized cutover can result in thousands of irate customers and substantial internal costs to a telephone company.

To the business customer without service for a couple of days, the loss can be momentous. Pacific Bell estimates every customer trouble report costs approximately $75, so the liability is sizable.

Ideally, a cutover would yield no complaints (a completely transparent transfer), yet any cut generating less than a 0.5% problem rate is generally regarded as successful.

Conversions come in all sizes and switching system types. Most common are conversions from aging electromechanical systems such as SXS CDOs, #5 X-Bars and the predominant analog electronic 1/1A/2/3 ESS to the several digital systems currently being installed, such as the 5ESS, DMS-100 and EWSD.

Some cutovers are massive, consisting of 50,000 to 75,000 lines, while others may only cut a single customer (i.e. centrex) or office code (prefix).

Carl Olson is president of the CMS Group, Torrance, Cal. The CMS Group has conducted numerous data base purification projects for several telcos including Pacific Bell, Nevada Bell, Ohio Bell and Indiana Bell.

▶ **The apprehension**

A lot of anxiety precedes a cutover. Millions of dollars and tens of thousands of customer lines are riding on a successful, synchronized conversion. Most any cutover from electromechanical to digital switches will be successful for 98% of standard service telephone lines. However, even a customer complaint rate of 1% can be unacceptable. Identifying mismatches—before the cutover takes place—for that 1% of the data base is the difference between a successful, cost-efficient cutover and a problematic one. The difference between a 98% and 99% successful conversion rate can mean $100,000 in service calls to the telco and a lot of grief to the cutover manager.

What if the vendor made a small error, or if the data in the old switch isn't completely compatible with the new switch? While some switch vendors are proposing the convenience of simplified, one-call-does-it-all services, reliance on a single source to install and test equipment may be risky. How can the performance of a cutover be audited before the cutover takes place and while there is still time to eliminate potential customer complaints?

The solution may be to "check the checker" by using an in-house process or an independent vendor to obtain a different perspective on the switch data base comparison.

Since all comparison tests are not the same, the independent or in-house analysis might pick up discrepancies missed by the vendor's comparison.

Also, the re-check provides peace of mind. After the cutover is not the time to be uncovering discrepancies.

The cost savings associated with automating data base comparisons can be documented—assuming a value to each customer complaint can be established. If it costs $75 to remedy every customer complaint after a central office cutover, multiplying this number by the number of customer complaints avoided—shown in management reports—will equal estimated cost savings that can be substantial.

Reducing customer complaints prior to conversions usually involves numerous hours of manually comparing old switch data with Cosmos or a similar data base. Before the actual cutover, as many discrepancies as possible are "scrubbed" from the existing switch and/or administrative data bases that may include systems such as LMOS, CRIS and Cosmos. Once the data base is loaded into the new switch, mismatches between old and new data bases are identified and rectified.

While most cutover managers attribute the majority of problems to the inability to identify inconsistencies with the actual service, existing switch and new switch data, that's often not the case. Many times, plenty of data is available for comparison, but it is disorganized, incompatible or the wrong analysis method is used.

▶ **Methods**

CO cutovers require data base comparisons that efficiently identify and eliminate line variances before the cutover takes place, effecting a transparent transfer to the new CO. Some conversion programs can quantify discrepancies, but to correct data base discrepancies before cutover, specific problems need to be reconciled.

Which management reports will be useful and which are superfluous? What data base comparisons can be completed in-house, and which require an outside vendor? If the telco uses an outside vendor, how does it determine which data base tests are needed, and which are not cost effective?

Just because a comparison process is automated does not mean it's efficient. For example, when comparing multiline hunt groups between dissimilar office types, a discrepancy report may provide little value since most of the data that could be compared would be different between the machines. A more practical solution might be to provide multiline hunt group listings in the old and new switches and conduct a manual check.

Another example of unnecessary data could be touch-tone variance listings between two switches. Many telcos, based on regulatory direction, are providing the touch-tone feature on a default basis. In this case, the status in the old switching system may be irrelevant. A better approach would be to list only those lines without the touch-tone feature in the new switch.

Preparation is essential to the transparent transfer. It entails a multistep process of data base comparisons before the actual cutover *(Figure 1)*.

First, the existing customer records should be purified prior to preparing the data base for loading to eliminate as many discrepancies as possible. This step, considered a standard step by many Bell operating companies, has proven to be cost effective.

Once the switch has been loaded, the telco should conduct (or have a data base analysis vendor conduct) a post-load comparison or comparisons of both switch data bases and, as needed, the Cosmos or administrative data base. The number of comparisons—from as few as one to as many as five—would depend on the size and complexity of the switch system data and the quality of the initial

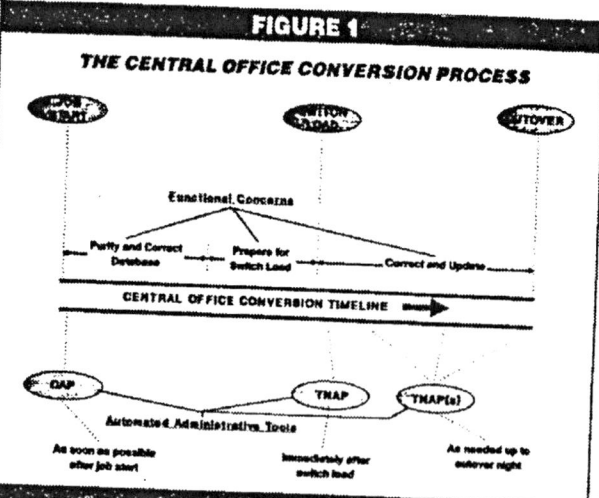

FIGURE 1
THE CENTRAL OFFICE CONVERSION PROCESS

load. Here is an ideal place to "check the checker" by internally comparing the vendor's work or conduct one or more comparisons through an independent contractor.

Phase 1—pre-load analysis. A successful comparison analysis, called the Cosmos analysis program (CAP), has been designed to be utilized in the initial preparation stages of a dial conversion project. The CAP validates and compares the accuracy of customer/switch assignment records in multiple data bases (Cosmos, LMOS, CRIS and the existing switch system). It helps to ensure the magnetic tape extractions—such as TMART or TODA tapes—are accurate for loading into the new switch *(Figure 2)*.

Phase 2—post-load analysis. Another comparison analysis provides an analysis of the old and new switch as well as line assignment data from Cosmos. The telephone number analysis program (TNAP) allows the telco to verify that the telephone numbers and ancillary data (IEC-PIC assignment, hunting, custom calling features, etc.) are properly configured in the new switch *(Figure 3)*.

▶ **Variance reports**

The reports generated in these stages should include comparisons between all desirable data bases that may include the old switch, Cosmos (or equivalent system), LMOS, CRIS, and after the load, the new switch data base. If most or all discrepancies are identified and resolved in the CAP, then the TNAP will be simplified, with most discrepancies involving tape translation errors or error due to continuing recent change activity.

For the older electromechanical office conversions, desirable reports would include variances in the working/not working status in each data base for each telephone number being transferred. While this may be somewhat routine for a small conversion, it still makes sense to automate the process to reduce manpower costs and assure a higher degree of accuracy than a "stare and compare" method of manual data base checking.

For new feature-rich switches (such as centrex, custom calling features, etc.) the process of data base validation becomes quite complicated and beyond the capability of a manual check. For these systems, several additional variance reports would prove valuable:

■ *Series completion/multiline hunting*—a line-by-line analysis of variances in hunting sequences. This is especially valuable if variances in the system require differing line treatment in the old and new offices.

■ *LEN/OE assignments*—a check of the line assignment in the new switch against the line data base (usually in Cosmos). This step can prevent customer complaints by detecting missing jumpers, crossed assignments and other problems.

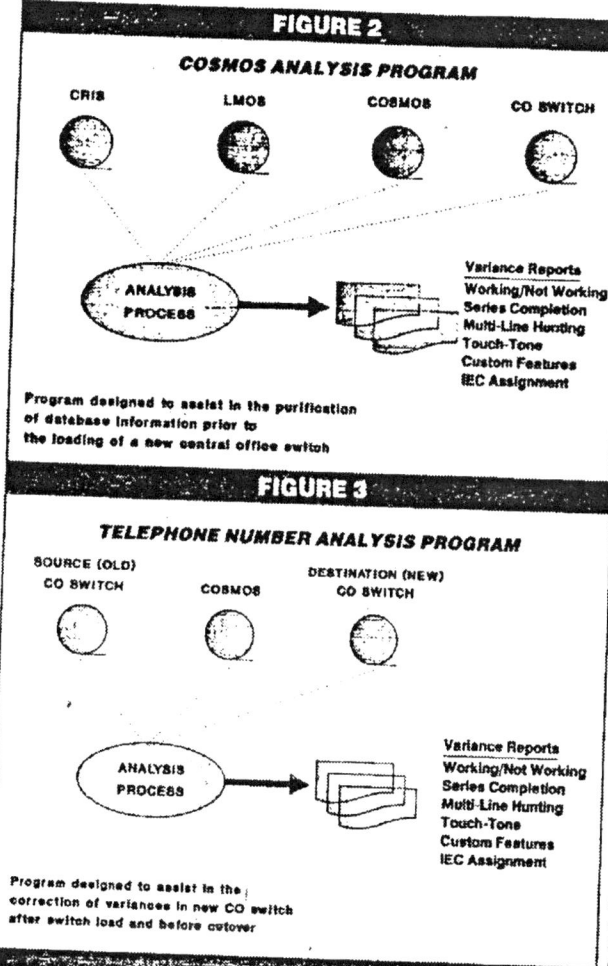

FIGURE 2
COSMOS ANALYSIS PROGRAM

Program designed to assist in the purification of database information prior to the loading of a new central office switch

FIGURE 3
TELEPHONE NUMBER ANALYSIS PROGRAM

Program designed to assist in the correction of variances in new CO switch after switch load and before cutover

■ *Custom calling features*—feature-by-feature comparisons of old, new and, if desired, the Cosmos. Any missing or incorrectly assigned feature could potentially result in a customer complaint. With the almost constant introduction of more complicated features in the new digital switches, this area requires close attention. Feature variance reports should also include line related data such as IEC-PIC assignments, essential service flags and remote call forwarding.

Comparison of the line data is only one of several steps used to reduce customer complaints and assure a smooth cutover. In addition to hardware checks, such as board-to-board testing, call-through validation testing also is common. This has been—and with many telcos, continues to be—a manual process involving a number of clerks dialing and recording results. Like data base comparisons, this process has been successfully automated in several telcos. Using an automated call though test set for validating, routing and changing trunk data bases is as important on the trunk side of the switch as the automated data base comparisons are on the line side of the switch.

▶ **Pacific Bell**
After deregulation, and faced with the equal access requirements established by Judge Greene, many operating telcos initiated the expensive dial conversion process to replace electromechanical switches with digital switches.

Pacific Bell undertook a massive project to meet the equal access requirements.

The bulk of the project, titled "Project 87," involved replacing #5 Xbar units with either DMS-100 or 5ESS digital switches. Within the Orange/Riverside area of southern California, 15 dial conversions and 19 equal access conversions, impacting more than 698,000 access lines, had to be completed by the end of 1987.

Considering the quantity of work involved, and the quality and accuracy essential to make the project a success, the undertaking appeared insurmountable without work force additions and extensive overtime hours.

However, the parameters of the project dictated no work force additions because after completion of the project the workers who maintained electromechanical switches would be without an assignment. Overtime levels of 20% were budgeted. The other parameter involved service, in which customer trouble reports were not to exceed 0.5%.

PacBell senior managers examined the processes involved in performing a dial transfer. The significant tasks were labor intensive and seemed to be candidates for automation. They included the following:
1) Purification of customer data bases in preparation of either TMART or TODA tapes, involving scrubbing Cosmos, LMOS and CRIS.
2) Verification of all vacant telephone numbers that would be manually bashed against the new switching machine.
3) Verification of number group frames or switch data bases to determine hunting configurations.
4) Physical checks of the existing switch to validate what was really working against what the Cosmos records reflected.
5) Call-through testing to ensure bil-

ing and routing translations are correct.

6) Generate management status reports to describe dial transfer activity.

Having identified these tasks, PacBell established three goals for a successful transfer:

- An ideal cutover would be achieved if everything working in the old switch was duplicated in the new switch.
- Reduce as much as possible the manual purification process since labor-intensive comparisons have been proven to create errors.
- Working under time constraints, it was not feasible to develop automated processes within the company.

PacBell consulted with an outside vendor to automate many of the labor-intensive processes. The only labor required was resolving the true discrepancies identified by the automated comparison of various data bases.

The end result was an analysis service aimed at verifying and purifying data bases prior to extraction of the TMART and TODA tapes. The service involved comparing as many as four data bases (Cosmos, CRIS, LMOS and the switching machine data bases where available) against each other for discrepancies.

The next concern was reconciling accurate telephone number counts between the old and new switch and Cosmos. In the past, most management status reports relating to cutovers were at best, a guess. To eliminate the "crystal ball" forecasting and its inherent problems, another analysis program was developed, which compared the telephone numbers transferred to the new switching machine—usually a DMS-100, 5ESS or 1AESS—with the old switching machine and Cosmos.

The program identified working and disconnected telephone line discrepancies. Hunt group and line equipment (OE, LEN) mismatches were clearly identified for resolution. Finally, a management summary report was prepared identifying the number of working lines by prefix and data base.

Using this report, accurate counts were made and variances accounted for with a minimal amount of labor, providing an accurate indication of the progress and activity of the program.

The last tool used to update the cutover process was an automatic telephone number dialer. The call-through testing requirements for billing and routing validation tests, which typically involved up to five clerks manually dialing, listening for the proper response and recording the results was essentially eliminated. In total, 14,000 test calls were made in the routing and validation process for each central office switch. The test took eight hours per switch to complete, compared to the manual process, which required 1000 hours to complete 5000 test calls.

▶ **Indiana Bell**

Of course, every cutover does not involve 700,000 lines. But automated data base comparisons are still cost effective in single switch conversions, as well as single prefix moves, area transfers and even single customers, such as centrex customers moving from one switch to another switch—if the telco already is set up to handle the comparisons internally, or has access to an outside data base analysis service.

In February 1990, Indiana Bell completed a 1AESS to 5ESS conversion for a business area in Indianapolis. The cut involved 53,000 lines, 56 centrexes and 4500 trunks. Indiana Bell conducted a thorough data base scrub of the 1AESS, and several switch comparisons for mismatches after the switch vendor's dump. The result was a total of 15 customer reports after the cutover, or a 99.96% success conversion rate.

"Using a data base analysis service provided cheap insurance," according to Fred Lewis, cutover manager for Indiana Bell. "We assured the success of a multimillion-dollar project with a $5000-$10,000 data base bash."

Switch cutovers involve a great deal of coordination and testing, and require synchronization. A cutover usually occurs at midnight and is performed on a slash cut basis, with all new customer lines activated at the same time. If the process is not adequately pretested and discrepancies are not resolved, problems will invariably occur. Conducting automated data base comparisons prior to cutover can eliminate the majority of customer complaints. ■

© Reprinted from TELEPHONE ENGINEER & MANAGEMENT, December 1, 1990

CASE STUDIES

SUMMARIZATION STRUCTURE & CONCLUSION

"Let your attitude be gratitude"

It should be made clear, that the three models presented are not to be used to evaluate people in an organization. The models define for everyone the type of people we prefer to work with in our organizations. People that love things and use people (to get things) need the good people in their life in order to fulfill their goals. However, good people really don't need bad people to accomplish their goals. Studying the companies that I worked for while working to earn my college degrees lead me to develop and modify these three models. Heroes are the people we prefer to work with more often than people who use people for the love of things. Fred Smith and Ron Taylor both had a brilliant idea and pioneered new services. Fred Smith provided an innovating service in the package and document delivery service, and Ron Taylor (President of the Pyxis Corporation) provided outstanding products and services in the health care industry. During the start-up phase of their operations, both leaders personally interviewed new employees. During my time with Federal Express, Fred Smith showed his gratitude to his employees by providing bonus programs, open door policies, and a wide variety of programs for employees to be promoted in the organization as well as be rewarded for doing good work. When you became a ten-year employee at Federal Express, you are flown to Memphis to spend time with Fred Smith to receive the royal treatment. Fred Smith always made himself available for the people he loved, the employees of Federal Express and his customers. Ron Taylor (Pyxis Corporation) did the same thing. He would take all the employees out of the field (annually) for a week of rest and relaxation. Service teams would meet with Ron Taylor (personally) and he would listen to our complaints and success stories. Ron Taylor would place a phone call to all of his employees at home during the Christmas holidays to talk and say thank you for your service. The highest bonuses I have ever received, came from Ron Taylor. The people that were involved in the Pyxis start-up were all heroes. So are the people that participated in the Federal Express start-up. It is not easy to start an enterprise. Very special people of high caliber must be involved in order for it to work.

A myth in management begins to emerge when mangers do not understand the concepts of interfering and tampering. Mangers think they have to have a management style or fake it till you make it philosophy, but heroes are managers that manage things and lead people with their genuine character ethic. Anytime we tamper with people, it always worsens the alignment of the team, the team of people who share values. The commonality of purpose and a vision come from the team of people sharing values. Ineffective managers are like actors who forgot that they are playing a role. They become trapped in the theater of their thoughts. The words theater and theory have the same Greek root *theoria* meaning to look at. Reality may change but the theater continues. We operate in the theater, defining problems, taking action, solving problems, and losing touch with the larger reality from which the theater is generated. Our theater is all of the tasks that are put forth on the team to develop and maintain the enterprise. Using dialogue and removing fallacies (as presented in this book) any group of people became observers of our own thinking and sound thinking (removing fallacies) continues to become more active.

When Ron Taylor sold the Pyxis Corporation to Cardinal Health, everyone was excited that the company was bought out for $1,000,000.00 per-employee. At this time Pyxis had approximately 360 employees. Employee stocks of Pyxis were converted to Cardinal Health stocks. The downside was Ron Taylor left and Cardinal Health replaced many managerial positions with new people. Middle management implemented an MBO (Management by Objectives) program that reflects one person's view not the successful view of the team workers. The management team functions well with routine issues listed in the MBO program, but when complex issues outside the MBO program rise to the occasion, the management team becomes less proficient, keeping themselves from learning new ideas concerning customer service at the local level. During the five years I worked under Ron Taylor, I had one manger during those five years, John Beale. John Beale is a hero, an outstanding individual. There was no change in the management team for those five years. The Southeast Regions Vice President was another outstanding individual, Steve King. There were no MBO programs, but there were evaluations done that fostered development. The following six years when I was under the Cardinal Health Pyxis, I had 11 different managers (within a six-year period) and Cardinal Health Pyxis constantly reorganized. This created changes that produced tampering with processes. Before the MBO program implementation, field service employees were given the autonomy to make decisions concerning customer service at the local level. The local team's time was spent at the customer location and the team worked as a partner with the customer to solve customer issues, set policy and procedures, as well as routine preventative maintenance on the computers located in their hospitals. As a result management would evaluate the installation processes as well as the team's actions with the customer. Managers under Ron Taylor's leadership, were involved in ways that supported the teams, not destroy the team.

Because of this business structure under Ron Taylor, everyone was familiar to the installation and support processes. This required management to take an active role in learning what their local teams were doing to raise the customer service level at the local level. After Ron Taylor, the managers did not have to take that active role. Managers could care less about having employees PARTICIPATE (Model #2); managers only TOLD employees what to do. The MBO program established a list of objectives that field service employees must complete in order to have a high performance review. This list of MBO objectives had nothing to do with improving customer service. In fact many of the listed objectives are oriented around an easy management evaluation of "did you complete this objective or not." This very process blocks out any new understandings which might threaten the management teams MBOs for field employees.

SUMMARIZATION STRUCTURE AND CONCLUSION

When the organization allows these types of learning disabilities to persist, along with their consequences of not directing people to serve others, customer complaints will be the demise of any large market share. There is a difference in adaptive learning and generative learning. An MBO program is an adaptive learning program only for an organization, it means taking in information only. Managers need to become adept learners in the customer service process and encourage generative learning that enhances the team's capacity to create new customer service processes. This process of teaching and learning reacts well to the ever event driven world of customer service. We all live in a learning society, but the new President of Pyxis took away the organization's will to be a learning culture. Once again, not understanding the processes, they were tampered with.

There is a difference in people management and project management. The difference is managing things and leading people. People's Express Airlines is an example of the perils of being the first to do something, but an unsuccessful way of doing a start-up enterprise. The pioneers always get the arrows. Even though People's Express Airlines got off to a great start, declining customer service, quality and standards, lead to a bankrupt company. The business structures generally consist of three customer consciousness. These structures are price consciousness, quality consciousness, and service consciousness. A business should never let only one of these structures be their competitive advantage or the business will be vulnerable to fail. Organizations must organize with a belief in something that is greater than the organization itself. Any relationship between co-workers, customers, or friends will thrive if the people in the relationship share values. When we put feelings before values we all loose. When people put feelings before doing the right thing first, we all miss opportunities. Values are all about doing the RIGHT thing first and then the feelings will follow. When we put feelings first, feelings then destroy our values. Values are all about doing the right thing first and the feelings will follow. It should never be done in the reverse order.

A creative person is one who can process in new ways the information directly at hand. This information appears as ordinary sensory data available to all of us. However, a creative individual intuitively sees possibilities for transforming ordinary data into a new creation, transcendent over the mere raw materials. There is a difference between the two processes of gathering data and transforming data creatively. My research studies as well as personal experience has determined that creative managers (Heroes) look toward the conceptualizing with science (looking for the facts) to supply their metaphors and images (models). Heroes study to determine what are the initial conditions of a start-up company? Cause and effect become dependent on a contingency event driven system that have sensitive dependence on the contingency rather than the cause and effect. During start-up competition, whether Beta vs. VHS or FedEx vs. a competitor; there is a period of complexity, a convoluted nonlinear relationship that appears to be impossible to analyze by classical methods. Only heroes overcome the difficulties of the evaluation of such relationships.

Schools of thought give everyone a feeling of being informed but we are not really being informed. There is a difference in feeling informed and being informed. In quantum mechanics we have an infinite number of degrees of freedom (not to be confused with degrees of freedom in statistics). With probability we often include the analysis of the possibilities. When we study a process such as the migration of brain cells in humans, we see that there are infinite possibilities in a finite space but we cannot always calculate the most probable outcome. We cannot necessarily find the facts that lead to truth, but many times we can claim a very high quality of understanding. Many times people think they are pursuing the truth and claim to have complete understanding, but there is danger when we do not participate with others and when we allow others to tell us what to think.

Even when we think we are conceptualizing with science, science continues to improve the analysis of systems. An example of this improvement to scientific thought is the science of chaos. Chaos science understands that classical science has discovered a great majority of the linear relationships that exist (universal truths) but science must continue to understand the non-linear (quality answers) that make up the rest of the science of gauged fields and other systems. When we use movement or school of thought to conceptualize solutions or to define what we think is a better process, leaders will often create confocal vulnerabilities in our organizations. A confocal vulnerability is one in which a single attack or devastating event can hurt or destroy more than one thing at the same time, because they are located at the same physical place (confocal). This is what happens when we tamper with processes and have to deal with managers that "just don't get it." These are the ungrateful complainers that steal from the company and never consider others. To give you an example, while at Federal Express, a director of the region just didn't get it. He would travel to many of the Federal Express stations to talk to employees. He often acted as if this was an inconvenience in his life. If an employee asked a question concerning improvement, the director's response was "If you don't like it here McDonalds is hiring." Many people in the region didn't care for his management style. Shortly after the director's comment, the corporate office had determined that he was not open to employee suggestions and was stealing from the corporation. Once this person was fired, the employees at the Nashville FedEx Office sent him a McDonald's application for employment. Everyone knew this person would not last long under the watchful eye of Fred Smith.

The ungrateful complaining people are often the people that blame others for the issues they created. By shifting the burden to others causes an eroding goal dynamic. Eroding goal dynamic is when standards in the overall system begin to decline. The longer the deterioration goes unnoticed, or the longer people wait to confront the fundamental cause of lower standards, the more difficult it is to reverse the situation.

The cases presented in the book are examples of four different enterprises that were presented with a new experience. In any new experience, people have a tendency to take in and remember only the information that reinforces ones existing mental models thus limiting ones ability to change. The Arkansas bid is an example of this concept. Managers only wanted to see the EDS model, even though there was no real product to do the reality modeling. We live in a world of self-generating beliefs that remain largely untested. As with the case of religion; many claim to give you eternal life, fake faith healers trick people into following them and giving money, as well as the obvious that very few people actually read the book or books they consider holy. The core task of the discipline of mental models is to bring tacit assumptions and attitudes to the surface so people can explore and talk about differences and misunderstanding with minimal defensiveness. Once a group defines and agrees to a model that fits the system, our individual models are no longer distorted. Everyone's vision is focused on a shared concept (model-science, shared values, and people) that all have agreed to see. The discipline of shared values is the set of tools and techniques for brining all of these disparate aspirations into alignment around the things people have in common. In building shared values, a group of people build a sense of commitment together. Developing images of "the future we all want to create together," along with the values that will be important in achieving our goals. Without a sustained process for building shared vision, there is no way to articulate a sense of purpose.

Team learning should not be based on the concept of agreement, rather alignment.

Alignment has the connotation of arranging a group of scattered elements or entities so they function as a whole, by correctly orienting a common awareness, a common purpose, and a common reality. An essential part of team learning is dialogue. By starting a dialogue the group learns to think together-not just in the sense of analyzing a shared problem, but in the sense of occupying a collective sensibility. The word "system" descends from the Greek word *sunistanai*, which originally meant, "to cause to stand together." The nature of a system includes the perception with which the observer sees what causes something to work in synchronization to stand together. The discipline of systems thinking is the study of the structure and behavior of the agent that sustains events and how can leverage effectively make improvements. Systems thinking is enriched by a set of tools and techniques that have developed over the past thirty-five years, particularly out of the computer industry. People who have experience in systems thinking can act more effectively using leverage than the short attention span of our present culture generally permits.

Aristotle suggested that morality cannot be learned simply by reading a treatise on virtue. The spirit of morality, said Aristotle, is awakened in the individual only through the witness and conduct of a moral person. John Dewey argued that at the pre-critical, pre-rational, pre-autonomous level, morality starts as a set of culturally defined goals and rules, which are external to the individual and are imposed or inculcated as habits. But real ethical thinking, said Dewey, begins at the evaluative period of our lives, when, as independent agents, we freely decide to accept, embrace, modify, or deny these rules. Dewey maintained that every serious ethical system rejects the notion that one's standard of conduct should simply and uncritically be an acceptance of the rules of the culture we happen to live in. Even when custom, habit, convention, public opinion, or law are correct in their mandates, to embrace them without critical reflection does not constitute a complete and formal ethical act and might be better-labeled "ethical happenstance" or "ethics by virtue of circumstantial accident." According to Dewey, ethics is essentially "reflective conduct," and he believed that the distinction between custom and reflective morality is clearly marked. The former places the standard and rules of conduct solely on habit; the latter appeals to reason and choice. The distinction is as important as it is definite, for it shifts the center of gravity in morality. For Dewey ethics is a two-part process; it is never enough simply to do the right thing, which could be wrong.

Many of the best decisions made by individuals and groups were made by those who are statistical thinkers or they work with statistical thinkers. Today's good decisions are driven by data. In all aspects of our lives, and importantly in the business context, an amazing diversity of data is available for inspection and analytical insight. Business managers and professionals are increasingly required to justify decisions on the basis of data. They need statistical model-based decision support systems. Statistical thinking enables all of us to intelligently collect, analyze and interpret data relevant to our decision-making process. We are able to reduce guesswork (avoid availability errors), solve problems in a diversity of contexts, and add substance to our decisions. But we all need to be reminded that variation is inevitable in life. We must understand the difference in special cause variation and common cause variation. Statistics don't lie, people do. Statistics determines if a system is controlling us or are we controlling the system. Just like the weather, if we cannot control it, then we should learn how to measure and analyze it in order to predict the variation patterns effectively. What we cannot change or control, we can learn how to escape the time the system produces a harmful pattern.

Let your attitude be gratitude.

Many people in business and throughout the world talk about attitude. There is positive mental attitude, aggressive attitudes, dress to impress attitude, the fake it till you make it attitude, and many other attitudes we are told to develop. Different concepts of attitude application, but everything written about people's attitudes are that attitudes becomes one's mental filter for how we interact with others throughout life and how we perceive life's events. If we agree that one's attitude becomes one's mental filter, then let us agree to perceive the filter as one's beliefs. Beliefs are combinations of a person's convictions and opinions (our talk), where as our values are demonstrations of what is important to us (our walk-what we really do). The mental filter is a memory storage area that contains the collaborative opinions and convictions of an organization, household, or any associating group of people. The filter separates important information from interesting information. Values are the walk, which is the implementation of our beliefs. When our beliefs and our filter for important information are closely coherent, then the outcomes that foster development are our accountabilities. It is important because a demand (from management) without definition equals no accountability and bad behavior. You cannot manage people without an understanding of a persons filter. As a result let your walk talk loader than your talk talks.

The purpose of this book has been to bring exposure to many of the concepts of business management. It was also to bring to others the destructive effects of tampering with processes. Stephen Covey said it best, "First seek to understand, then be understood." Just as the illustrations and cases presented in this book, if leaders are to be heroes, then they will first understand the processes of their organizations rather than practice bidding for political power to be understood first. We have the cart before the horse if we make others understand the one person's idea rather than seeking understanding of others first.

Our educational institutions tamper with processes, our religious enterprises tamper with people's beliefs, they interfere when in reality their holy scripts teach intercession not interfering. The removal of a small component and failure to understand caused Federal Express millions of dollars because a small group of people built an expensive self-serving empire and took advantage of others by tampering with a process. And what can we say about our government institutions that collaborate to tamper with what is legally supposed to be a fair and unbiased bid process. Their myopic intention for years was to single source this bid and pretend to solicit computer hardware and software for over two years in an advanced planning document. Then these public servants created the illusion of placing computer hardware and software out for competitive bid, the bid required a demonstration of computer hardware and software, and then public officials purchased vaporware at the taxpayers' expense. What were people thinking? But during all of my experiences, every situation had heroes and zeroes.

This book has presented several concepts, but the focus is to make a public awareness of the pitfalls that occur when zero people tamper with processes. Everyone looses when leaders are not trained to understand both the implicate order as well as the explicate order. We live in an information age, therefore we should understand how to better evaluate information and understand fallacies and false positives. Humans in general do much more than just process information, we understand it. In general it is the process that fails us and not people. It is only when we have a tested process of time that produces results or failures. If the process has been tested and proves to produce results, then if bad outcomes manifest themselves, then we know that people are failing to follow the process (tampering).

In K.C. Cole's book, The Universe and the Teacup, she refers to *the tipping point* of systems and processes. Tipping points are a result of emergent properties of simple interactions between system parts that over time add up to far more than the sum of their parts. She states in her book that time may well be the ultimate emergent property of many systems. Often we do not allow processes to finish and complete, so we never have an understanding of a true end result. A simple example of tipping point is the old saying about the straw that broke the camel's back. At some point, more changes everything. Also small changes make a difference. One degree in temperature change (33 degrees Fahrenheit to 32 degrees Fahrenheit) changes liquid water into a solid. This tipping point of one degree moves water from one transitional phase to another. In her book she also discusses this concept as it refers to social policy. Cole suggests that we shouldn't jump to conclusions about the effectiveness or failure of a social policy without taking the tipping point into account. We shouldn't conclude that the welfare system doesn't help people get out of poverty because it hasn't accomplished that goal yet. We should not necessarily conclude that money spent on inner city schools is wasted because it hasn't shown results comparable to money put into the programs. It could be simply that these processes have not reached the tipping point. I also highly recommend her book as excellent reading material. In chaos theory, chaotic systems have a tendency to self-organize due to chaotic attractors. Attractors live in mathematical constructs known as phase space. Phase space is an imaginary space that turns numbers into pictures, making a flexible map of all the information available. When impatient people advocate changing the system and abandoning the present process, it is apparent that they are tampering with the tipping points and attractors of a system that could free all of us to a new transition. Many times zero people are too impatient to let time be the emergent property to guide improvements. Heroes will continue to look for tipping points that could be a threat to organizational stability (the straw that broke the camels back). Heroes also look for tipping points that will take the organization out of chaos in order to enter a new transition of stability. Heroes find the attractors in chaotic systems that cause other heroes to gravitate toward shared values and greater accomplishments. Strengths, weaknesses, opportunities, and threats (SWOT); these are the tipping points and attractors that need to be identified in every organization in order to avoid tampering with people and processes.

Why are we so quick to abandon a particular belief, science, or process that is obviously producing results? Heroes are patient to first understand and then be understood. Zeroes invade our organization with preconceived ideas, not conceptualized in science, but school of thought or movement strategies. I have recently read another book that expounds why we often are too quick to abandon sound practices. I highly recommend this book. My father, Dr. Richard P. White, wrote this book. The title is <u>Bibles, Science, and Sanity-The Case for Modernism.</u> This book is loaded with examples of insightful accounts of the endless conflicts between science and religion that are a result of poorly taught science and the failure of religious extremist to teach the sound practices of the science of textual criticism (hermeneutics).

I want to end with a story that someone once told me. A young man was looking for a part time job in Cincinnati, Ohio. He applied to be a waiter at one of the finest restaurants in the area. The interview process was conducted differently. The manager of the restaurant took the applications and reviewed them. He then had a personal conversation to determine if the candidate was an interesting person. The manager then put the new employees in a room. In this room was a table, well prepared with beautiful dinner ware. The manager sat at the table and talked to each of the new employees as a group, treating them as if they were royalty. The waiters and waitresses provided a wonderful atmosphere. The food was excellent and the service was the best the new employees had ever received. The new employees at the table had never been treated this well by anyone in their life. The manager then asked, "Did you like the service you received?" Everyone answered yes. He then asked, "Did you feel like someone special, as if you were important?" Everyone answered yes. He then asked, "Did you like the way you were treated?" Everyone said definitely yes. The manager then asked, "Will you be able to server others in the same way you were served?" Those that answered yes and became an employee for this manager learned a valuable life long lesson. How true, we always want others to treat us with respect and courtesy, but we should stop and ask ourselves, "Are we willing to serve others as we have been served?" The moral to this story is treat others in the same way you want to be treated. Pay it back and pay it forward. Treat others the way you want to be treated and let your attitude be gratitude.

THE END

Printed in the United States
73813LV00002B/551-580